Naguib Mahfouz

Mohamed El-Hindi Series on Arab Culture and Islamic Civilization

Naguib Mahfouz
1988 Nobel Prize Winner for Literature

Photograph by R. Neil Hewison and used by permission of American University of Cairo.

Naguib Mahfouz

FROM REGIONAL FAME TO GLOBAL RECOGNITION

Edited by
MICHAEL BEARD
and ADNAN HAYDAR

SU SYRACUSE UNIVERSITY PRESS

First Edition 1993
93 94 95 96 97 98 99 6 5 4 3 2 1

A modified version of Mona N. Mikhail's essay appears in her book, *Mahfouz and Idris: Studies in Arabic Short Fiction* (New York University Press, 1992).

This book inaugurates the Mohamed El-Hindi Series on Arab Culture and Islamic Civilization.

The paper used in this publication meets the minimum requirements of American National Standard for Information Sciences—Permanence of Paper for Printed Library Materials, ANSI Z39.48-1984.∞™

Library of Congress Cataloging-in-Publication Data

Naguib Mahfouz : from regional fame to global recognition / edited by Michael Beard and Adnan Haydar. — 1st ed.
p. cm. — (Mohamed El-Hindi Series on Arab Culture and Islamic Civilization)
Includes bibliographical references and index.
ISBN 0-8156-2567-7 (alk. paper)
1. Maḥfūẓ, Najīb, 1912- —Criticism and interpretation.
I. Beard, Michael, 1944- . II. Haydar, Adnan, III. Series.
PJ7846.A46Z716 1992
892.7'36—dc20 92-8144

Manufactured in the United States of America

For Paula and Victoria—
cardinal points

CONTENTS

MAP

ACKNOWLEDGMENTS

We have been fortunate to have help from more than one quarter of the map. The genesis of this collection was a symposium at the University of Massachusetts recognizing Naguib Mahfouz's receipt of the 1988 Nobel Prize. The more we thought about it, the clearer it became; Mahfouz is of greater than occasional importance, and it seemed necessary to widen the dialogue beyond the scope of a single symposium.

Many people came onto the scene to help us at this point. We had help from a remarkable editor, Cynthia Maude-Gembler, who knew the difficulties of editing a multiauthor book and encouraged us through the process at every turn. Both the University of North Dakota and the University of Massachusetts at Amherst helped us pay travel expenses for connecting two editors separated by a big map. Ayman A. el-Desouky provided the original version of Gaber Asfour's "Naguib Mahfouz's Critics." Roger Allen gave us extensive help with the bibliography. Mona Mikhail translated the chapter from Gamal al-Ghitani's "Naguib Mahfouz Remembers." And Samia Mehrez brought us ideas and contacts that have reshaped our cartography more than once. If we listed everyone who gave us directions and good advice, we would need to compile a who's who of the field.

Indeed, Mahfouz's writing enlarges the field. His innovations as a novelist are important enough in a global perspective to encourage a readjustment of our traditional literary map. We hope our mosaic of commentaries will make that project more possible.

CONTRIBUTORS

ROGER ALLEN is the author of *A Period of Time: al-Muwaylihi's Hadith 'Isa ibn Hisham* (2d ed., 1992), *The Arabic Novel: An Historical and Critical Introduction* (1982), and *Modern Arabic Literature* (1987). He has written numerous translations and articles on modern Arabic fiction and drama and on Arabic language pedagogy. His translations include Mahfouz's *Mirrors* and *Autumn Quail.* He teaches Arabic language and literature at the University of Pennsylvania.

GABER ASFOUR is a prominent Egyptian literary critic and theorist and a contributing editor to *Fusul* magazine. He teaches Arabic literature at the University of Cairo.

MICHAEL BEARD is the author of *Hedayat's "Blind Owl" as a Western Novel* (1990), on the Iranian writer Sadeq Hedayat. With Adnan Haydar, he wrote *Naked in Exile,* a study of the Lebanese poet Khalil Hawi. He and Haydar collaborate frequently on translations and commentaries of Arabic literature, most recently *In Forbidden Time* (1991), an English version of poems by Henri Zoghaib. Beard teaches English literature at the University of North Dakota.

MIRIAM COOKE has written *The Anatomy of an Egyptian Intellectual: Yahya Haqqi* (1984) and *War's Other Voices: Women Writers on the Lebanese Civil War* (1988). She has translated Haqqi's stories under the title *Good Morning!* (1987). She coedited *Opening the Gates:*

100 Years of Arab Feminist Writing (1990) with Margot Badran and *Collateral Damage: Gender and War* (forthcoming) with Angel Woollacott. Her current research focuses on gender, postmodernism, and war in the Arab world. She teaches Arabic language and literature at Duke University.

GAMAL AL-GHITANI is an Egyptian novelist and a protégé of Naguib Mahfouz. He edits the cultural supplement to *al-Akhbar* newspaper in Cairo, and his novel *Zayni Barakat* has been published in English (1988).

ADNAN HAYDAR is the author of a forthcoming book on Lebanese *zajal* poetry and *New Words to Old Tunes,* an analysis of musical and poetic meter in Bedouin and Palestinian poetry, as well as numerous articles on classical and modern Arabic poetry. Besides his collaborations with Michael Beard—*Naked in Exile* (1984) and *In Forbidden Time* (1991)—he has translated, with Roger Allen, Jabra Ibrahim Jabra's *The Ship* and *The Search for Walid Masoud* (forthcoming). He teaches Arabic language and comparative literature at the University of Massachusetts.

SALMA KHADRA JAYYUSI is a well-known Palestinian poet and critic, and the director of PROTA (The Project of Translation from Arabic). Among her books are *Trends and Movements in Modern Arabic Poetry* (1977), *Modern Arabic Poetry: An Anthology* (1987), and *The Literature of Modern Arabia: An Anthology* (1988).

SARAH LAWALL has recently completed editing "Reading World Literature: Theory, History, and Academic Practice" (forthcoming). Among her writings are *Critics of Consciousness: The Existentialist Structures of Literature* (1968) and an edition of Euripides' *Hippolytus* (with Gilbert Lawall, 1986). Since 1977 she has edited the modern section of the *Norton Anthology of World Masterpieces.* She teaches comparative literature at the University of Massachusetts.

FEDWA MALTI-DOUGLAS has published extensively on classical and modern Arabic literature and Islamic civilization. Her books include *Structures of Avarice: The Bukhalâ' in Medieval Arabic Literature* (1985), *Blindness and Autobiography: al-Ayyâm of Tâhâ Husayn* (1988), and *Woman's Body, Woman's World: Gender and Discourse in Arabo-*

Islamic Writing (1991). She is professor of Arabic, semiotics, and women's studies and chairperson of the Department of Near Eastern Languages and Cultures at Indiana University.

SAMIA MEHREZ is the author of *Spoken Egyptian Arabic* (1985) and of articles on contemporary Egyptian and Palestinian literature and on francophone writing in North Africa. She teaches English and comparative literature at the American University in Cairo, where she is currently writing a biography of Naguib Mahfouz.

MONA N. MIKHAIL has published *Mahfouz and Idris: Studies in Arabic Short Fiction* (1992), ʿAraʾis fi al-mawlid: dirasat hawl al-marʾa al ʿArabiyya (Brides at the feast: Studies on Arab Women, 1978), and *Images of Arab Women: Fact and Fiction* (1979). She has received the P.E.N. Prize for the translation of short stories and the Columbia University Center Award. Among her translations is the Egyptian novel *Seeds of Corruption* (1980), by Sabri Musa. She teaches Arabic literature and Islamic studies at New York University.

CAROLINE WILLIAMS is an art historian, formerly of the School of Architecture and the Center for Middle East Studies at the University of Texas at Austin. She has written extensively on Islamic architecture, notably in the third edition of *Islamic Monuments of Cairo: A Practical Guide* (1985).

1

MAPPING THE WORLD OF NAGUIB MAHFOUZ

ADNAN HAYDAR AND MICHAEL BEARD

BEFORE THE NOBEL PRIZE in literature was established, how did readers validate the reputations of great writers? In our regimented century we persistently rely on the Swedish Academy to determine who the world-class imaginations are, at the rate of one a year. There must have been a time when we were left to our own devices on these questions. Chances are that readers in the great age of the novel did pretty much what Mahfouz's Egyptian readers did before 1988: looked for new books according to their subjects, talked about them with friends, and searched out writers whose style seemed congenial, however defined.

Naguib Mahfouz was a widely read, popular novelist in Egypt—indeed all over the Arabic-speaking world—long before his stock rose on the international market through external stimulus. Since receiving the 1988 Nobel Prize in literature, he has had the other kind of popularity too, the kind that enshrines a writer in translations and critical anthologies. This book bridges the gap between the regional importance Mahfouz has had since the 1950s and his significance as a world writer—to find the common terms behind the two varieties of popularity.

The first task is to acknowledge that before the Nobel Prize there were comparable cultural abysses to bridge. When Mahfouz speaks of himself in his Nobel acceptance speech as the child of two cultures, he underestimates; he is the child of many more. We acknowledge the importance of mixed cultures every time we spell his name in the accepted English transcription, which combines an indigenous dialect and French. In standard Arabic transcription, one would write Najib

Mahfuz, with long marks over the *i* and *u* and dots under the *h* and *z*. The standard Arabic *j* is compressed in Egyptian dialect (in a more archaic pronunciation) into a *g*. Thus we say "Gamal" rather than "Jamal" when pronouncing Jamal 'Abd al-Nasir, or Nasser. The *u* in Naguib (sign of a hard *g* in French orthography), like the *o* in Mahfouz (the French *ou* representing a long *u* sound), reminds us that the French were the first Europeans to leave their mark on Egypt, during Napoleon's expedition of 1798.

Comparable cultural mixing stands in our way as we cite Arabic titles and phrases. Mahfouz writes in modern standard Arabic about characters who are obviously thinking and speaking in a dialect that differs from the narrative voice not just in lexical items but also in pronunciation and syntax. Nor is it simply a matter of regional dialect. Should we transcribe the Arabic title translated as *Children of Gebelawi* by its classical Arabic equivalent, *Awlad haratina,* or should we reproduce the graphemes of spoken, cultivated Arabic (not just Egyptian) and call it *Awlad haritna?* We have chosen the former, with the understanding that total consistency may be impossible. We have decided, for instance, to call Mahfouz's neighborhood al-Gamaliyya rather than al-Jamaliyya, though most of our transcriptions are based on standard, rather than colloquial, Arabic. Compromise seemed our only alternative, since even within the Arabic context, his culture is multileveled. There is not a single, "real," originary Mahfouz, despite his fascination with roots and stability.

Mahfouz's range of narrative styles has become notorious. It includes the three romances in pharaonic settings; the realistic, or naturalistic, novels (particularly *The Trilogy* [*al-Thulathiyya,* 1956–57], for which he is most famous); the allegory of *Children of Gebelawi* (*Awlad haratina,* 1959); and the series of experimental short forms that followed.[1] Through these changes, Mahfouz's fascination with the urban setting, with the way that life in the Cairo streets molds a characteristic sensibility, has persisted. When he writes as a realist, the traditional sense of novelistic stability is linked with his experience of the city. When he experiments with surrealism, in "Taht al-mizalla" (1969), for instance (described in Mona Mikhail's contribution to this collection), he continues to rely on closely observed details of city life.

No extensive critical tradition exists that might help us understand the emotional commitments that underlie the choice of settings in literature, but Mahfouz makes us feel the need for one. For other contemporary writers, a conflict of settings has generated innovations in style. The dichotomy between village life—with its folkloric, exuberant modes of storytelling—and city life—with its routine and its bureaucratic style (and its impoverished modes of expression)—has generated what we call magic realism. For Gabriel García Márquez, a city is impersonal, the result of a nomadic experience in which various Latin urban settings are more or less interchangeable. The composite capital of Márquez's *Autumn of the Patriarch* has features borrowed from numerous centers of authoritarian power. The novel's vision is made distinctive by the composite voice of uninitiated observers, who constitute a Greek chorus of citizens cunningly woven into those famously long, protean, lyrical sentences.

Mahfouz's cities are, instead, particular, recognizable places, such as Cairo or Alexandria. They are not just any cities, and they are certainly not interchangeable settings. If one of his cities is perceived in opposition to something, its other is itself at a different moment in history. In characteristic dialectic of change, the city both is and is not its former self. The nostalgia behind it is not nostalgia for village life but a need for a stable focus—for the kind of stability and trust found in a solid setting—and for a dependable narrator's voice, which characterizes the realistic novel.

A comparable distinction sets Mahfouz apart from recent novelists writing elsewhere in the Arab world. Edward Said has characterized the writing that evolved in Lebanon during the last two decades as a response to a society in a state of disintegration.

> In some Arab countries you cannot leave your house and suppose that when and if you return it will be as you left it. For another, you can no longer take for granted that such places as hospitals, schools, and government buildings will function as they do elsewhere, or if they do for a while, that they will continue to do so next week. For a third, you cannot be certain that such recorded, certified, and registered stabilities in all societies—birth, marriage, death—will in fact be noted or in any way commemorated. Rather, most aspects of life are negotiable.[2]

The battered apartment blocks of Beirut stand behind the style of, say, Elias Khoury as distinctly as the Cairo skyline stands behind the stable contours of Mahfouz's writing. In Egypt "the Arabic novel has flourished especially well . . . because throughout all the turbulence of the country's wars, revolutions, and social upheavals, civil society was never eclipsed, its existence was never in doubt, was never completely absorbed into the State." (Said, xii)

What Heinrich Schliemann did for Troy, what James Joyce's readers could do for Dublin, Mahfouz permits us to do with Cairo. The dichotomy that drives Mahfouz's writing is within city walls. It juxtaposes disparate historical moments inside the city setting. At times the pathos of history is intense, as in his vision of Nasser's Egypt in *The Thief and the Dogs* (*al-Liss wa al-kilab,* 1961), in which a former convict considers the postrevolutionary world a betrayal of its own principles. But underlying that pathos we feel a complacency, not an unhealthy one, that trusts the stability of some current in the society. For example, in the recurring scenes at the Sufi *Sheikh*'s house where Said Mahran seeks shelter, some values of city life persist.

In Mahfouz's work the aesthetic of the city saturates the grain of his narratives. It is his subject; it also colors his style, whose unobtrusive stylelessness is a source of its distinction. James Joyce, away from Dublin, transforms the city of his youth into a series of polished, exact, and balanced scenes; his distant love for the city burnishes it, makes it glow. The will to aesthetics transforms Joyce's vistas of that colonial capital with an intensity that Mahfouz channels elsewhere. Mahfouz, writing from up close, takes for granted the physical specifics of the cityscape. His surroundings await the characters to breathe life into them. In *The Thief and the Dogs,* when Said Mahran looks at the spot where he was arrested four years earlier, the scene is dark until he gives us a meaning. "When I traverse this street . . . I swear I hate you . . . the windows of houses which tempt, particularly when they're empty, scowling walls with their peeling plaster [*al-judran al-mutajahhima al-muqashshafa*], and this strange lane, al-Sayrafi Lane, the dark memory where the thief stole and vanished in the blink of any eye. Woe to traitors."[3]

Figurative language attends the scene, but not with the leisure we would expect in a Joycean cityscape. The building's human meaning is attendant upon narrative motion. Said Mahran's vision makes it incidental; we push on past it into his memory. We might oppose to Joyce's aesthetics of the leisurely a Mahfouzian restlessness. Mahfouz's favored neighborhoods are those on an edge, where the city backs against its walls and graveyards or against an outcropping of rock, the Moqattam hills.

His narrative voice is likely to sound unproblematic and stable, but readers familiar with Mahfouz may start to hear in it something comparable to his landscapes—a search for complexity, for tangles and edges, for extremes of emotion and intensity; a voice that flirts with chaos and abuts on experiences inaccessible to language. The vehicle of that restlessness is an unornamented, colorless, plain style.

The passage cited above, for instance, contains a syntax without a prominent center, a list of impressions strung together by a feeling ("I swear I hate you"). The windows, the walls, and the lane continue the list of objects until the memory of his arrest materializes.

Such is not the poetic prose of, say, Jabra Ibrahim Jabra or Yahya Haqqi, who press the resources of the language in a different way. In comparison, Mahfouz's writing is indirect, submerged. Egyptian readers have observed that his use of modern standard Arabic, formal on the surface, evokes in its rhythms the colloquial language of Cairo. In his dialogues the Egyptian reader senses the spoken language underlying the words on the page; in his narrative style one feels a very traditional rhythm. By Mahfouz's own account he does not plan his style in advance.

> As for the history of my style, it is related to my personal experience. I choose my style, or my style chooses me, according to the particular situation. . . . I remember that I wrote *Midaq Alley* [Zuqaq al-Midaqq, 1947] the way I wrote it, though I had read Joyce, Kafka and Proust. Criticism was directed at me by Professors Badr al-Dib and Yusuf al-Sharidni, that I was writing in the style of the Nineteenth Century, but I found the courage to write *The Trilogy* in the same style because I felt that it was the style appropriate to the experience I was presenting. . . . After that, my feeling changed and I was no longer interested in the individual as an individual, possessed of particular characteristics in a particular time and place.[4]

The elements of style which matter to Mahfouz are visible in translation, but the impatient reader is likely to find his work boring. The pace speeds up and slows down without regard for the demands of suspense, restlessness that leaves narrative gaps. Even in a leisurely, full canvas like that of *Palace Walk* (*Bayn al-Qasrayn*, 1956), we start to wonder, as we pursue Amina's point of view for long, single-minded narrative stretches, what is happening to her son Karam. We follow the individual's point of view so insistently that it can become a prison. In the more compact style Mahfouz developed after *Children of Gebelawi*, as in *The Thief and the Dogs*, his narrative makes sudden gear changes. In chapter 7 Said Mahran plans and carries out his attempt on Ilish Sadra's life in one uncanny, concentrated page, which does satisfy the reader's sense of anticipation but makes us feel that we have missed something in the rush. Indeed we have because he turns out to have shot the wrong person.

This narrative restlessness and its attendant gaps contribute to the reader's sense of an unspoken level of meaning in Mahfouz's writing. Readers acknowledge this level when they speak of characters with an archetypal dimension and when they distinguish between realistic and symbolic novels. Mahfouz can seem enigmatic, but he can also provide his own clues. In the scene in *The Thief and the Dogs,* when Mahren tells his companion, the prostitute Nur, that he hates dogs but adds that he does not mean it literally, Mahfouz is also looking over Nur's shoulder and instructing the reader how his figurative language works.

> "Most Egyptians neither fear nor dislike thieves," said Said as he bit into a piece of meat. Several minutes passed in silence while they ate, then he added: "But they do have an instinctive dislike for dogs."
>
> "Well," said Nur with a smile, licking her fingertips, "I like dogs."
>
> "I don't mean that kind of dog." (115)

Nur's response, an anecdote about a dog she had at home when she was a child, tells readers they are privileged as interpreters of the narrative's internal logic. In the context of this novel, dogs have been used by the authorities to track Mahran down, as they will track him down again in the concluding scene. Dogs are the embodiment of an illegitimate regime, and we, who know the title of the novel, have an advantage over Nur. And yet the effect of such moments is not to distance us from her. Her mistake, after all, makes her more human than Mahran. Rather the reader is drawn to her naïveté, while Mahran bobs to the surface of the fictional world and floats somewhere half in and half out of the created environment, becoming less of a character in the process.

This self-conscious undercurrent of meaning is typical of Mahfouz's writing in the period following *The Trilogy.* These works feature a bifurcation of voices in which we feel that significance is layered, that the reader is invited to see patterns the characters only glimpse or (like Nur) miss altogether. It is traditional to call this style symbolic. Following Jameson, we might also call it, national allegory—with the understanding that it is not a style confined to writers of the Third World.[5] Elias Khoury, a Lebanese novelist who writes unmistakably from outside the stable settings of Mahfouz's Cairo, assesses Mahfouz's style as a struggle for an inclusive vision, a wider, more complete horizon. Khoury suggests a dialectic tension between two elements: Mahfouz's uncontested achievement of objective realism, "his meticulous portrayal of the accession to power of the petty and middle bourgeoisie . . . their philosophic, social and intellectual concerns";[6] and a challenge to go beyond portrayal, to acknowledge a wider ethical and international context—which peeks in even against Mahfouz's will, particularly in the works that follow the 1967 war.

We know that Mahfouz is truly sensitive to the world of politics. The revolution of 1919 is the central event behind *The Trilogy,* the revolution of 1952 fundamentally revised his conception of his mission as a writer, and the response to the 1967 defeat was a profound personal and professional crisis in his career. Khoury focuses on Mahfouz's response to that defeat, and in his analysis he gives us still another way to characterize Mahfouz's "symbolic" styles—as various attempts to reconcile the fragmented values that are the organizing principles of Mahfouz's vision (faith and reason, authority and innovation). The reconciliation, Khoury argues, is often premature, sometimes forced: "Are we confronting symbolic stories, and if so, why is movement absent to this extent? The symbols move by themselves, without revealing the relationships between them" (Khoury, 40). Khoury links the values that collide in the problematic period with class affiliations. Mahfouz's characters and situations are drawn from the classes he knows, and after 1967 the range of his familiarity may have become unrepresentative. The test case for Khoury was the then recently published *al-Hubb taht al-matar* (Love under the rain, 1973), in which the reader is to identify with the characters of the intellectual, petite bourgeoisie. For Khoury, meaning emerges through the use of parallel situations, accident (or fate, *qadr,* a key word since Mahfouz's first novel, *'Abath al-aqdar* [The absurdity of the fates], 1939), the distribution of narrative commentary and dialogue, and what Khoury calls the author's complicity (*tawatu'*) with the reader, in which a particular character is presented as exemplary and provides a privileged point of view. Through Mahfouz's techniques of identification, Khoury traces a pattern of sympathy with the nonaligned, the intellectuals who film the 1967 Israeli-Arab war rather than the classes who fight in it.

The response to the brute realities of 1967 is crucial. We cite Khoury because he writes from outside—as a novelist, as an observer of Arabic culture from a vastly different setting, as a committed participant in the political realm as well. As such, he is able to escape falling into parochial issues. In fact, all writing about Mahfouz may require some conscious act of analogous distancing to establish a context against which that massive corpus and its warring values can be measured. The authors in this collection suggest various ways to make that shift of perspective, to step back and see Mahfouz from a distance. In the process they engage in a dialogue without explicitly acknowledging one another's essays—with the exception of this one. Asfour implicitly distances himself from such readings as Khoury's; Miriam Cooke's assessment of the character of Nur in *The Thief and the Dogs,* in the course of her examination of Mahfouz's women, shines a feminist light on that book, which adds another dimension to what we have said above.

One context which allows the stepping back is the Nobel Prize itself, which provides a starting point for Salma Jayyusi, Roger Allen, and Sarah Lawall to rethink Mahfouz as a global phenomenon. Mona Mikhail argues for the relevance to Mahfouz of philosophical contexts grounded in existentialism, an existentialism not necessarily either Western or Eastern in its application. Michael Beard searches Mahfouz's characteristic scale of action for readers' responses that make the approach to Mahfouz problematic or difficult for Western readers.

Local backgrounds and perspectives on issues of particular concern to Egyptian culture and Arabic literary history illuminate Samia Mehrez's account of the social and political pressures that have shaped Mahfouz's career. Gaber Asfour's critical analysis of Mahfouz's commentators, similarly grounded in Egyptian contexts, surveys the local critical scene and demonstrates the widespread interest in Mahfouz that prevailed long before he received the Nobel Prize. Asfour's survey is particularly important because it introduces Western readers to specific issues of the Egyptian debate over Mahfouz's writing. The Egyptian magazine *Fusul,* from which Asfour's analysis is extracted, has been a major forum in Arabic for intellectual discourse on world literature. Asfour's analysis is as much a tentative theory of reading, based on criticism of Mahfouz, as it is a reaction to specific social and aesthetic issues raised by the novels.

Asfour's terminology presents distinct translational dilemmas, because it tests, in a new context, the relevance of critical tools familiar in Europe and the United States. Despite the pioneering work of such scholars as Magdi Wahba (whose *Dictionary of Literary Terms: English, French, Arabic* is indispensable for students in the field), there are still no widely accepted systems of equivalence between Arabic, English, and French critical terms. Western critical terminology is itself in flux. For instance, when Asfour speaks of *isqat* (rendered here as "reduction") or *istijwab* (rendered as "interrogation"), he is improvising terminology that may not necessarily become standard. In context, it will serve its purpose, like those striking images he has devised to describe the systems developed by Mahfouz's critics. Asfour reassesses the commonplaces on Mahfouz, laying them out visibly and exposing ideological habits and trends of thought behind the critical tradition. In other words, he gives shape to an otherwise amorphous and shadowy world of opinion.

The Egyptian novelist Gamal al-Ghitani, in an excerpt from his book *Najib Mahfuz yatadhakkar* (Naguib Mahfouz remembers, 1987), provides us with an evocative visual portrayal of the neighborhoods that have been Mahfouz's concrete inspiration. As Mahfouz's acknowledged disciple, al-Ghitani shows a Mahfouzian fascination with place—a trait visible in his famous novel *al-Zayni Barakat*.[7] Caroline Williams adds an additional historical perspective, mapping a background to the same places that inspired Mahfouz's works and al-Ghitani's personal memoires.

The process of stepping back can be achieved in the analysis of a single work as well. Fedwa Malti-Douglas studies a little-known, relatively recent, experimental work of Mahfouz to show the relevance of classical Arabic styles. Her study makes us aware of how little has been written about Mahfouz's recent work and reminds us that Mahfouz has never stopped building and retrofitting new structures onto his original novelistic plan.

Our task at this point is to step back. The Nobel Prize has afforded us the occasion for this dialogue. Let us grasp that occasion by allowing our contributors to guide us through Mahfouz's world, not just to celebrate his global recognition but, in Sarah Lawall's words, to provide "a space of exchange and shared inquiry."

2

THE ARAB LAUREATE AND THE ROAD TO NOBEL

SALMA KHADRA JAYYUSI

THE AWARD of the Nobel Prize to Naguib Mahfouz finally confirmed a truth that Arabs and non-Arabs had long ignored: that contemporary Arabic literature is of a high standard not only in the art of poetry, which critics worldwide have so far conceded, but also in the new and rapidly developing art of fiction. The idea that poetry is the only literary art in which Arabs excel has long been dominant and was shared by the Nobel Academy itself until 1985.

Historically, poetry has been the greatest verbal art of the Arabs. It is the medium that expresses the Arab spirit not only in its modern transformations but also in its stubborn continuities: the pervasive nostalgia, the passion for the heroic, the grand sweep of self-assertive rhetoric, the resistant spirit, and the persistent memories. These continuities have hindered poetry's true achievement of modernity in general, although some leading modernists, poets, and writers alike have insisted that all poets should embrace modernity and cut themselves loose from the inherited idiom and the persistent conventions of Arabic literature.

These hindrances were stronger in poetry than in fiction, although it has been the poets and their critics who have led the campaign for modernity, calling, with much loud rhetoric and argumentation, for an open form for Arabic poems. No matter how hard poets of the 1950s, 1960s, and most of the 1970s tried to emerge on the modernist scene, the great poetic tradition of their ancestors held them back. The Egyptian poet Salah ʿAbd al-Sabur, definitely the most modernist of the poets of the pre-1980s generation, wrote poetry that truly expressed the spirit of humankind in the latter half of the twentieth century, where heroism and rhetoric had very little place. When ʿAbd al-Sabur described people in the age of the machine as victims and as tools in the social order, he was not quite popular with poetry's general audience.

While all these gallant and vociferous efforts to modernize a well-rooted art of poetry went on—rhetorical assertions, self-exhibitionism, flagrant heroic demonstrations, medieval defiance, and affirmations in which the poet saw himself as prophet, seer, teacher, judge and master—the newly established art of the novel was quickly developing in the direction of a more modernist apprehension of experience. The novel was to express the spirit and to chart the experiences of modern man in the Arab world, proving its capacity for a greater freedom and for a closer affinity with the rhythms, temper, vision, moods, and realities of contemporary Arab life.

In its modern form, the novel is the product of the twentieth century. There is no room here to go into the history of Arabic fictional genres, such as *The Arabian Nights*, well known to all students of literature, and the *maqama* (assembly), a particularly Arab invention.

During the first few decades of the twentieth century, the Arabic novel was highly experimental, imitative, and unsure of itself. In its growth toward modern maturation, it depended on Western examples and on the intermittent efforts of a handful of experimentalists, mainly in Egypt. Because of its hesitant beginnings, it took more than half a century for the novel to become a serious genre employed by many writers and sought by a good-sized reading public. But during the last two or three decades a great burgeoning of the genre has occurred, with a sudden rise of many novelists all over the Arab world, from Morocco to Bahrain, some of whom are very good indeed.

Following the initial period of almost complete dependence on Western methods and styles, the Arabic novel has sought, and in good measure found, its own identity as an expression of a people whose particular experiences are different from those of peoples living in Western cultures and whose rich literary heritage can lend inspiration even to a fictional genre initially built, in its modern form, on Western models. This radically changed situation of the Arabic novel must be assessed against its arid background only three and a half decades removed from the contemporary scene. It will be realized then that this new wealth, this unprecedented activity, this supreme literary assertion, this fantastic explosion of the Arab fictional genius, this unbounded aventure, this flourishing productivity, this liberation, this courage, and this ambition are indebted fundamentally, and in no uncertain terms, to the genius and diligence of a single man: Naguib Mahfouz. He established the novel's inception in the Arab world; in the course of three decades, he transformed a hesitant, rather naïve art into the preeminent literary form of our time.

The movement, action, and moods of modern people in the Arab world are more adequately translated through the novel than through the epic or platform poems more suitable to a heroic age. Of course, many aspects of contemporary Arab life are still conducive to a poetic apprehension of experience: distortions of the rhythms of living, uprooting of human relations through external aggression, people wrenched by brutal force from their homes and land, whole cities and villages destroyed, freedom suffocated, terror and fear and anger, and heroism and revolt and strife. A silent conflict is in fact taking place between poetry as an answer to contemporary needs and an assertion of the traditional creative art of the Arabs and the novel as a new, encompassing, more realistic, more modernist expression of contemporary Arab life.

During the first half of this century, and in the prime of their own careers, various writers, mainly Egyptian, made a few limited attempts at the genre; some wrote a single, concise, autobiographical novel, as did al-ʿAqqad. Some wrote more, as did Taha Husayn. But to establish the novel as a major genre in Arabic required a dedication to, and a fascination with, the genre. It required a concentrated effort to conquer its yet untrammeled boundaries, to enter its domain armed with knowledge and artistic instinct, to preserve, yet at the same time invade, its sanctity, and to fling open doors to a familiarity hitherto unknown. The novel was established by the disciplined dedication of Naguib Mahfouz, who was prepared to sacrifice years of his life and creative energy to prove that it was time for the novel to become a major genre in Arabic literature and that it would do so at his hands. In him, a creative flame burned with unrelenting zeal.

In 1951, Mahfouz had already published eight novels, gradually establishing the form in Arabic. But the turning point in contemporary Arabic fiction was the publication of his famous *Trilogy,* a novel of 300,000 words in three volumes (*Bayn al-Qasrayn, Qasr al-shawq, al-Sukkariyya*), published in 1956 and 1957. *The Trilogy* is a saga describing the intimate life of a middle-class family in Cairo over three generations. It spans the time from near the end of World War I in 1917 through 1944. It not only compressed the time needed for the Arabic novel's inception as an established art form but also represented the most striking example of artistic courage yet known.

Mahfouz had spent six years writing it, working during his free time, for he kept a regular job all his live. *The Trilogy* was an immediate success. It was hailed as a great literary event, and Naguib Mahfouz was acclaimed as the greatest novelist in Egypt and the Arab world.

The Trilogy radically changed the whole balance of Arabic literature. The former intractability of the novel was broken, and the old timidity and sense of alienation that Arab creative talent had felt toward that medium were gone. Mahfouz proved its accessibility, and after *The Trilogy* many writers began writing novels, quickly learning the craft and realizing the possibility of a novelistic achievement. From this time on, the novel became an ever more desirable form. Although people still flock, with the same zeal as before, to listen to poets declaim their poetry, it is the novel that is now read on a large scale. Mahfouz made all this possible. Very rarely in the history of literature does a single writer herald the advent of a whole literary era and, at the same time, introduce a hitherto alienated medium as the preeminent literary genre of the future.

By making the novel accessible to millions of people, Mahfouz fulfilled a crucial role in changing their tastes, basic sensibilities, concentration, and emphasis by objectifying emotion, stilling undue passion, and painting life in slow motion. Mahfouz probes all aspects of Egyptian life through the accurate description of locales and characters. His description is illuminated by a universal outlook on the human condition. He reflects on the problems of time and change, human suffering, injustice, alienation, cruelty and loneliness, and corruption and stupor—on all aspects of the human condition, finding a meeting place in his work for the criminal and the saint. He always presents the other side of the coin, the other possible interpretation.

Mahfouz regards the novel as the poetry of the modern age, an age dominated by science and technology. During his career, which has stretched from 1939, and from the publication of his first novel, *ʿAbath al-aqdar* (The absurdity of the fates), to the present, he has passed through the stages that represent the historical changes characterizing the development of the novel as an art. Meanwhile, he read all the world masters: Flaubert, Stendhal, Shaw, Wells, Huxley, Tolstoy, Dostoyevsky, Chekhov, Mann, Kafka, Joyce, Proust, and many others. As one peruses the list of writers that Mahfouz read and enjoyed (he never liked Balzac or Dickens), one notes that his readings in Western fiction did not invite a haphazard, experimental career in which the influences of certain writers were reflected in his works according to his readings. Instead, his readings filtered through him to carry him over the historical stages of the novel, from romanticism to realism and then to the modern apprehension of experience. This movement tells us something about him and something about the nature of art; Mahfouz's talent is authentic, sound, and resistant to deviations.

The history of modern Arabic literature furnishes us with numerous examples of nonresistant talents that deviated from the natural course of literature into chaos and failure. But Mahfouz kept his literary instincts alive and vigilant. Because he was no heir to a great novelistic tradition in his own language, he had to learn the world tradition of the novel through his readings, superbly guided by an instinct that avidly absorbed artistic knowledge. About the nature of art, this progress tells us that artistic growth cannot be induced haphazardly. We cannot, for example, become symbolists before we have comprehensively passed through other stages of artistic development. It takes great, clear-sighted talent to find the right path through the numerous experiments in novel writing achieved by the great modern writers of the world.

The romantic stage of Naguib Mahfouz centered mainly on ancient Egypt. After *ʿAbath al-aqdar,* Mahfouz wrote two more historical novels: *Radubis* in 1943 and *Kifah Tiba* (Struggle of Thebes) in 1944. In the mid-1940s he turned to the contemporary scene, writing realistically about modern Cairo: *Khan al-Khalili* appeared in 1945 and *Zuqaq al-Midaqq* (Midaq Alley) and *al-Qahira al-jadida* (The new Cairo) in 1947. By then Mahfouz had embarked on his realistic phase, which culminated with *The Trilogy* in the mid-1950s. And with the appearance of his wonderful novel *al-Liss wa al-kilab* (The Thief and the Dogs) in 1961, the new modernist phase was established. He wrote several novels in this modernist vein, with an emphasis on modern techniques in dealing with characterization and the sequence of events; his progress is clearly marked in *Miramar* (1967).

His later novels rely heavily on symbolism. In several of them, the characters are social archetypes chosen, usually, from city life: government officials (symbols of bureaucracy), policemen (symbols of the coercive authority), prostitutes and servants (symbols of the exploited underdog), thieves and murderers (symbols of city corruption), and affluent middle-class characters conscious of their class status. Most of the heroes lack a healthy, constructive attitude toward society and thus reflect the great social upheavals of city life in Cairo at the time. Very often Mahfouz's characters are antiheroes caught in the mechanism of the social order and in the web of their own mistakes. In *The*

Thief and the Dogs, Said Mahran suffers a double betrayal on his release from prison: his wife has deserted him, and his old friend Rauf Alwan, a journalist, has abandoned his former radical stance regarding society and the rights of the downtrodden poor. Mahran becomes obsessed with avenging himself against those who have betrayed him, and his attempts turn him into a fugitive from the law, a fugitive still planning ways of taking revenge and killing the enemy. He is helped by a prostitute who loves him and gives him shelter and by a sympathetic holy man he knew as a boy. He revolves in vain around the pivots of love and faith, as he tries to flee a treacherous world in which even a thief and a murderer can be a victim. At the end, the prostitute who gives him love and the holy man who gives him pity become unattainable, and he is again left alone with the police dogs, who tear him apart.

His novel *Tharthara fawq al-Nil* (Chatter on the Nile) is a novel of the absurd (if we can accept the suggestion that the absurd need not be socially uninvolved, for there is a very deep social critique running through the novel). One can easily feel the influence of Kafka, and probably of Jean Genet and Beckett, in Mahfouz's superb treatment of the deadlock in the deeply alienated life-style of the middle-class city dwellers who frequent a houseboat *('awwama)* on the Nile. Mahfouz delineates the thinking and activity, or rather inactivity, of a group of pseudointellectuals who can find no redeeming hope in the existing system and seek oblivion, sedation, and solace by smoking hashish, practicing sex, and chattering, with a certain amount of a detachment, about the various aspects of contemporary Arab life. Every night they meet on the houseboat, where an ageless servant looks after them and procures both narcotics and women. Their female compatriots are exactly like them, lacking any healthy, constructive attitude toward society. Sex is given and taken freely, but it is devoid of love and tenderness, exchanged almost with ennui. Ennui is indeed a basic attitude in the novel, and the whole work is a magnification of human impotence.

Many of Mahfouz's characters are alienated, either because of their acts or because of their own frame of mind. But they differ from the alienated poets of the same period because their alienation is egocentric and cool and does not embody the anger and social commitment found in the poets. The latter are invariably concerned with society rather than the private individual, but a number of Mahfouz's characters are asocial or antisocial.

Unlike the characters of *Chatter,* however, not all his characters, even when alienated, withdraw from the social world. Many of them are looking for something. In *al-Tariq* (The path), the main male character, Sabir, is looking for a father whom he has never seen and whom he never finds. In *The Thief and the Dogs,* Said Mahran is looking for a shelter where he can find safety and peace. ʿUmar in *al-Shahhadh (The Beggar)* and ʿIssa in *al-Summan wa al-kharif (Autumn Quail)* are looking for a solution to big questions. There is always a quest, but it is almost never realized. Even the virtuous, innocent village heroine in *Miramar* (one of the few village characters Mahfouz introduces to us) does not reach her goal, and we see her at the end of the novel leaving the hotel where she had been a servant and had known disappointment in love, to look again for her future. Although the novel ends on an optimistic note, the quest is still unrealized. *Chatter on the Nile* symbolizes the end of all questing. Even the woman journalist who comes in quest of information is corrupted by the characters of the boat and loses interest in her objective. Time has stopped completely in this novel. Only the accident that kills the innocent, unknown pedestrian brings any action, and that action is negative. In deciding to go to the police about the accident, Anis Zaki carries out not an act of conscience but an act of revenge intended to destroy even the static, uninvolved world of the houseboat where he and his friends had found sedation and false peace.

In these novels, Mahfouz does not make statements that portray his own view of life. The meaning he is trying to convey to the reader is hidden behind the experience he delineates. The heroes in *The Thief* and *The Path* are antisocial and live dangerously. The hero in *The Beggar* tries all kinds of experience and eventually rejects society, flouting bourgeois standards and expectations.

What, then, is Mahfouz's stance toward society in these later novels? He primarily draws pictures of social and individual behavior in particular circumstances, such as alienation, loss, betrayal, and failure. His highly controlled objectivity helps him to give full expression to his characters and themes as he imagines them enacted on the social scene, and he fanatically avoids adding a sympathetic note to his characterizations. Although many of his characters do not arouse our sympathy or affection, they nevertheless increase our consciousness by their actions. In some of these novels *(The Path, The Thief,* and *The Beggar),* Mahfouz opens our eyes more to the human condition in its universal aspect than to its particularity in present-day Egyptian society. Even in the novels that focus on Egyptian experience, such as *Miramar* and *Autumn Quail,* a universal dimension shines through.

The work of Naguib Mahfouz is characterized by an utter lack of sentimentality, mawkishness, and verbiage and by a passion for justice and harmony, although the harmony is often shattered by the impossibilities of contemporary life. In an age of frenzy, Mahfouz has provided a powerful equilibrium in the literary field, introducing poise and a capacity for pity and fear for others, for those many characters in his novels who never find a solution to the dilemmas of their lives.

Among all the major writers of the Arab world, Naguib Mahfouz is the only one I have never met. He is a private man and has kept his personal life in prosaic anonymity, shunning the growth of any legends around his name. I think that everyone respects this dignity. Whatever Mahfouz wanted to say to the world, he said unobtrusively through his characters. He never played any games with his ideas. One cannot help having the highest respect for him, his work, his persistence, his honesty, his artistic and moral integrity, his unrivaled discipline, his humility and unassuming manner, his respect for his reader's sensibility and intelligence, and above all his civilizing role in contemporary Arabic literature. The word *pioneer* is perhaps too weak to describe that role. He engineered the novel's inception in Arabic as a major art form and established it as an ever-thriving continuity. Without him, the history of contemporary Arabic literature would have to be written in a completely different way.

What events led the Arts Committee of the Nobel Academy to select Mahfouz as the recipient of the 1988 prize? Considerable activity took place, especially in 1988, to draw the attention of the committee to the Arabs. Some of Morocco's most prominent ministers and high-ranking men made a concentrated effort to nominate Morocco's well-known thinker Muhammad Aziz Lahbabi and acquired signatures on the nomination form from distinguished representatives of numerous cultural institutions all over the world. Many such approaches have been made to the Academy. The Lund Conference in October 1984—planned by the University of Lund and the Swedish Institute in Stockholm (whose main aim is the dissemination of Swedish culture), with the energetic help of Mrs. Sigrid Kahle—was organized not only to bring together a number of well-known Swedish and Arab poets and critics but also to attract the attention of the Academy to Arabic literature, particularly to Arabic poetry. Mrs. Kahle, the daughter of the well-known Swedish Orientalist Henryk Nyberg, himself a member of the Academy, had involved herself, heart and mind, in a campaign to introduce Arabic poetry to the Swedes and to help remedy the neglect which the Arabs had so far received from the Academy. She cooperated fully with the Institute and the University of Lund in the preparation for the conference, and with the help of two young Tunisian poets, Muhammad al-Ghuzzi and al-Munsif al-Wahaybi, who assisted with the Arabic, she translated selections from Arabic poetry into Swedish and selections from the poetry of the famous Swedish poet and member of the Arts Committee at the Academy, Ostën Sjöstrand, into Arabic. Mrs. Kahle's translations were presented to the participants at the Lund conference, and translations from Arabic poetry into English were presented by the Project of Translation from Arabic Literature (PROTA).

Clearly, at the time of the Lund conference, the concentration of the interested Swedes was not on Arabic fiction but on Arabic poetry, of which there were then few translations in the Academy's library. There were very few translations from the other genres as well, as Muhammad al-Ghuzzi, al-Munsif al-Wahaybi, and I discovered when we visited the Academy's library in Stockholm before the conference. The few cards in the archives representing Arabic culture could not have given the members of the Arts Committee any genuine clue to the fine status of the contemporary Arabic literature. At the time, the Academy accepted the idea that fiction was not among the genres mastered by contemporary Arabs. This I personally knew from the chief librarian of the Academy, Mr. Anders Ryberg. During the ensuing years, however, the Academy must have become convinced of the high status of contemporary Arabic fiction and of the fine contribution of Mahfouz.

What were the main qualities in Mahfouz which supported his nomination? We have first of all to think of the recent accessibility of some of his work to the Academy. Mahfouz himself said that the appearance of his *Trilogy* in French must have been a factor. Moreover, more books on Arabic fictional genres had been published since 1985. When I visited the Academy on December 12, 1988, two days after the prize ceremonies in Stockholm, Mr. Ryberg led me to a hall where the translated works of the new laureate, Mahfouz, were put on display; but side by side with them were other works of and about Arabic literature. Included were the two large PROTA publications, *Modern Arabic Poetry: An Anthology* (1987) and *Literature of Modern Arabia: An Anthology* (1988); Roger Allen's book entitled *The Arabic Novel: An Historical and Critical Introduction* (1982); and the second volume of my critical work, *Trends and Movements in Modern Arabic Poetry* (1978, acquired by the Academy in 1988); and several other works. I feel that the Lund conference must have sharpened the Academy's interest in contemporary Arabic literature, and some of us have become a little more outgoing and have made sure that the Academy had the new books dealing with Arabic literature. But these efforts would have been to no avail if the qualities of Mahfouz had not imposed themselves on the minds of the Arts Committee members.

In his opening speech, Professor Lars Gyllensten, chair of the board of the Nobel Foundation, emphasized the importance of a writer vigorously and actively pursuing his career, naming Eliot and Schopenhauer as two fine examples of this kind of dedication, a dedication celebrated and attributed to Mahfouz by Professor Sture Allén, permanent secretary of the Swedish Academy, and member of the Nobel Committee for Literature in his address on Mahfouz at the ceremonies.

On more than one occasion, the academy noted that Mahfouz "has formed an Arabian narrative art that applies to all mankind." In that statement, the academy signaled two important achievements at once: the novel's inception in Arabic, and Mahfouz's capacity to treat his subject in a manner that rises to the level of universality. Another attribute mentioned by Professor Allén is Mahfouz's variety and versatility. Standing on the wide stage of the great Music Hall in Stockholm, Professor Allén addressed Mahfouz, who was watching the ceremonies via satellite in Cairo:

> Mr. Mahfouz, your rich and complex work invites us to reconsider the fundamental things in life. Themes like the nature of time and love, society and norms, knowledge and faith recur in a variety of situations and are presented in thought-provoking, evocative and clearly daring ways. And the poetic quality of your prose can be felt across the language barrier. In the prize citation you are credited with the forming of an Arabian narrative art that applies to all mankind. On behalf of the Swedish Academy I congratulate you on your eminent literary accomplishments.

Another quality that the academy upholds, reiterated by Professor Gyllensten in his opening speech, is that the work of its laureates should "confer the greatest benefit on mankind." Mahfouz worked relentlessly toward opening people's minds to the human condition in his country. He always stood on the side of the common man and against all the forces that usurp his freedom, dignity, and happiness.

He never meandered in his ideas, and the changes he underwent were only the normal changes that happen to intellectuals during times of huge upheavals and great stress. More importantly, despite his critique of stagnation and backwardness, he held an evenhanded outlook toward cultures in general and never demonstrated an inordinate disrespect for his own culture. This kind of dignity appeals to intellectuals who must assess a writer for the most important cultural prize in the world. While self-criticism is a sign a maturity, courage, and dignity, there is always a clear line between rebellion against, and rejection of, coercive religious, social, and political establishments and rejection of one's whole cultural identity.

Mahfouz's humility, his aloofness and great dignity, his almost fanatical rejection of self-exhibitionism, and his intellectual and artistic honesty—all of which have had a civilizing influence on his contemporaries in the Arab world—must have also impressed the committee greatly. For these are the qualities of the true mind and heart. The Nobel Prize is not given for merely one aspect of a writer's genius but for his whole *oeuvre*. And in the case of the 1988 laureate, it was not given to Egypt alone but to the whole Arab world.

3

NAGUIB MAHFOUZ AND THE NOBEL PRIZE

Reciprocal Expectations

SARAH LAWALL

THE EXPECTATIONS AND REACTIONS surrounding the award of the 1988 Nobel Prize to Egyptian novelist Naguib Mahfouz have drawn attention to the ambiguous connotations of a prize that is supposed to mark both global fame and authentication of a writer's work as "world literature." The geographic globe in its entirety and the essence of human experience represented in language—such ambitious universal horizons narrow uncertainly when the award is seen as a belated recognition of Arab culture or if the Nobel Prize is accepted as a rite of passage for a Third World writer. What cultural expectations are in play, what criteria are used, what ideas of literature are implied, and what understanding exists of the way a literary text operates?

The Nobel Committee confirms a writer's fame, consecrate a writer's work in a noble posture, and suggest ways in which it should be read. Mahfouz, for example, is conveyed simultaneously as the voice of Arab culture and as a developer of the Western tradition of the novel, an Egyptian Dickens or Balzac (two comparisons that have been repeated in the popular press). The glory of being received into the canon of world-class literature must carry some risk if it entails the stamp of definition along with the imprint of approval and if the spate of reprintings that follows an award tacitly provides a framework and guidelines for how the writer's work should be read.[1] An initial difference celebrated as the recognition of Third World literature becomes, if not harder to maintain, at least harder to communicate.

Clearly, the Nobel Prize is recognized around the globe—we specify the audience as those who can read and who value a particular "civilized" and universalist literary tradition. Inside this tradition, however, we should not allow *global* as a geographic term to be substituted for the infinitely richer and more ambiguous word *world.* The implications of the Nobel Prize are that a *world-class* writer has been identified, someone whose work has meaning for readers at any point on the globe because of the common humanity that unites us all. This claim is a claim of value; it draws upon its unique tradition and definitions of "common" human experience, and brings with it its own canonized way of asking "essential" questions.

Even if we use the more secure term *globe,* it is still necessary to ask where the global vantage point is and who decides what is "reaching out" and what is a "central" perspective. This difficulty has not been ignored by the Nobel Committee, which has recognized from its very first years the awkwardness of speaking for the whole world. Clearly, the horizons of global recognition shift according to the position of the viewer. Studies by the Dutch comparatist Brandt Corstius and the French Etiemble have shown how the canon of world literature varies from region to region, according to who is deciding what is world class.[2]

Commenting several years ago on the influence of location in awarding prizes, Wole Soyinka asked, "If Africa creates a prize similar to the Nobel, will she wait eighty years to bestow it on a European?"[3] Northern perspectives also vary. Responses to the election of Rabindranath Tagore in 1913, reported in the *New York Times,* demonstrated "surprise and resentment that Occidental writers were passed over in favor of a 'Hindu bard' with 'a name hard to pronounce'." But in Ireland the *Irish Citizen* drew its own conclusions from Tagore's mysticism and rejoiced in an award that vindicated the traditions of Irish literature as represented by the country's native son William Butler Yeats.[4] Regional perspectives are conspicuous, and they do not disappear: after Mahfouz's election, the German magazine *Der Spiegel* complained that a Nobel Committee of old men (ages fifty-four to eighty-four), in their "obscure urge to open up new regions," had repeated its whimsy of two years previous by going outside Europe again while such greats as Friedrich Dürrenmatt, Graham Greene, and Günter Grass still awaited their prize.[5]

In what map projection, with what centering, does Mahfouz appear? The broader geographical range of recent prizes indicates the Nobel jury's desire to encompass the globe, but the direction of this expansion calls into question the centered geometry of the jury's judgment. If a Nobel vantage point is tacitly accepted, the jury's aim for global recognition carries the same Eurocentricity that the award of the prize to non-Western writers was intended to eliminate. Archimedes wanted to find a place for his lever so that he could move the world, but history does not record that he found it in northern Europe.

In a less geographic sense, however, *world* points toward the imaginary world of the writer, the constructed world of the work, the world as it is perceived by the reader, or the referential network set into play as readers impose their familiar worlds on the imaginary horizons of the text. The literary world is not easy to get at or to define. We know that intertextual complications draw out meaning in a series of referential networks. The multiplicity and change that characterize experience (and, according to philosopher Hans-Georg Gadamer, define the concept of worldview)[6] are not easily captured in critical theory or in any one pattern of reading. Moreover—and this element is particularly visible in cross-cultural interpretations—any given reading necessarily tends to redefine a work's otherness in accordance with the reader's own needs and experience.

Through its very principles of selection, the Nobel Prize suggests a particular aim and manner of reading, with its committee seeking works of universal scope and essential humanity, no matter how rooted the writer may be in a specific cultural tradition. According to the statutes of the Nobel Foundation, which cite the will itself, the literature prize is to be given to "the person who shall have produced in the field of literature the most outstanding work of an idealistic tendency."[7] The Nobel interpretation of the word *idealistic* (the Swedish *idealisk*) has been much debated. William Riggan prefers to translate *idealisk* as "ideal" in "The Swedish Academy and the Nobel Prize in Literature: History and Procedure." He notes that both *ideal* and *idealistic* exist in Swedish and English, and that "the word used in Nobel's will is *idealisk* (ideal) and not *idealistisk* (idealistic) . . . widely varying interpretations have been offered."[8] *Ideal* certainly allows for a wider range of literary achievement, and Nobel's friend Mittag-Leffler reported that "by *idealisk* he meant anything that comprehends a polemic or critical attitude toward religion, royalty, marriage, or social organization in general." According to Lars Gyllensten, " '*idealisk* is about as bewildering in Swedish as *ideal* is in English' (letter of 1 April 1981),"[9] which suggests that any investigator of the Nobel *idealisk* will be faced with patterns of interpretation.

Since Alfred Nobel's will specified that the prizes were to be awarded to people who had, during the preceding year, "conferred the greatest benefit on mankind" through their work, it is not surprising that *idealisk* was interpreted in such a way as to reward positive and visibly constructive views. The committee was aware, for example, that Nobel had detested Émile Zola's work and (like many of his generation) considered it crude and degrading. Although Zola's name was presented to the committee, there was no chance that he would be awarded the prize for an *idealisk* work of literature. Tolstoy himself was rejected in 1902, not because his novels were not good literature but, in the words of one of the jurists, because in his other works "he has condemned all forms of civilization and urged instead a primitive mode of life divorced from all forms of higher culture. . . . Confronted by such expressions of narrow-minded hostility to all forms of civilization, one feels dubious."[10] Rabindranath Tagore's victory over literary historian Émile Faguet followed a recommendation that "his poetry contains nothing debatable or disturbing, nothing that is vain, worldly or petty, and if ever a poet may be said to possess the qualities which entitle him to a Nobel prize, he is precisely the man. . . . We have finally discovered an idealistic writer of really great stature."[11] Thomas Hardy never overcame his novels' reputation for a "deep pessimism and inexorable fatalism" that were incompatible with the spirit of the prize.[12] Even if the definition of *ideal* or *idealistic* has become less narrow, the Nobel citations continue to mention the national writer's universal significance, and most Nobel lectures respond to a presumed global audience and speak in broad terms about human concerns.

Such an image of global significance and idealized world-class standing invites readers to interpret the Nobel texts on a level where lesser distinctions disappear, as though the Nobel collection reached a degree of achievement so powerful that its literature must always be read in roughly the same way. Prizewinners themselves—including those most aware of their local circumstances—tend to develop the same worldview—with its framework of national essences, Eastern and Western cultures, and common humanity—as part of their opportunity to reach a worldwide audience.

Many writers have taken the occasion of the award to speak as representatives of regional culture inside the world community or to speak in the name of a common constituency that goes beyond regional boundaries. The overtones are generally those of the celebrated (European) Romantic notion of world history or world literature—the vision in Herder and Goethe of a great concert of nations, of a conversation among civilized men from different lands. Surely this sense of representativeness is one of the more familiar and more important elements in the history of the prize. George Seferis (1963) described his predecessors in Greek literature and accepted the award in the name of Greek culture past and present.[13] Gabriel García Márquez (1982) used the prize lecture to describe the political and economic misery of Latin America and to appeal for worldwide support: "I dare to think that it is this outsized reality, and not just its literary expression, that has deserved the attention of the Swedish Academy of Letters."[14] Joseph Brodsky (1987) saw himself not as an Occidental but an "accidental" writer, representing the tragic generation of Auschwitz and Stalin's repression. Elias Canetti (1981) celebrated the grand tradition of European culture through the example of four modern German writers. Mahfouz said, "The Arab world also won the Nobel with me."[15] Czeslaw Milosz (1980) accepted the prize

> on behalf of all men and women for whom I am not so much an individual as a voice, and someone who belongs to them. First of all, I think of those who cherish the Polish language and literature, wherever they live, in Poland or abroad; I also think of my part of Europe . . . and particularly my thoughts go to a country where I was born, Lithuania. Moreover, since I have lived a long time in exile, I may be legitimately claimed by all those who had to leave their native villages and provinces because of misery or persecution and to adapt themselves to new ways of life; we are millions all over the Earth, for this is a century of exile.[16]

Jean-Paul Sartre, refusing the Nobel Prize in 1964, commented that if it had been awarded during the Algerian war he would have accepted the prize because it could have been associated with a political cause whose representative he then was.[17]

It is not always easy to decide who represents whom, however, or to have one writer represent a whole continent or culture. The debate was strong over Soyinka's prize,[18] and discussions of Naipaul and Salman Rushdie often show little sympathy for the writers' divided allegiance or ambivalent representation. Yet as more and more writers express the nonhomogeneous worlds of cross-cultural experience and the difficulties of living inside clashing layers of internationality, it will be interesting to see the effect on definitions of representativeness—both local and universal—and to interrogate what representation means both to the society that selects and awards and to the culture that accepts representation.

The question of representativeness is not new to Nobel deliberations. It used to be phrased in terms of "major" or "minor" writers and directed at small European countries, such as Finland or Greece, in contradistinction to their larger siblings, Germany, France, and England. An important address in 1900 by the director of the Swedish Academy, Esaias Tegnér, responded to public debates about the viability of the awards and took up the issue of biased selections. He concluded that the Swedish perspective was neutral and objective because Sweden was a small country and out of the mainstream—that the view from the margin was truer than that at the center. "If there are drawbacks to being a small nation situated on the outskirts of the civilized world, there are also certain advantages. . . . A person living on the border of a province is better able to decide which peaks inside it are the highest than an observer standing amidst the mountains themselves. In a different sense, this is also true of us. And in the fact that we are a small nation we have, in a way, a safeguard against partiality which the big nations lack."[19] You may note the implied center of civilization if Sweden is on the margin. I do not know whether it is amusing or alarming to hear Tegnér referring to Sweden as situated on the "outskirts of the civilized world," but this image of the Nobel jury as situated in a special removed location is recapitulated ambiguously in Mahfouz's Nobel lecture.[20]

For Mahfouz, Sweden is not so much the "outskirts of the civilized world" as its center—the literate representative of Western society as an "oasis of culture and civilization" to which others make appeal and are occasionally admitted. At the same time, however, Mahfouz invokes the other civilizations still alive in him as an Arab writer: "I am the son of two civilizations that at a certain age in history have formed a happy marriage. The first of these, seven thousand years old, is the pharaonic civilization; the second, one thousand four hundred years old, is the Islamic one." Several images of civilization overlap in Mahfouz's lecture; and even if they are occasionally at odds, they illustrate the themes of universality and local roots, of art and humanity, and of the artist as representative figure that are familiar from preceding Nobel awards. There is the civilization of humanity, where the leader is to be measured by "the universality of his vision and his sense of responsibility towards all humankind"; the civilization of art, literacy, and intellect, where authors of sufficient merit are admitted to the company of the best international writers, [21] and where "intellectuals ought to exert themselves to cleanse humanity of moral pollution"; and the final, most developed image of a scientific or "developed world," the "civilized world" inhabited by "the able ones, the civilized ones" who are responsible for the miseries of Africa and the

West Bank, as opposed to the presumably less civilized Third World from which the "moans of mankind" resound into the oasis.

The Egyptian Mahfouz, speaking as one of the "children of the third world," pleads: "Be not spectators to our miseries. You have to play therein a noble role befitting your status. From your position of superiority you are responsible for any misdirection of animal, or plant, to say nothing of man, in any of the four corners of the world." Mahfouz's stance is a strangely ironic mixture that turns various notions of world and civilization against each other so as to interrogate the whole. It is ambiguous because Mahfouz clearly privileges the notion of cultural oasis at the same time that he attacks it. Thus the only thing of which we can be sure is that the posture of humility is a complicated and effective strategic approach.

Perhaps the jubilation over a Third World writer's receipt of the prize should be accompanied by a certain interrogative stance. One would thus scrutinize not only the foundation of any prize claiming global status but, more importantly, the complicated signifying practices, claims of representation, and subtly offered schemas of value that are bound up in the award itself and to which the prizewinners tacitly respond. It is the old question of canon, seen cross-culturally: of who can fit into the canon, whose canon it is, and who knows how to read it; of the necessary complications of cultural identity and representation to the other (which becomes, in circular fashion, representation to the self).

Finally, we might use the occasion of Mahfouz's lecture to move beyond the always-debated question of the intrinsic value of the Nobel prize as a clue to an author's worth. Perhaps it is time to describe the Nobel Prize—or any prize—not as a reward or a mark of distinction (even though it is) but as a *point of attention*, a space of exchange and shared inquiry in which the writer's work focuses our attention in two ways. First, by turning attention inward and provoking a vertical dialogue inside the writer's own tradition about art, representativeness, and cultural values, especially as they are related to awards that "open international doors . . . for [in this case] Arab literature." Second, by developing a lateral dialogue between cultures, dialogue that entraps the whole question of self and other on a shifting but common ground of different traditions and value systems. In this way, the much-sought-after prize could work as a speculative instrument rather than as a stamp of approval.

4

NAGUIB MAHFOUZ AND THE ARABIC NOVEL

The Historical Context

ROGER ALLEN

> Naguib Mahfouz is acknowledged throughout the entire Arab world as the great pioneer in the mature Arabic novel, and he has achieved that distinction by dint of sheer hard work, tenacity, patience in adversity (both political and medical), and a disarming humility. He is recognized as the Arab world's leading writer of fiction because he has . . . turned the novel into an accessible and accomplished medium. His is a nomination which, the normalities of Arab politics aside, would be welcomed throughout the Arab world.[1]

UNTIL I REACHED the end of that quotation, one could be forgiven for imagining that I was commencing an encomium of this year's Nobel Laureate in literature. However, it comes from an article, "Arabic Literature and the Nobel Prize," which I wrote at the request of the editors of *World Literature Today* in October 1987. They had been asked by the Nobel Committee to repeat a project first done a decade or so earlier, namely a survey of Nobel Laureates over recent years compared with writers from other cultures which had not been represented thus far. My article appeared in a special issue of the journal entitled "The Nobel Prizes in Literature 1967–1987: A Symposium," published in March 1988. That issue was sent to the Nobel Committee in Stockholm and was a small part of the evidence at their disposal in making their colossally difficult and controversial annual decision. It also seems clear that the recent publication in French of the first two parts of Mahfouz's much discussed *The Trilogy* was also an important factor in the Nobel Committee's decision. In any case, Naguib Mahfouz, an Arab novelist from Egypt, *is* the 1988 Nobel Laureate in Literature, and we can all rejoice in the award on behalf of Mahfouz himself (although, based on contact with him during a visit to Egypt in January 1989, I wonder whether he will survive the amount of attention he is currently receiving), of Egypt and the entire Arab World with its many litterateurs, and of Arabic literature studies in both the Middle East and the West.

It is the last of these categories which provides the focus of the present study. Clearly, the Nobel Prize places its winners into a fairly exclusive literary canon where the company includes Tagore (1913), Anatole France (1921), Yeats (1923), Mann (1929), Galsworthy (1932), Pirandello (1934), Pearl Buck (1938), Gide (1947), Eliot (1948), Faulkner (1949), Churchill (1953), Hemingway (1954), Camus (1957), Pasternak (1958), Steinbeck (1962), Sartre (1964), Beckett (1969), Solzhenitsyn (1970), and Márquez (1982). I hasten to point out that even this list omits several significant names. It is an exclusive group indeed, but the complete list of winners of the Nobel Prize in Literature also includes Rudolf Eucken (1908), Roger Martin du Gard (1937), and Halldor Laxness (1955). While it may be purely my own ignorance which makes the second group sound less familiar than the first, I would like to suggest at the very least that some of these names resonate on the stage of world literature to a considerably lesser degree than others. Thus, while the Nobel Prize award certainly affords a temporary position in the limelight, it equally clearly does not *guarantee* an enduring world focus; factors other than this clear certification of literary merit play a role. So where does this leave us with regard to Naguib Mahfouz and Arabic fiction?

Such a literary-historical question presents us with at least one major dilemma. I can insert at this point that a writer such as F. W. Bateson might here comment that, since literary history *is* a "non-subject *par excellence*," it serves me right. But a scholar such as Northrop Frye is at hand to provide the comforting thought that, while we should not attempt to use literary history to prescribe, all humans like to use categories and organization to clarify, if not to classify. The primary issue here is, of course, the lack of historical perspective; Mahfouz is still writing. While the Nobel Prize is awarded to a living writer, Mahfouz will not merit an entry in the first printing of the second edition of the *Encyclopedia of Islam* precisely because he is still living; and unfortunately they have already passed *Ma* in assigning articles; "you win some, you lose some."

In a radio interview with colleague critics in Saudi Arabia, both Trevor Le Gassick and I expressed a certain diffidence in discussing Mahfouz's works written since 1970, a point on which Fatma Moussa-

Mahmoud picked up in a persuasive presentation at the series of panels on Mahfouz held in conjunction with the annual Cairo International Book Fair. How are we to evaluate the stream of fictional works which Mahfouz has published in the last twenty years since the 1967 June War? I should make it clear at this point that I have chosen the year 1970 as *my* dividing point so as to include within my first grouping the series of short stories written in the years immediately after the June War. For me at least, it is *al-Maraya* (Mirrors, Serialized 1971, published 1972) which marks the beginning of a new phase in Mahfouz's literary career. For it is in that work that I detect a significant narrowing of the narrative distance between the speaker in the literary work and the author himself; it is almost as if, within the recriminative atmosphere of the early Sadat era (marked by the publication of several sensational accounts of the Nasser years), Mahfouz had decided to emerge from his carefully crafted ironic distance and enter the sociopolitical fray for himself. I am, of course, aware that many critics have identified—quite rightly—separate phases in his earlier writing career, based on an analysis of both themes and techniques, but what I am addressing here is the larger issue of the modes of evaluation of his total oeuvre. More recently, it seems to me, we find a concentration on particular issues of local Egyptian political and cultural life. I would like to emphasize immediately two points: first, that such a posture has tended to reflect the broader political situation as far as Egypt is concerned, most particularly since the signing of the Camp David Accords; and second, that it is Mahfouz's perfect right as a creative writer to focus on whatever subjects he chooses. However, what I personally miss in these works is that broader philosophical vision which was so characteristic of his earlier novels, though many may wish to see that too as a product of certain historical moments. A further literary-historical point which needs to be emphasized here is that in my opening quotation I used the term *pioneer* to describe Mahfouz, a status that I propose to investigate later in this chapter. On the basis which he has provided, a younger generation of Arabic novelists throughout the Arab world has begun to write in this complex genre and to do so in startlingly experimental ways: one need only mention the Algerian al-Tahir Wattar; the Palestinian Emile Habibi; al-Tayyib Salih from the Sudan; Jabra Ibrahim Jabra also from Palestine and now resident in Iraq; and from Saudi Arabia via Jordan, Iraq, and France ʿAbd al-Rahman Munif. To this list must also be added the name of the Egyptian Gamal al-Ghitani with his creative use and parodying of historical and religious source texts. In treatment of point of view, use of time, psychological insight, invocation of traditional sources and style—for example, combinations of prose and poetry—these writers (and many others) have followed the lead prepared for them by "the master." They have experimented with the novel, that literary genre which, without experiment and change, ceases to fulfill, I would suggest, its primary generic purpose.[2] During these years Mahfouz has expressed his opinions, in both newspaper articles and fictional forms on issues confronting his country. A particular focus has been his antipathy to Sadat and his policies, most especially *infitah* (economic "opening up of markets") and its drastic effects on the poor. He has watched as the rich classes have become ever richer and the poor ever poorer (in the latter case leading to food riots), while the middle class has been torn in two in its attempts to pull itself out of the uncomfortable middle position between the other two. In this frenzied attack of the Western suburban ethic of "keeping up with the Joneses," there have been winners and losers. A particular focus of loss has been the crisis in housing, well captured in Mahfouz's story, *al-Hubb fawq hadbat al-haram* (*Love on Pyramid Plateau,* 1979). No one would wish to doubt either the veracity of Mahfouz's vision in these works nor the depth of his frustration. Indeed, during this period, he and a number of other writers have also felt the pressures of political opprobrium (he was temporarily removed from the ranks of the Writers' Union in the early 1970s, along with Tawfiq al-Hakim, Yusuf Idris, and Lewis ʿAwad) and of the increasingly forceful presence of fundamentalist Islamic elements (e.g., the temporary banning of *The 1001 Nights*). However, in writing these works it seems to me that Mahfouz has tended to make direct use of subjects and techniques which have provided only the building materials for earlier works. There is, for example, the focus on the cultural sector and the multinarrator technique in *Afrah al-qubba* (1981; *Wedding Song,* 1989); a concentration on generations, in particular, the thug gangs in both *Hikayat haratina* (1975; *Fountain and Tomb,* 1988) and *Malhamat al-harafish* (The epic of the riff-raff, 1977); and the use of an alphabetized listing of characters in *Hadith al-sabah wa-al-masa'* (Morning and evening talk, 1987). There is even a return to the focus of *The Trilogy* itself in *al-Baqi min al-zaman saʿa* (There only remains one hour, 1982), chronicling the life of an Egyptian family during the Sadat era, with the 1973 October crossing of the Suez Canal as a major focal point. It seems more than likely that, in *Layali alf layla* (The nights of thousand nights, 1982) and *Rihlat ibn Fattuma* (The travels of ibn Fattuma, 1983), both works having titles strongly evocative of well-known works from the Arabic tradition of the past, Mahfouz is paying tribute to the writings of his younger Egyptian colleague and acknowledged disciple, Gamal al-Ghitani, as well as other novelists who have made similar experiments in the creative use of texts from the classical heritage of Arabic writings. In December 1988, Edward Said wrote an article which is essentially a review of recently published translations of novels by al-Ghitani and Elias Khoury as well as the earlier published translation of Emile Habibi's brilliant novel *al-Waqa'i' al-ghariba . . .* (1974; *The Secret Life of Saeed, the Ill-fated Pessoptimist*). He too makes the point that these latter novelists have shown more innovation in their recent writings. The title of his article is "Goodbye to Mahfouz."[3] In the current historical context, I myself would prefer to propose that, while the short survey that I have just essayed certainly suggests that a younger generation of novelists throughout the Arab world is fulfilling the function of keeping the novel genre alive and lively through the necessary processes of innovation and experiment and that Mahfouz's recent works thereby emerge as both local and self-imitative, it is still too early to make any definitive literary-historical judgments about Mahfouz's works as a whole.

Bearing in mind the problems associated with literary history noted above, it should be clear by now that my critical instincts have in a sense led me into a trap of my own making. In essaying the above comments on Mahfouz's recent output, I should make it clear that my interest is in the continuing development of the novel genre throughout the Arab world and indeed (dare one say it after the award of the Nobel Prize) in the context of world literature. A survey of more recent critical writings about the Arabic novel shows clearly, I believe, that, while his works continue to attract a great deal of attention within Egypt itself, such is not the case in most other Arab countries and certainly not to the extent that was the case during the 1950s and 1960s. The award of the Nobel Prize to an Arab was certainly greeted with enthusiasm in most countries of the Arab world, albeit guarded in certain cases, and it was marked by interviews with, and articles on, the Laureate. In the coming years it will be interesting to observe whether this symbol of world recognition will lead to a wider interest in Mahfouz's more recent works to match that shown for his earlier (i.e., pre-1970) works. I would like here to underline once again that we are dealing with a target that is still moving. Only Mahfouz himself knows what he has in store for us; as I write, he has another novel and short story collection in press. I will therefore adopt the French adage *reculer pour mieux sauter* and devote the rest of this chapter to the factors contributing to Mahfouz's "pioneer" status, first venturing a few remarks on the initial stages of the novel's development in the Arab World.

Few scholars would deny, I believe, that the novel genre comes to the Arab world from the West. I hasten to add that the obverse statement, to the effect that the Arabic novel owes nothing to the classical tradition of Arabic, is not the case. Presumably the *language* of modern Arabic fiction, for example, has a provenance within the earlier tradition. It is to be hoped that, now that Western scholars have begun to study the corpus of classical Arabic narrative as literature rather than fodder for Western exoticism, we will be able to see more clearly the role of language use in the development of Arabic fiction. In discussing the origins of the Arabic novel, Edward Said summarizes the situation most usefully:

> The twentieth-century novel in Arabic has a variety of forebears, none of them formally and dynastically prior and useful, as, say, in the rather directly useful way that Fielding antedates Dickens. Arabic literature before the twentieth century has a rich assortment of narrative forms—*qissa, sira, hadith, khurafa, ustura, khabar, nadira, maqama*—of which no one seems to have become, as the European novel did, the major narrative type.[4]

Within such a scenario, literary historians investigating the beginnings of the Arabic novel seem to have been more concerned with identifying who wrote in the genre first rather than in the more complex process of analyzing how the concept of generic purpose was to develop within the various subgenres of the novel. It is certainly true that the romantic, historical, and philosophical fiction written in Arabic during the nineteenth and early twentieth centuries played a crucial role in arousing a public's consciousness regarding the genre, and no more so than in the case of Jurji Zaydan (1861–1914), who, in a series of historical novels, created a public for a genre which would take on serious topics, fashioned a prose style which was immediately accessible, and, equally significant, used episodes from Islamic history as a means of rousing and fostering an emerging Arab nationalist consciousness. That very Western source, however, which had provided exemplars of the novel for translation and imitation, did not allow Arabic fiction the luxury of time in order to develop its interest in, and understanding of, the novel genre. World War I and its aftermath were to present the Arab World as a whole with some new and unpleasant realities. The same cultural traditions whence the novel had come were now represented by the Mandate Powers, the French and British, whose incursions had to be challenged and resisted through a series of local nationalisms. It is hardly surprising that the novel, in Philippe Sollers's words "la manière dont cette société se parle," now shifted its focus to the genre's primary target, the writer's own society and the process of change.[5] Within this perspective, some early pioneer works, such as Muhammad al-Muwaylihi's *Hadith 'Isa ibn Hisham* ('Isa ibn Hisham's story, 1898–1902, 1907), Mahmud Tahir Haqqi's *'Adhra' Dinshway* (The maiden of Dinshway, 1906), and Muhammad Husayn Haykal's *Zaynab* (1913—each one of which chose to focus on contemporary Egyptian society—assume a historical importance within the development of modern fiction, a process which is replicated mutatis mutandis within the literary traditions of other Arab nations. This is not to maintain, of course, that the historical novel disappeared overnight. Indeed, in the case of Egypt, the impact of the ancient tradition, abetted to a considerable degree by the discovery of the Tutankhamon treasures in the early 1920s, was to fuel a view of historical continuity known as Pharaonism, which is found at its most obvious in the famous novel *'Awdat al-ruh* (Return of the spirit, 1933), written by another famous Egyptian litterateur of this century, Tawfiq al-Hakim (1898/1902?–1986) and also in one of Mahfouz's early essays in the short story form, entitled "Yaqzat al-mumiya" ("The Mummy Awakes").[6]

Naguib Mahfouz himself began writing while still an undergraduate student during the 1930s, one of the most turbulent and therefore stimulating decades in Egypt's cultural history this century. As Sasson Somekh shows in his authoritative study of Mahfouz (*The Changing Rhythm*), Mafhouz too was drawn into this intellectual milieu. An interest in ancient Egypt led him to translate a popular work on the subject in English by James Baikie (translation published in 1932 and republished in 1988) and to formulate a plan for a number of historical novels set in that period. Indeed, three such novels were published between 1939 and 1944. However, events now ensued which were to transform the world map and especially the Middle East, as the World War II once again brought the armed might of the West tramping across the region. The aspirations of Arab nations, already thwarted in the wake of the World War I, were now pushed aside yet again. As we look back from the perspective of the Nobel year of 1988, it seems to have been a clearly momentous decision when Mahfouz decided to abandon his earlier plans—so carefully laid out then as now—and to turn his attention to the circumstances of his fellow-countrymen during this appalling period of political chaos, rampant corruption, and threat of imminent invasion. Having established his course, Mafhouz now set about expanding upon his knowledge of fictional genres and techniques. He was already an admirer of some of the major early figures in Egyptian fiction, such as Taha Husayn (1889–1973), Tawfiq al-Hakim, Yahya Haqqi (b. 1905), and Mahmud Taymur (1894–1973), but now set himself to expand his horizons by reading examples of the fiction of novelists in almost every Western literary tradition. The list of authors read by Mahfouz is enormous.[7] It is no exaggeration to say that the course and standards of Arabic fiction were transformed by this single-minded, methodical, and thus utterly typical attention to every aspect of the novelistic craft, making the series of social realist novels, which he completed before the 1952 Revolution in Egypt, a completely new phase in the development of the modern Arabic novel. Indeed, the appearance of the much-discussed *al-Thulathiyya* (*The Trilogy,* 1956–57)—three novels tracing the course of change within Egyptian society through a lovingly detailed portrait of three generations of a single family—is a milestone in modern Arabic literary history. With its publication in 1956, not only Egypt but the entire Arab world found within its pages a faithful reflection of their tribulations and aspirations during the prerevolutionary era, a period which was to be decisively transformed by the 1956 Suez invasion and the subsequent withdrawal of European forces. Nasser's authority was consolidated, and optimism was at its height. Mahfouz's own reputation was also enhanced in the following year when he was awarded the State Encouragement Prize for Literature for *The Trilogy.*

To those readers who admire the neat symmetry of chronological presentation, it will by now be clear that, in attempting to trace the current dilemma of the scholar specializing in the modern Arabic novel in the wake of the Nobel Prize award, I have taken a leaf out of the volume of fiction itself, namely, fractured time. As I noted at the outset, my aim here has not been to summarize Mahfouz's career as a whole but rather to analyze his significance within the development of modern Arabic fiction. Having now attempted to place him within the *development* of the novel genre in Arabic, I would like to suggest that the enduring strength of his great masterpieces of the 1940s, 1950s, and 1960s is in the care and devotion with which he manages to encapsulate the trials and ambitions of the urban middle class, the novel's great subject. But alongside his carefully developed craft in depiction of place and time and in portrayal of character, there is also a concern with broader themes. It is useful to recall that, in his educational background, Mahfouz differs from many other earlier writers of fiction because he studied philosophy. The question "What is madness?" begins the title story of his first collection, *Hams al-junun* (The whisper of madness, [1938?]).[8] Alongside a concern with the mundane but crucial issues of survival in the inimical environment of the modern city, Mahfouz shows a continuing and particular concern for such questions as the nature of madness, the alienation of modern man and his search for consolation, and the role of religion in contemporary societies dominated by humanistic values. His choice of venue for the various fictional worlds he has created has been the city, with a particular concentration on Cairo but also involving a number of "excursions" to his beloved Alexandria. Unlike other Egyptian novelists like ʿAbd al-Rahman al-Sharqawi and Yusuf Idris, he has not used the countryside and its peasant popularion as a focus for criticism of the course of socialist policies in his country. He has concentrated instead on the sector with which he is extremely familiar, the bureaucrat class in the city. And, as the majority of countries in the Arab world have themselves witnessed processes of change and development involving widely varying degrees of disruption, the characters who people Mahfouz's novels have served, in Lionel Trilling's useful phrase, as "most effective agent[s] of the moral imagination."[9]

I hope that this study has made it abundantly clear that the name of Naguib Mahfouz already holds an enduring place in the history of modern Arabic fiction, not only for his rȯle in bringing the genre to a level of artistry from which it might best serve its generic purpose within the Arab World, but also for crafting and developing it into such an expressive instrument for the analysis of his own society. On that larger world stage opened up by the award of the Nobel Prize will the name of Mahfouz remain familiar (once people have learned how to pronounce it!), or will it suffer the fate of several other winners of the prize, both Western and nonWestern? I hope that I have been able to show that Mahfouz's greatest contributions to the novel genre deal with issues which are of universal interest. Advances in technology and communication have shrunk the size of our world to the extent that the Middle East, so designated by us because it intervenes between us and the Far East, preoccupies our attention on an almost daily basis. If nothing else, the award of the Nobel Prize to an Egyptian novelist tells us that Arabic literature can no longer be hidden behind the skirts of exoticism. In terms of world *literature* at least, "us" and "them" should be one.

5

FROM "NAGUIB MAHFOUZ REMEMBERS"

GAMAL AL-GHITANI

Translated by Mona N. Mikhail

THE PLACE

I HAVE NEVER come across anyone more attached to his place of birth than Naguib Mahfouz. He lived in the Gamaliyya Quarter for the first twelve years of his life and then moved to the ʿAbbasiyya Quarter, but he has always remained drawn to the quarters and the narrow streets of al-Husayn and al-Gamaliyya. He has remained attached to the people he came to know and who came to know him. This place has become the setting for his most important and greatest works.

During the summer, Naguib Mahfouz stops writing until the beginning of autumn, primarily because his eyes are subject to allergies in the summer air. On the first week of vacation, he goes to al-Husayn and to al-Gamaliyya, and I often accompany him there and observe his various reactions. We walk through the streets and alleys where I myself grew up and lived for thirty years.

We started in Maydan al-Husayn and stopped in the center of it for a few moments. Naguib Mahfouz looked serene and confident; he appeared resigned to the surge of memories. He looked at the Azhar administration building. "The Khalil Agha Secondary School used to be here," he mused.

"In recent years the landmarks of the square have changed a number of times," I observed, "since some governor issued an order to demolish the famous Fishawi Café as well as a series of old buildings close to it."

"There used to be a clock standing in the middle of the square, and then they built a fountain, which was renovated and then surrounded by a small garden. About thirty years ago this same place used to serve as a terminal for the horse-drawn carriages bound for al-Darb al-Ahmar and al-Husayniyya." Pointing to the *waqf* buildings[1] to the west of the mosque, he said, "There used to be a green door here, a huge vault leading to a narrow alley that was the headquarters of the dervishes, the *majadhib*[2] of the Husayn. You could see them sitting on both sides of the aisles."

I also recalled Maréchal 'Ali, the lunatic who wore a military uniform with many old decorations and Pepsi-Cola bottle caps, and the way he would carry a stick to shoo people away with. Naguib Mahfouz laughed out loud as he reminisced.

From Maydan al-Husayn, we proceeded to a spot that served as the inspiration for one of his greater novels, *Zuqaq al-Midaqq (Midaq Alley).* To reach Midaq Alley from the side of the Azhar, we first had to go through Sanadiqiyya Street, which was covered with dirt and the refuse of the stores and houses. Naguib Mahfouz noted regretfully, "These streets and alleys used to be swept clean twice a day: they used to sprinkle them with water. I personally still remember the famous mule belonging to the municipality, the garage for carts, the stable of mules that was next to the judge's home." Mahfouz pointed out some buildings erected in the 1930s and recalled old homes surrounded by gardens that stretched out to Midaq Alley. The alley is very narrow, no wider than five meters, and no longer than twelve. The coffeehouse was closed, because it was Sunday. There were three shops on the other side. "I remember that there was only the coffeehouse in the alley," he added. "I don't remember that house." In the middle of the alley stood a spice shop. Three elderly men sat in front of it.

"Is there still a bakery inside?" Mahfouz asked them.

"Yes. It seems you still remember the old times," the oldest answered. Mahfouz climbed the steps leading to the bakery, new steps now, built on the dirt road he had described in his novel. He looked at the bakery where Zaʿita, the "maker of deformities," used to live.[3]

"This is Naguib Mahfouz, the great writer," I whispered in the ear of one of the three old men.

After some hesitation he replied, "Is he the one who portrayed our alley in the movies?" I nodded yes. "*Ahlan wa sahlan!* Welcome!" he burst out, then lapsed again into his silence. We left the alley and the coffeehouse where Naguib Mahfouz used to mingle with his friends in bygone days.

So the idea behind *Midaq Alley* was born in this very spot—taking shape scene by scene, event by event—giving this narrow, forgotten place notoriety and fame. I recall one day when I accompanied an orientalist who insisted on seeing Midaq Alley. He came to the place, stood there contemplating it, and said laughing, "If Naguib Mahfouz wrote that extraordinary novel about this narrow, confined place, can you imagine what he could have accomplished if he had written about a thoroughfare like Shariʿ al-Azhar?"

THE SOUKS

We proceeded to al-Hamzawi Souk, where the small shops of spices and perfumes still stand—where the souk still occupies the same spot it used to. It was a typical nineteenth-century Egyptian marketplace, without a counter between buyer and seller. Had this marketplace existed in any European country, someone would have intervened to renovate it and turn it into a tourist attraction. From there we headed to the Gold Market. Mahfouz stopped at the entrance of the Salihiyya Alley. Overhead stood the minaret of al-Salih Najm al-Din Ayyub, one of Cairo's oldest minarets, distinguished by its *mibkhara,* or "incense-burner," shape.[4] It is considered a particularly early minaret design, from a period when the forms were first taking shape.

Naguib Mahfouz lingered for a few moments in front of a closed door and asked, "Is this still a coffeehouse?"

A passerby volunteered, "Yes, but today is Sunday."

"You know," he said, "this is the strangest coffeehouse—a long narrow alley with chairs on each side placed so that the customers almost touch the ones facing them. Things were different in our day."

We returned to the street of Muʿizz li-Din Allah. He pointed in the direction of an old house almost in ruins. "Some beautiful young women used to live in this house, and some of the rich, prominent men used to sit here, and just lift their eyes up to them and wink, twisting their proud moustaches. These were the accepted norms for flirtation and courtship in the 1920s and 1930s," he said, chuckling.

We moved through the copper market (Suq al-Nahhasin), where Mahfouz conceived of the place for Ahmad ʿAbd al-Jawad's shop in *The Trilogy.* I noticed that he stared at some length into some corners, while he walked slowly by others. In most instances he would lift his head as if meditating. At this point, I did not wish to disturb his memories with too many questions.

We walked past the historical monuments of Qalawun, the hospital, the bathhouse, the mosque, the dome of the mosque of al-Nasir Qalawun, and the mosque of Barquq. The minarets, especially those of Qalawun and Barquq, towered over the souks.

I turned to Naguib Mahfouz and said, "You have described this place where the house of Ahmad ʿAbd al-Jawad stood in *The Trilogy*. If we go strictly by your description, there is no house standing here, but rather the mansion of the prince Bashtak." Mahfouz agreed. We walked past the sultan's famous bathhouse, and he wondered, "Is it still standing?"

"Indeed it is," I replied, "and still in working order." I added that most of the Gamaliyya bathhouses are still in working order. We reached the ʿAbd al-Rahman Katkhuda public fountain and stopped for a few moments while Mahfouz pointed to the alley of al-Timbakshiyya.

"This side used to be a souk exclusively for Syrian merchants. They used to sit in front of their stores, wearing huge yellow turbans, smoking their water pipes and displaying their merchandise: apricot paste, almonds, nuts, pistachios and walnuts." He pointed to the remains of an old and spacious building. "This," he said, "used to be the mansion of the Muhaylimis, an important family. Some of them took part in the July 23d revolution." [5]

"Let's head toward the Bayt al-Qadi Square," I suggested. "We can pass by either the vaulted passage of Qirmiz or Bayt al-Qadi Alley."

"I was there a week ago," he said.

I added, "Then let's go to the other vaulted passage."

THE QUR'AN SCHOOL (al-kuttab)

We started in the Bayt al-Qadi Quarter. "We used to call it al-Kababji Alley," he remarked. We walked past the historical tunneled passage where the family of Ahmad ʿAbd al-Jawad had taken refuge during a World War II air raid, after which the hero of *The Trilogy* died. As the alley began to curve, Mahfouz pointed out some tall buildings. He said that they had not changed. He picked up his pace and went ahead of me toward the bend, where a historical fountain stood. I caught up with him, noticing that he appeared revitalized. "This is the *kuttab* (Quʾran school) where I studied," he said. "The fountain still stands, but unfortunately the kuttab has been destroyed. It was on the upper floor, number nine." He pointed to the dilapidated upper floor, looked through the door, and turned to say that the stairs were still standing, though they were leading nowhere. At this point an old man approached him, asking, "Where are you from? Who are you looking for?"

I just said, "We are visitors."

He repeated his question. "Who are you? Who are you looking for?" I realized then that he was hard of hearing, and I remembered Shaykh ʿAbd al-Samad, a character in Mahfouz's *The Trilogy.* We left the Kuttab, and we came closer to Bayt al-Qadi Alley, closer to the place where Mahfouz was born.

THE OLD HOUSE

Mahfouz's steps quickened toward Darb Qirmiz. "I remember our house was number eight," he said. I looked toward the house on the corner and said, "It still carries the number eight." "House numbers don't change," he said, but the house itself had. The house where Mahfouz was born had been leveled. It used to be three stories high—a vertical rather than a horizontal structure. His novel *Hikayat haratina* (Stories of our alley; translated as *Fountain and Tomb*) contains a detailed description of his house, but the one standing now is only two stories high. The first was occupied, while the second floor, made of red brick, was unfinished, an unattractive structure. Naguib Mahfouz expressed dismay and sorrow at the sorry state of his birthplace.

"The windows on our house were made of hard carved wood," he said. It overlooked Darb Qirmiz on one side and the Maydan of Bayt al-Qadi on the other. The square used to be full of trees. From my balcony I could reach out to touch the leaves of the trees we used to call pasha's beard trees." He circled the only remaining tree, which stood next to the public lavatories, in the middle of the square. The lavatories had been built recently. Next to them there used to be an elongated cement basin where the mules and donkeys would drink. This was gone.

"I don't know what kind of tree this is, but surely this is not a pasha's beard," he insisted. "Dr. ʿAbd al-ʿAziz's house was next to ours. It had a splendid entrance, a clinic, and a spacious garden. The house itself was inside. The house of Bayt al-Sukkari occupied this whole area on Darb Qirmiz, yet none of these houses exists now. To the right of Bayt al-Sukkari used to be the meeting place of the dervishes. In my time the square had a huge, imposing mansion, and next to it were the houses where the poor used to live." He fell silent for a few moments and added, "I used to watch the street bullies gather at the Gamaliyya police station after their fistfights in the open spaces. I would also watch the demonstrations of the 1919 revolution. From here I could clearly see the demonstrations by the women (*banat al-balad*), who rode on open donkey-drawn carts. I could hear the flying bullets. This is when arguments would erupt between my mother and me. She would pull me away from the windows, and I wanted so much to stand and watch."

Mahfouz pointed at the entrance of Bayt al-Qadi. "I often watched the demonstrations," he said, "and the British soldiers trying to stop them. I have witnessed quite a bit of history." He turned to look at the square, and the monument of al-Qadi Mamay [6] that stands in the middle of the square, and he pointed to two tall buildings. "I remember those buildings were erected while we lived there, and a great fuss was raised about them, for they were very high by the standards of the time."

As we passed under the gate of Bayt al-Qadi, he remembered, "A candy seller used to sit here. His name was al-Shabkhurli." At the thought of this, Naguib burst into his high, resounding laughter. "Can you guess the meaning of his name? Al-Shabkhurli! What a name."[7]

We left Bayt al-Qadi, where Mahfouz was born at house number eight. We walked past Khan Jaʿfar Primary School and the Egyptian Club hotel, where Mahfouz saw the very first moving pictures in Egypt. Then we came to the streets of Mashhad al-Husayni where al-Husayn Mosque faces the historic fountain of Uthman, and right above it sits Bayn al-Qasrayn Primary School. "I studied here for several years," he said. He stared at the front of the school for a long while, and then we proceeded to the old Fishawi Café, which had been pulled down in 1969. Not much remained of the original structure. When he was an employee at the Ghuri dome and the Waqf Ministry, Mahfouz used to spend long evenings and many hours here, smoking a water pipe and seeking inspiration for the heroes and events of his novels. "In those days," he noted sadly, unveiling his nostalgia, "the water pipes were enormous and tobacco came in many varieties and grades. Ya salam!" (Those were the days).

I had no idea what was going on in the mind of our great author, what far-off images were being conjured up. I only know that this place had marked him deeply, and that no other place had had such a great hold on his life as al-Gamaliyya Quarter, al-Husayn, and this whole area, in spite of his residence in other parts of Cairo, in such quarters as al-ʿAbbasiyya or al-Nil Street. He has never reflected on those areas with the same intensity with which he portrayed al-Gamaliyya, whose alleys remain the center of his world.

THE ALLEY

In 1924, when Mahfouz was twelve years old, his family moved from the old house in Bayt al-Qadi to the house in ʿAbbasiyya (for which his father paid a thousand pounds). Naguib Mahfouz, however, remained drawn strongly to the Gamaliyya Quarter, often visiting the Midaq Alley Coffeehouse, al-Fishawi, and one friend in particular who was a merchant in the Ghuriyya Quarter.

Mahfouz got married in the mid-1950s, moved to al-Nil Street in the suburb of al-ʿAguza, and lived in a small, first-floor apartment overlooking the Nile. But he never lost his connections in al-Gamaliyya. His yearnings for old Cairo remained powerful and overwhelming, and this old world and these ancient alleys formed the core of his works. He succeeded in refracting its spirit forcefully and truthfully, immortalizing the area in his writings.

When I was flying over on my way to Morocco two years ago, I happened to sit next to a Moroccan professor from Muhammad al-Khamis University. He was wearing the Moroccan national costume, a white *ʿaba* with a hood. He was good company during those five long hours of the flight. He explained that he had just ended a vacation in Cairo, and that his primary reason for the trip was to visit the old Cairo of al-Muʿizz, where he could see the old quarters that Naguib Mahfouz had written about. He wanted to visit the sources of Mahfouz's inspiration for the characters of *The Trilogy,* and how gratified and happy he was having done just that.

Some time ago, the French cultural attaché invited me to a dinner party, along with a few other colleagues whose works have been recently translated into French. There we met a few French intellectuals who were involved in translations and who also worked in the French Research Center for Political and Strategic Studies, recently established in Cairo. One of those present, a novelist who spoke Arabic well, informed me that he had once rented a room in the al-Husayn hotel overlooking the square adjacent to the famous Khan al-Khalili bazaar, and that he had spent two months in the area, studying it stone by stone. He wanted to experience life there through the Mahfouzian characters he came to know, and all the while Naguib Mahfouz's works were constantly at the back of his mind.

INTO THE DEPTHS

Those twelve years spent in al-Gamaliyya sank deep into Mahfouz's psyche. They were forcefully reflected in his fictional work. ʿAbbasiyya, where he spent all of his youth and early manhood, appears only as a secondary locale that can be reached from Gamaliyya, as we follow Kamal, one of the heroes of *The Trilogy,* who visits the mansion of the Shaddad family by going from Gamaliyya to ʿAbbasiyya. Al-ʿAguza and al-Nil Street do not even figure in his work. The modern thoroughfares and tall buildings left no impression on him. He considered these merely convenient places to live, work, and sleep in.

I feel the same way, because I lived for thirty years in the alleys of al-Gamaliyya. Only when I got married did the critical housing problem force me to move to Hilwan. I left al-Gamaliyya physically, but never for a moment spiritually or emotionally. I must confess that I felt no affinity with the suburbs of Hilwan. I am incapable of making connections there or personal relationships; I take no pains to establish ongoing contacts with it. I am always haunted by the thought that I am there only temporarily, and that one of these days I will return with my family to live in al-Gamaliyya.

The alley where Mahfouz lived in the 1920s differs from the alley where I lived in the mid-1970s. During Mahfouz's time old Cairo was a center for the petite bourgeoisie, the successful merchants and civil servants. The alleys of Gamaliyya had a rather strange social structure. In the same alley one could easily find a mansion surrounded by a beautiful, spacious garden and right next to it the modest house of a merchant. In the vicinity there would be a large *rab*ʿ, a tenement for dozens of poor people. Typically the *hara* (alley) housed all social classes. One could see that unique structure in Harat al-Tablawi, in the area of Qasr al-Shawq, where I used to live. There stands the famous palace of Musafirkhana, or the guest house of the dynasty of Mohammad Ali Pasha, in one of whose rooms the Khedive Ismail was born. This palace still stands today as a museum and as the headquarters for artists and painters. The mansion of the Shams al-Din family still stands as one of the great structures of its kind. The house of the sheikh of the Sufi order al-Ahmadiyya al-Marzuqiyya stands next to Sidi Marzouk. In the same alley there are modern multistory buildings inhabited by middle-class tenants and houses occupied by poor families.

Until the mid-1950s one could find in the Darb al-Asfar Alley large houses surrounded by pretty gardens. These houses were built by the Suhaymi and the Mustafa Ja'far family: the Suhaymis' own house is now a museum and the Ja'fars' is now occupied by the Egyptian Antiquities Office. The other houses and mansions, with their celebrated gardens, are now in ruin, and since the early 1930s they have begun to disappear. The great families began their migrations from al-Gamaliyya to the new suburbs in Cairo. Some of these alleys became the dwellings of the lowest social classes. Neglect took over completely. I can still remember when our alley, Darb Tablawi, was swept and sprinkled with water twice a day. The street sweeper arrived in the mornings and at midday. He collected and placed the garbage on the sides of the wall for the garbage cart to collect. Now I am filled with sadness and dismay when I see the open sewers, which make it hard to walk around or visit the old mosques and the historical mansions.

Most of the alleys in Gamaliyya were paved with colored cobbles, like the old streets of Paris. Unfortunately, the shortsightedness of the current employees of the Cairo governate was evident when they replaced the cobblestones with asphalt. No sooner had they done so than potholes appeared. This is exactly what happened in Darb al-Tablawi Alley, along with everything else that happened to alter the original topography of the area, most notably the demolition of Fishawi Café. This short-sighted decision destroyed one of the most elegant, authentic coffeehouses of old Cairo. Now only a few remnants of it still exist.

THE SYMBOL AND THE REALITY

The alley functions in Naguib Mahfouz's work on two levels, realistic and symbolic. The realistic level is found in *Midaq Alley, Khan al-Khalili,* and *The Trilogy.* The alley in these works has distinctive features, especially if we compare it with the modern alley. Its inhabitants move in clearly defined spaces. Mahfouz was true to the structures of reality in the area of al-Gamaliyya, and we can easily trace the striking affinities of the characters with the topography of the area and its characteristics.

One can in essence consider *The Trilogy, Khan al-Khalili* and *Midaq Alley* to be meticulous, reliable references to the area during the time in which the events took place, reviving such extinct landmarks as the coffeehouse of Si ʿAbduh, which was underground and had a water fountain surrounded by booths. This was the coffeehouse where Kamal ʿAbd al-Jawad, the hero of *The Trilogy,* used to meet his friend Fuad al-Hamzawi. I have retraced the steps and movements of the characters of Mahfouz's works and concluded that there was a close and precise correlation between the descriptions in his books and the reality of the surroundings. If we were to visit Midaq Alley today, we would find the coffeehouse, the barber shops, and another store gone out of business. The inhabitants of the alley say that the stout man who used to sell *basbusa* (a dessert made out of semolina) is none other than ʿAm Kamil of *Midaq Alley.* The midaqq (pestle) itself is still there, and so is the bakery. During the realistic phase of his writing, Mahfouz made the alley a true reflection of the area as he had actually experienced it.

The symbolic level is seen clearly in *Awlad haratina* (*Children of Gebelawi*), *Malhamat al-harafish* (The epic of the riff-raff), and many short stories. In these works we experience the *hara* as a mixture of dream and reality—as distilled reality. This distinctive alley has its own vocabulary and symbols. Here we see the houses, the hyacinth trees, the coffeehouse, the vaulted roofs and arches, and the open, deserted places. Here we find the serenity and the isolated spots where the men of God congregate secluded and unseen, dedicated to Sufi prayer. Their prayers and mysterious invocations echo, sometimes in Turkish, sometimes in Persian. Open space is the ultimate goal. It is as wide and as vast as Earth itself; it suggests nothingness. On the horizons the minarets and domes emerge, and in the sufi enclaves mulberry trees grow.

In the alleys of Naguib Mahfouz, the days succeed each other, redolent with their secrets; new characters appear, while others disappear forever and still others depart for far-off places. Brawls erupt, and heads are broken. Bullies are enthroned, while others are ousted. Generations succeed one another and people and lives come to an end, while the fences of the Sufi meeting places remain intact and the voices of dervishes reverberate from behind them.

The alleys of Naguib Mahfouz are in this way transparent, summarizing all that life contains and reflecting the features of humankind in all its phases. In short, it is a distilled vision of our world and our lives, which Mahfouz has admirably recorded with great sensitivity and poetry, and with a great love for all Cairo.

AL-ʿABBASIYYA AND THE COFFEEHOUSE

The ʿAbbasiyya Quarter has grown bigger and has changed greatly since the 1920s and 1930s. Then the desert stretched out at the edge of the Sarayat thoroughfare. In one of its two sections, the eastern ʿAbbasiyya, mansions stood surrounded by luxuriant gardens. In spite of the changes that have taken place in the area, the image conjured by Mahfouz in the second book of *The Trilogy* remains the predominant one of al-ʿAbbasiyya. Whenever I visit it, a whiff of the old times envelops me, those times when Kamal ʿAbd al-Jawad shuttled back and forth between the palace of al-Shaddad and Bayn al-Qasrayn, when his heart throbbed with passionate emotions on his way to the house of his beloved ʿAyda Shaddad, on Sarayat Street. There she glowed, radiant before him in the garden, and his emotions were in turmoil. Under a tree in this street, Kamal stood watching the lit window in the palace of the Shaddad family, on the eve of ʿAyda's wedding. He was trembling with cold and pain, in this love experience where pain and love mingled. This event has influenced me profoundly, and I have often asked Mahfouz about the features and personality of ʿAyda in real life. She was older than him, and if she lived today she would be around eighty years old. Strangely one of her relatives currently lives in an apartment in the same house where Mahfouz spends his summers in Alexandria.

"ʿAyda, my destiny, my fate," Mahfouz wrote in *The Trilogy*. "If I hadn't known ʿAyda I would have been a totally different person, and the universe would have been a different universe." When I ask him about ʿAyda, whom he fell in love with in real life, his features relax and become more tender. He seems immersed in memories—distant memories, for more than fifty years have elapsed since this love that shook him at the beginning of his adult life. It was perhaps the ultimate love experience of his whole life. "This relationship has affected me profoundly, to the extent that in my twenties I tried to emulate and relive the events of this earlier love story. Love for love's sake, with no hope of a happy ending."

Mahfouz spent his youth in al-ʿAbbasiyya, after his family moved from al-Gamaliyya in 1924. He remained there until his marriage in the 1950s. After that he went back to al-ʿAbbasiyya every Thursday to have lunch with and spend the day with his mother. At exactly six o'clock every Thursday, he would head toward the old ʿUrabi Café to meet with his childhood friends. I used to see Mahfouz in this coffeehouse in the late 1960s.

THE OLD COFFEEHOUSE

The ʿUrabi Café was one of Cairo's most renowned coffeehouses in the first half of the twentieth century. The owner was one of the better-known gangsters of Cairo. Mahfouz describes him as someone with an imposing stature, "as if born to be a leader." He was such a formidable person that the chief of police of al-Dahir precinct once asked him for protection. ʿUrabi, however, was demoted from his position as the supreme gang leader after beating an English constable and stripping him naked. The constable appeared before his superior undressed, and ʿUrabi was arrested and put in jail. After serving his sentence, he abdicated his position, and his whole life was centered around the coffeehouse. I came to know about ʿUrabi, through Naguib Mahfouz, when I began frequenting the coffeehouse to meet Mahfouz. ʿUrabi had been dead for several years. In the café one could detect remnants of the grandeur of days gone by. Today the space it occupies has been reduced to a new oblong space overlooking al-Jaysh Street.

In this coffeehouse I came to know Mahfouz's old friends and a totally different Mahfouz from the one I had known in the weekly literary meetings that met every Friday evening at the Café Riche.

At the Café Riche, Mahfouz was a listener more than a talker. Occasionally, he would participate in the conversation, and he appeared eager to get to know the new young authors. Sometimes he would engage in debate, but most of the time he just listened attentively. The famed weekly meetings ended at Café Riche rather strangely, when the proprietor decided to renovate the café and chose Friday, the day the weekly meeting was held, as his day off. It seems that the man preferred his peace of mind, for often these heated discussions turned to politics. From there the meetings moved to one of the casinos on the bank of the Nile.

Looking back, I think the Thursday gatherings at the ʿUrabi Café were distinguished by their vitality, marked by the loud laughter of Mahfouz as he exchanged sarcastic repartee with his childhood friends. I soon became part of these warm, friendly, inner-circle gatherings.

Mahfouz used to leave promptly at eight-thirty every evening. His old friends would insist on keeping me around longer at the coffeehouse or would continue the evening at one of their homes in al-ʿAbbasiyya. It was not difficult for me to recognize in these men many of the characters that I have read about in Mahfouz's novels.

AL-KARNAK BORN HERE

At the ʿUrabi Café in al-ʿAbbasiyya, I witnessed the birth of the novel *al-Karnak.* One day I saw a fair-skinned, white-haired, small-statured man with strangely askew eyes and thin, elongated fingers that were pointed at the tips like a bird's claws. The minute he entered the coffeehouse, a strange silence fell. The waiter was quick to produce a water pipe and set it beside him along with a chessboard. He and one of the patrons began to play a game of chess. It was normal that the stranger would attract our attention, and Mahfouz turned to me, asking, "Who is this man?"

I did not know him, so I asked the waiter who the man was. "That's Hamza al-Basyuni, former warden of the military prison," he replied. Mahfouz's eyes widened and glanced stealthily at the man. I can still recall Hamza al-Basyuni's demeanor—the way he held the water pipe, how he stooped over the chessboard—and the heavily laden atmosphere his presence caused in the coffeehouse. He had just finished serving a prison sentence after having been arrested in the aftermath of the 1967 war.

He did not show up the following week. Mahfouz's friends told many stories about him, especially about the military prison. A few days later, I read in the papers a small news item about the death of Hamza al-Basyuni in a car accident on the Cairo Alexandria rural highway.

That Thursday afternoon, Mahfouz saw in al-Basyuni the torturer and taskmaster of the military prison. That afternoon, he conceived his novel *Al-Karnak,* which was published a few years later.

THE MEMORIES

About seven years ago, Mahfouz stopped going to the ʿUrabi Café, and the weekly Thursday meeting broke up. The reason was transportation. Mahfouz does not own a car. He travels by taxi. It became

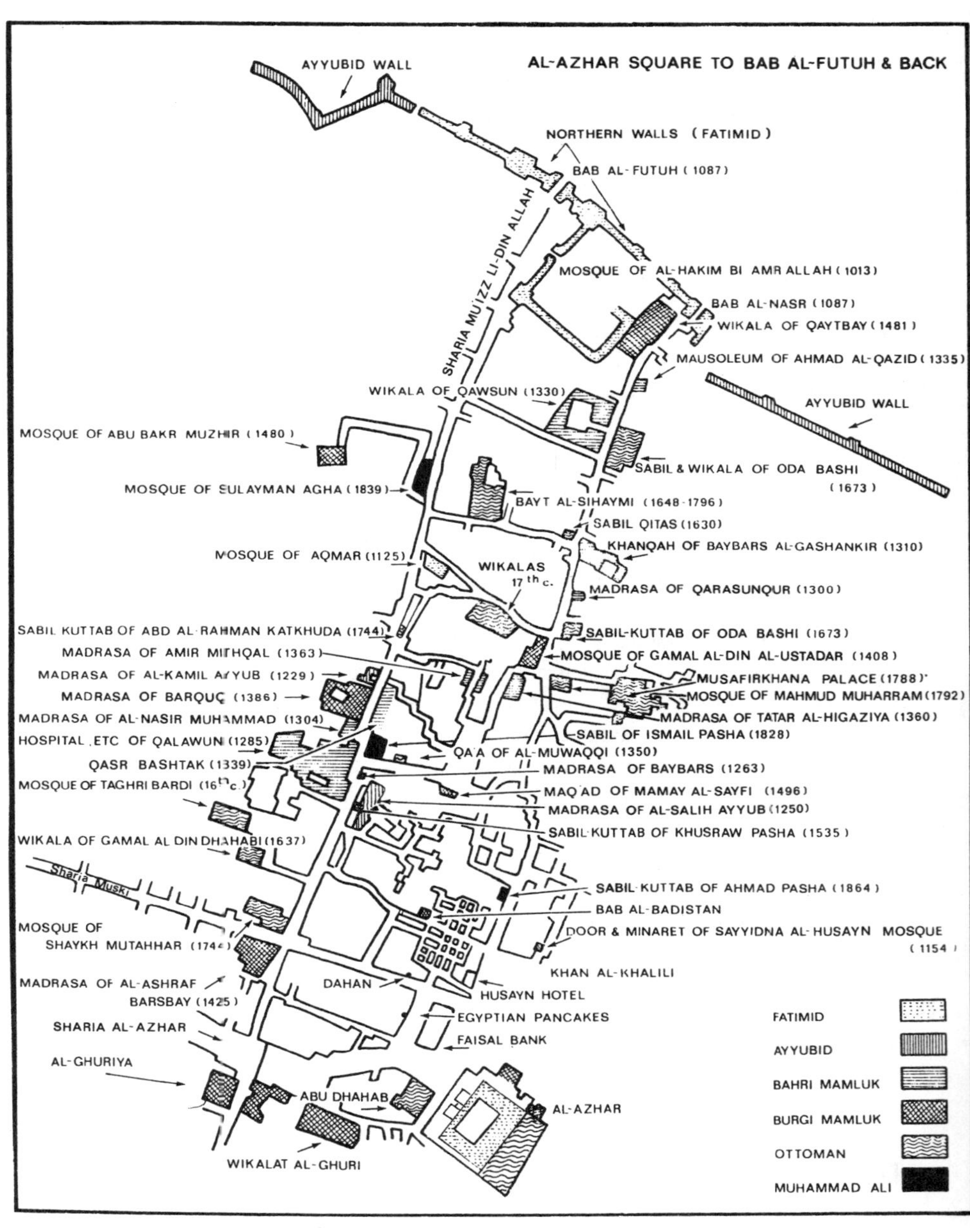

Al-Azhar Square to Bab al-Futuh and back.
Courtesy of American University of Cairo Press.

difficult for him to get a taxi to take him from al-Nil Street to al-ʿAbbasiyya. Also, his mother passed away in the early 1970s. The ʿAbbasiyya regulars themselves no longer frequented the coffeehouse. Some had passed from this world, and some were prevented by illness. Mahfouz has said with despair, "Imagine that I cannot carry out the responsibilities of condolence because of transportation. How often I have been forced to send a telegram instead."

Naguib Mahfouz was, and still is, faithful to his lifelong friends. His dear friends are still those whom he has known from early childhood. His closest friends were Mukhtar Nuwayri and Fuad Nuwayri—brothers of the artist ʿAbd al-Halim Nuwayri—ʿAbd al-Hay Al-Alfi, and Dr. Adham Rajab. I used to see them in ʿUrabi Coffeehouse, and when I went to Café Riche early in the morning, I would find Mahfouz reading the obituary page carefully, checking off the names of some of the deceased. Then he would send telegrams of condolence.

In Naguib Mahfouz are embodied basic values: faithfulness, courtesy, and the preservation of old friendships. There is no doubt that the breakup of the weekly Thursday meetings with his dear friends was painful for him. But work and time are unstoppable forces, and time, in the absence of a true hero, lurks behind Mahfouz's greatest literary works.

6

PLACE AND TIME IN MAHFOUZ'S AL-QAHIRA

CAROLINE WILLIAMS

AL-QAHIRA—MEDIEVAL CAIRO, the city where Naguib Mahfouz was born—has for more than nine hundred years occupied a central place in Cairo's urban history. From A.D. 969, when it was founded by the Fatimids, an alien dynasty from North Africa, until 1871, when the Khedives of Egypt moved their courtly entourages closer to the Nile, al-Qahira has been successively a palatial-administrative enclave (969–1171), a ceremonial-monumental center (1250–1450), and a commercial-artisanal district (1517–1850). Throughout this period it has also been the religious-spiritual nucleus of the city. Today this area of only one square kilometer[1] continues to be the historic, traditional, Islamic heart of the Cairene megalopolis, which in 1991 covered an area of more than 250 square kilometers and contained almost sixteen million inhabitants.

An understanding of the place is thus important for the non-Cairene readers of Naguib Mahfouz's writings. The main setting for Mahfouz's social-realist novels of the 1940s and the 1950s—such as *Khan al-Khalili* (1944), *Zuqaq al-Midaqq* (*Midaq Alley* [1947]) and the three novels that form part of the great trilogy written between 1945 and 1952, *Bayn al-Qasrayn* (*Palace Walk*), *Qasr al-shawq* (*Palace of Desire*), and *al-Sukariyya* (translated as *Sugar Street*)—is very localized, specific, and restricted in area. The main characters live and operate in al-Gamaliyya and al-Ghuriyya quarters of al-Qahira. Al-Gamaliyya[2] lies between the eleventh-century walls that bound al-Qahira on the north (whose two gates, Bab al-Futuh and Bab al-Nasr, are prominent architectural landmarks) and Shariʿ al-Azhar, an east-west street that was carved through the medieval nucleus in the late 1920s. Within this area two important arteries run north-south: Shariʿ Muʿizz li-Din Allah, which begins at the Bab al-Futuh (the Gate of Conquests) and continues for more than two kilometers to the great Southern Cemetery; and Shariʿ al-Husayn, which parallels Shariʿ Muʿizz and connects the Bab al-Nasr (the Gate of Victory) with the western end of the great square in front of the mosque of al-Husayn. The southern half of al-Qahira is known as al-Ghuriyya, a name deriving from a group of buildings endowed by the sixteenth-century Mamluk sultan Qansuh al-Ghuri. Shariʿ Muʿizz li-Din Allah continues on the south side of Shariʿ al-Azhar to the eleventh-century Bab Zuwayla, the southern gate of the old court city. The quarter includes in its northeastern corner the mosque of al-Azhar.

Even within this limited area of al-Qahira, the action of each novel is primarily confined to only a few blocks. In *Midaq Alley*, the alley itself is a tiny capillary just off Shariʿ Sanadiqiyya. It runs east-west between Shariʿ Jawhar al-Qaʿid (or New Street, the eastern extension of Shariʿ al-Muski) and Shariʿ al-Azhar. Excursions away from the alley take place along Shariʿ Jawhar al-Qaʿid, where Hamida, the heroine, walks in the late afternoon; along the fringes of the Ghuriyya, where Kirsha, the coffeehouse owner, buys socks; and at the mosque of al-Husayn, where ʿAbbas, the barber, prays, and where Zaʿita, the maker of deformities, and Mrs. Afify, the landlady, separately, visit the Green Gate. This setting is no more than three blocks by three blocks. The cemetery outside the Bab al-Nasr is farther away, but it is only the scene of the furtive, nightly, and very irregular excursions that Zaʿita and Dr. Booshy, the "dentist," undertake. Bab Zuwayla, the main gateway at the southern end of the city, is mentioned only as the place where Kirsha and the boy part company.

Palace Walk is similarly confined to a very narrow locale. Its central locus includes those blocks that move east-west from Shariʿ Muʿizz at the point of the Coppersmiths' Bazaar, through Darb al-Qirmiz and the Maydan Bayt al-Qadi, to the mosque of al-Husayn. The north-south axis is along Shariʿ Muʿizz, south past the monumental complex of Sultan al-Ghuri to Bab Zuwayla, where the daughters Khadija and Aisha live when married, and north to Bab al-Futuh, where the father al-Sayyid Ahmad is impressed into service as a laborer for the British.

In the thirty to forty years since Mahfouz wrote these novels, particular houses and shops in his scenes have disappeared. But the main street names and street activities remain. Mahfouz's dramatis personae come and go within a circumscribed, descriptively recognizable, and still discernible context. Their spatial setting is clear, and even today it is not difficult to follow their movements. What Mahfouz does not make clear, however, is the temporal environment, and herein lies the second point about these particular novels, one that the foreign reader who has never been to al-Qahira, never walked the streets of these quarters, and never breathed in its atmosphere of continuing time will find difficult to visualize. The foreign reader has to appreciate that, although this area is relatively tiny by the urban limits of today's Cairo, the richest architectural heritage in the Middle East lies within its confines.

Naguib Mahfouz does not emphasize or delineate this spectacular legacy. He mentions it only as a name or two around which the daily events, the small happenings, and the emotions and involvements that propel his characters take shape. Mahfouz is not intentionally nondescriptive. Rather this architecture is such an intimate part of his awareness, such a natural and continuing part of his urban setting, that it remains a persistent, although silent, backdrop of the story. In order for foreign readers to savor the extraordinary worldly richness that overlays this seemingly restricted ambiance, they must understand this architectural context. Let us therefore consider the monuments of the Bayn al-Qasrayn that stand on either side of Shariʿ Muiʿzz li-Din Allah, a narrow, rectangular area no more than 250 meters long.

The name itself, Bayn al-Qasrayn, means "Between the Two Palaces" and refers to the tenth-century Fatimid palaces—the Great Eastern Palace and the Lesser Western Palace—that once stood facing each other across a wide ceremonial maydan, or square, in the middle of the court city. Over the centuries the palaces and the maydan have been replaced by monumental façades, themselves an architectural history of power and mortality.

On the east side of the street stands the *madrasa* (theological college) of Salih Najm al-Din Ayyub, the last ruler of the dynasty (1171–1250) begun by Salah al-Din. Salih's erstwhile concubine and later queen, Shajarat al-Durr, added a mausoleum after Salih died in 1250 while fighting in the Delta against the Crusade of Saint Louis of France. His widow was the only female to rule Islamic Egypt and the only female patron to build on the Bayn al-Qasrayn. She initiated a style of monument/tomb combination that persisted well into the nineteenth century. Next to Salih Ayyub's monument is the Madrasa of Sultan Baybars, Salih's former slave and the real founder of the Mamluk Dynasty. Baybars was a legendary figure. He ravaged the crusader lords and stopped the Mongols' advance at ʿAyn Jalut, or Goliath's Well, after they had plundered Baghdad and devastated the heartland of classical Islam. Not much of Baybars' monument is left—only a block of stones that made up the lower part of the west corner. The rest of the madrasa was destroyed in widening the road from Shariʿ Muʿizz to the Maydan Bayt al-Qadi (the square of the Judge's House), so named because here the four chief religious justices (*qudat*) heard cases referred to them from lower courts.

On the west side of the street are the monuments on whose minarets Amina looks from her balcony and her roof (e.g., *Palace Walk,* 2). When Qalawun, the freed slave of Sultan Baybars, became sultan in 1270, he built his complex of madrasa, mausoleum, and hospital across the street from that of his master. This monument with its impressive combination of dominating architectural elements—dome, minaret, and long façade—was a prototype for the Mamluk style that endured into the nineteenth century, when new styles from Ottoman Turkey and Europe were adopted. The whole complex, with its three components, was built in thirteen months, from June 1284 to August 1285, and visitors continue to agree with a fifteenth-century historian's exclamation that "when a spectator contemplates this huge edifice and hears it was built in such a short space of time, he often will not believe it."[3] Qalawun's descendants ruled Egypt for a hundred years. He was the only Mamluk sultan to establish such a long-lived inheritance.

Next to Qalawun's complex is the madrasa begun by an interim sultan and finished by Qalawun's son, Sultan Nasir Muhammad, whose reign from 1293 to 1340, in three stretches, was the highpoint of the medieval period. Unusual features are the doorway plundered from the crusader church in Acre when the Mamluks expelled them from the Holy Land in 1291 and the minaret sheathed in beautiful stucco tracery. Sultan Nasir Muhammad was the greatest architectural patron of medieval Cairo. He encouraged the prominent amirs of his court to build likewise. Mosques, madrasas, Sufi monasteries (*khanqah*), mausoleums, and palaces rose in many parts of the old city. The sultan himself was a prime developer and builder of the citadel. Thus his madrasa on Bayn al-Qasrayn is not a measure of his architectural grandeur but an affirmation of his presence on the city's major medieval thoroughfare.

The last building in this canyon of monuments is the complex of Sultan Barquq, who was the first in the line of so-called Burgi or Circassian Mamluk rulers. It was built in 1384 in the full Mamluk monumental style, which in its imposing scale and profusion of ornament carries on the standards set by Qalawun's complex. The names of Islamic architects are not often known, but the Amir Jarkas al-Khalili, who was supervisor-engineer for this complex, also gave his name to the bazaar area nearby—the Khan al-Khalili.

Five other monuments, three of which are landmarks in Mahfouz's novel, are located in this narrow, rectangular area. Protruding from the wall of the Madrasa of Salih Ayyub, between the minaret and the mausoleum, is the *sabil-kuttab* of Khusraw Pasha, built by the first Ottoman governor of Egypt in 1535. This combination of water dispensary (*sabil*) and Qurʿan school (*kuttab*) was especially popular for provincial rulers in Cairo (1517–1798), since it incorporated in an economical way what the Prophet Muhammad described as the two greatest mercies: dispensing water to the thirsty and imparting knowledge to the ignorant.

The next sabil-kuttab was built two hundred years later, in 1744, by ʿAbd al-Rahman Khatkhuda, the greatest patron of the eighteenth century. Its location is dramatic because it occupies a wedge in Shariʿ Muʿizz a few yards north of the complex of Sultan Barquq. This is the "cistern" onto which the ʿAbd al-Jawad house looks (*Palace Walk,* 2, 37) and around which the British soldiers encamp (370, 436).

The third sabil-kuttab is where Yasin, the oldest son, works as a secretary (57, 416). It was built by Muhammad ʿAli Pasha, who ruled Egypt during the first half of the nineteenth century, from 1805 to 1848. Although the pasha constructed his palaces along the Nile and used the citadel to proclaim his status in architectural terms, he also put his stamp on this great artery. His sabil-kattab of 1828, dedicated to the memory of his son Ismaʿil, who died in the Sudan putting down an insurrection, is opposite the funerary complex of Sultan Barquq. The traditional charitable aims of instruction and thirst quenching are present in this building, but they are arranged in a new way. The school (one for copper-working apprentices, not for Qurʾan learners) has been placed to either side of the sabil, not above it, as in earlier years.

To the north of Muhammad ʿAli's sabil-kuttab, at the corner of Darb al-Qirmiz (49, 50[4], 167), stand the well-preserved remains of the palace of Amir al-Bashtak. This palace, constructed between 1334 and 1339, was built by one of the powerful sons-in-law of Sultan Nasir Muhammad, and it offers a prototype for much of the secular architecture in Cairo during the seventeenth and eighteenth centuries, such as the house of Sayyid Ahmad ʿAbd al-Jawad, which no longer survives. Qasr al-Bashtak once stood five stories tall and had running water on all its floors. The *mashrabiyya* (wooden lattice) windows still look down over the street life below. It is through these interlocking wooden spools that the cloistered ladies of the house could look out without being seen, and the spools formed the aerial "closed cages" that were the house's main external feature (2, 23, 24, 137).

The presence of the palace is evidence that along with the minarets, domes, and façades located on this ceremonial route, this core area has also provided a traditional environment in which centuries of people have lived and worked. The "hammam of the Sultan" (50, 132)—the bathhouse ordered by Sultan Inal in 1456, built on the west side of the street, opposite Bashtak's palace—has provided a place for local residents to bathe and socialize. On the east side, between Qasr al-Bashtak and the Nahhasin School of Muhammad ʿAli, opposite the mosque of Barquq, is Ahmad ʿAbd al-Jawad's general store (36). Here the street takes on the localized name of Suq al-Nahhasin, the Coppersmiths' Bazaar. Shops and one-person stalls along the Suq al-Nahhasin continue to edge Shariʿ Muʿizz as far as the façade of the Madrasa of Salih Ayyub. The main change today is that the pots and basins sold here are aluminum more often than they are copper. As Shariʿ Muʿizz continues south, the activity in copper gives way to that in gold. Tiny stalls filled with glittering bangles and dangling earrings still offer the ladies adornment and investment (71, 91).

The intersection of Shariʿ Muiʿzz and Shariʿ Jawhar al-Qaʿid separates the stretch where gold is sold from that where heaped mounds of spices, herbs, roots, and incense beckon the buyer visually and aromatically. Dominating the scene is the monumental complex of the Sultan Barsbay, built in 1425. Barsbay turned sugar and spices into state monopolies to finance his architectural programs and foreign campaigns. He conquered Cyprus in 1425 and forced the Lusignans, the descendants of the crusader kings of Jerusalem, to pay him tribute. Opposite the mosque, on the east side of Shariʿ Muʿizz, and at the corner of Shariʿ Sanadiqiyya, is Sayyid ʿAli's coffeehouse. From a bench inside this coffeehouse, Yasin observes the house of the lute player Zanuba (71); and by the light that shines through its windows, Ahmad finds his way to the singer Zubayda's door (91).

Another block down, and across the Shariʿ al-Azhar, stand the buildings of Sultan Qansuh al-Ghuri, the last effective Mamluk ruler. He died fighting the Ottoman Turks outside Aleppo. Shariʿ Muʿizz stretches between al-Ghuri's double ensemble—a madrasa-mosque on the western side, a mausoleum and sabil-kuttab on the eastern side. Here the street was once roofed over to make a place for the Silk Bazaar, a scene painted often by nineteenth-century European orientalist artists. The silk merchants are gone today, but the sale of textiles, stacked as bolts of colorful yard goods or as finished articles floating like banners above the crowds, is still lively here.

Such is the palatial, ceremonial, and commercial ambiance of Mahfouz's *Palace Walk.* From the sabil-kuttab of ʿAbd al-Rahman Katkhuda to the street-straddling complex of Sultan al-Ghuri is a distance of no more than 475 meters. Each minaret along this path offers the call to prayer, but the real religious heart of this area lies 200 meters west, in the mosques of al-Azhar and al-Husayn.

The mosque of al-Azhar has played an important role in the religious and political life of Egypt over the centuries, and major patrons have added to and extended its physical dimensions. It was founded in 970 as the congregational mosque of al-Qahira. Later it became a missionary teaching center for Shiʿi propaganda, and it is thus one of the oldest surviving universities in the world. Amina's father, a religious scholar, received his education here (47). The traditional curriculum (grammar, religion, and rhetoric) is still taught here in the old way: the shaykh sits on a chair (*kursi*), and the students sit on the floor around him in a circle (*halqa*). The professorial "chairs" of later universities in Europe probably originated from this setting. Today al-Azhar is the foremost center of Sunni theology in Islam and the intellectual center of the religious community.

The center for emotional and popular Islam, however, lies across Shariʿ al-Azhar in the mosque of al-Husayn. Here the head of al-Husayn, the Prophet Muhammad's grandson by his daughter Fatima, is believed to be buried (48). Husayn was decapitated in Iraq in 680, when he led an ill-fated insurrection against the Umayyad Caliph in Damascus. He was martyred upholding the Shiʿi tenet that the only legitimate successor to the Prophet is a member of his own family. Thus he became the Shiʿites' first and supreme Islamic martyr, and they commemorate his death with yearly rites of penance and mourning. As the beloved grandson of the Prophet, al-Husayn is also a revered saint for the Sunnis, and they seek his intercession in many areas of their daily lives. For example, Kamal prays to him for help in exams (49), Amina wants him to bless Aisha the beautiful bride (252), and Yasin's mother goes to him when she is ill (430). On Fridays Ahmad ʿAbd al-Jawad, accompanied by his sons, attends the Friday prayer services at this mosque (411). During the Fatimid period, al-Husayn's head was found in Ascalon. When Ascalon was threatened by the crusaders in 1153, the head was brought to Cairo and reinterred in a special tomb within the Great Eastern Palace. Bab al-Akhdar, the Green Gate, is all that remains architecturally of this period, because the mosque itself was rebuilt from 1864 to 1873, during the reign of the Khedive Ismail.

The mosque is still home to a constant flow of worshipers and visitors. They sit, they chat, they nap, and they pray. On Fridays the sanctuary is not large enough to hold the men—local inhabitants, merchants from the adjoining Khan al-Khalili Bazaar, coffee and tea drinkers, and shoppers—who congregate there for the noon prayer. The spillover extends out into the Maydan al-Husayn in long parallel rows of multicolored and handsomely patterned mats and rugs on which the collectivity prostrate or squat (414). The loudspeaker booms out the main address, and all within hearing are included in the service.

Although Amina lives only a few minutes from the mosque (35), she has never visited it. Her excursion to the shrine of Sayyidna—our master—Husayn is an important incident in the novel (168–170). She enters the tomb chamber through Bab al-Akhdar and joins the dense milling mass of women and children who surge, crowd, ululate, and circumnavigate around the cenotaph, separated from the throng by a wooden lattice screen. As have a continuous stream of visitors and supplicants for more than eight hundred years, she presses her face against the screen, rubs her hands over the wooden rails, and invokes al-Husayn's intercession in her life and for her special needs. The attendant uses his fly whisk to keep her from lingering too long. This is one of the novel's scenes that can be relived today without change.

Naguib Mahfouz was born in al-Gamaliyya, in a house on the Maydan Bayt al-Qadi. The house was one block west and one block south of the fifteenth-century funeral complex of Amir Jamal al-Din Yusuf, the majordomo for the Mamluk sultan Faraj ibn Barquq, after whom the area is named. Mahfouz's earliest and most beloved memories are of living in this house that overlooked the Maydan Bayt al-Qadi. This area, which lies midway between the Bayn al-Qasrayn and the mosque of al-Husayn, is the backdrop that Mahfouz uses for his novels about place and time.

In his great *Trilogy*, the quarter of al-Gamaliyya becomes more than a physical setting for the varied, vibrant, frail assortment of humanity who lives, works, and disports along its side streets. It also represents a vivid metaphor for Cairo, for Egypt. Bayn al-Qasrayn embodies more than the space between bygone eponymous palaces, more than a place in which handsome architectural remnants of glorious times still look down on the passing, changing throng. The title also alludes to an Egypt in transition, to an Egypt that lies between the power of the past and the power of the future, between the traditional and the modern worlds. In this wider temporal application, the title becomes a symbol of a time between that which is known and secure—as encapsulated in the area and in the monuments of Al-Qahira—and that which is different and uprooting—as exemplified by the wholesale changes initiated by foreign states and by the two world wars. If readers can understand the range, the variety, the complexities, and the grandeur of Mahfouz's al-Qahira, they can appreciate his metaphor of place and time.

7

RESPECTED SIR

SAMIA MEHREZ

"SOMETIMES THE ARTIST finds it difficult to express himself, especially when we consider the state's position toward him. This is generally true in the Arab world where we cannot dissociate art and politics. . . . The artist's dilemma depends to a great extent on the state's position vis-à-vis freedom of expression. Should the state ignore the writer's voice, it alone is the loser, for his is the voice of truth . . . a voice that knows and offers what no intelligence apparatus is capable of providing."[1] This statement from Naguib Mahfouz, quoted in Gamal al-Ghitani's *Najib Mahfuz yatadhakkar* (Naguib Mahfouz remembers), reconfirms Mahfouz's acute awareness of the relationship between literature and politics in the Arab world and of its constraining, perhaps even compromising, effect on cultural production in general and on the creative writer in particular. The interest of the above passage does not lie solely in the relationship it establishes between literature and politics, however, but in the nonauthoritative position Mahfouz assigns to the creative writer. First, the passage assigns a passive role to the writer and an all-active role to the state. The state takes a position toward writers, takes a position regarding freedom of speech, and recognizes or ignores the writer's voice, while the writer can only write (or not write) and hope that the state will realize the importance of his or her voice. Mahfouz presupposes a writer who depends on the state for recognition and legitimacy, without considering alternatives to such a binding, even stifling, relationship. Second, implicit in this passive writer/active state relationship is a tacit agreement to self-censorship. Even though Mahfouz recognizes the relationship between writers and authority, he fails to encourage the writer to be the active participant he must be if freedom of speech, which Mahfouz advocates, is to be won.

Therefore, it is not surprising that despite this statement and others made by Mahfouz that suggest his constantly compromised position vis-à-vis authority, a general consensus in the Egyptian intellectual and literary milieu is that the Nobel Prize winner's life has been a long, quiet stream. For example, in his published series of interviews with Mahfouz, Ghali Shukri, a leading Egyptian journalist and literary critic who wrote one of the earliest long studies on Mahfouz's works,[2] describes the Nobel laureate as an ordinary man. "People expect a writer or famous artist to have an extraordinary life, but in fact Naguib Mahfouz's life is devoid of such unusual events."[3] Likewise, Luwis ʿAwad, one of Egypt's foremost intellectuals, has emphasized Mahfouz's wide appeal. "Never," he suggests, "have I known a writer to be so widely accepted by the right, center, and left—whose works are appreciated by traditionalists and modernists, and by those in between"—as has been the case with Naguib Mahfouz.[4]

There might seem to be a contradiction between what Mahfouz says about the writer's position and what his critics have to say about him—that is, between how he articulates his literary career and how others see it developing. But rather than view his statements and those made by others as contradictory, I argue that they must be read as complementary. Only by so doing can we begin to understand how Mahfouz came to occupy his present position in the literary and intellectual world. Indeed, it is only because of his careful navigation and constantly negotiated position that Mahfouz may seem to lead an uneventful life.

Throughout his career as a writer, Mahfouz has walked a fine line between sincere political commitment and an amazing disengagement from politics. Consequently, his literary history is punctuated with several interesting jolts and confrontations with the state and with religious authorities that have remained potentially explosive and disruptive. In fact, to say that Mahfouz is an ordinary man or that his life is devoid of unusual events is to ignore one of the more fascinating and complicated aspects of his life. The question then becomes how and why these politically charged moments in Mahfouz's career have been hushed so that he finally emerges, unlike many of his contemporaries, unharmed by the authorities, in relative peace with the multiple factions of the intellectual community, and one of the most popular writers in the Arab world. The details of some of these potentially explosive moments in Mahfouz's literary history indicate that the deleted eruptions in his career can be attributed to the creative writer's apparently separate yet intrinsically interrelated role as civil servant. The great writer was employed in the government for more than fifty-four of his seventy-eight years.[5]

In compiling an archaeology of confrontational moments in Mahfouz's life, one will discern certain patterns that will eventually lead to a rereading of his "uneventful" life. Perhaps one of the most striking characteristics of Mahfouz's literary biography is his increasing caution, not so much in what he writes as in how and when he circulates what he has written. Although his works are predominantly critical, on both a social and a political level, his career as a writer is marked with a politics of nonconfrontation that, in many instances, has subjected him to criticism. This careful attitude toward the written word is something Mahfouz has learned over the years, in more than one trying encounter with power.

Very early in his career, in an episode that marks his initial introduction into the world of narrative and its relation to authority, whether religious or political, Mahfouz came up against the first signal of possible confrontations with the religious authorities in Egypt.

His lifelong friend Adham Rajab told this story as an example of the long history of uneasy moments that Mahfouz has lived and survived. Mahfouz had just published his first novel, *ʿAbath al-aqdar* (The absurdity of the fates) in 1939, and took a copy of the novel to the home of his mentor in philosophy, Shaykh Mustafa ʿAbd al-Razik. There he encountered several sheikhs and religious authorities, one of whom took the novel, looked at the title page, and said disapprovingly: "What do I see? The absurdity of the fates? And can Fate be absurd, dear sir? Fate is of God's creation! How dare you associate absurdity with God?" [6]

As Adham Rajab indicates, this instance of "intellectual terrorism" was perhaps the first to which Mahfouz was subjected. But, in 1939, novelwriting was still a budding art, and Naguib Mahfouz was still an unknown writer; thus a good scolding from a respected religious authority was apparently enough to set him on the right track. Also, even at this early point in his career, Mahfouz was benefiting from considerable patronage, a factor that has recurred quite frequently in his life. *ʿAbath al-aqdar* had already been published when the sheikh attacked it, thanks to the interest that the towering Egyptian liberal intellectual Salama Musa had taken in Mahfouz's early writing attempts. Musa had read the manuscript, liked it, and serialized it in his literary magazine, *al-Majalla al-jadida,* thus becoming one of the young liberal writer's first patrons.

Mahfouz experienced another collision with authority—this time political—after the publication of *al-Qahira al-jadida* (*New Cairo*) in 1943. In this novel, Mahfouz critically depicts Egyptian society during the 1930s. He exposes political and moral corruption in a country submerged in poverty, hypocrisy and opportunism through the story of a government employee who becomes a pimp in order to advance in the bureaucracy. This particular story happened to coincide with a real scandal among the Egyptian ministers at the time. Because of this "coincidence," *al-Qahira al-jadida* earned Mahfouz an interrogation by the mufti of the Ministry of Waqf, Sheikh Ahmad Husayn (Taha Husayn's brother). But because Sheikh Ahmad Husayn was under the impression that Mahfouz was one of Taha Husayn's students, he wrote a report in the young writer's favor, thus saving him from the accusation. The sheikh also volunteered advice to the young writer: "Why don't you write about love, and stay away from these dangerous things?"[7]

Similarly, when Mahfouz recalls the publication of *Zuqaq al-Midaqq* (*Midaq Alley*) in 1947, he remembers being called in for advice by Ibrahim al-Mazini (the well-known writer, who was also responsible for the decision to grant Mahfouz the Arabic Language Symposium prize in 1946 for his novel *Khan al-Khalili*): "Realism is a bad thing, my friend, and we still don't understand either realism or romanticism. All the calamities in *Zuqaq al-Midaqq* will be dumped on you. So be careful."[8] And careful he was! Not about what he was writing, but how he would make the written word pass, or not pass, depending on the kind of danger it presented and the general political climate in the country.

Perhaps the example which best narrates the shifting strategies in Mahfouz's confrontation with, and manipulation of, the authorities is that of his banned novel *Awlad haratina* (*Children of Gebelawi*), published in 1959. *The Trilogy* had been published three months before the 1952 revolution and is considered a monument in social realism. For the seven intervening years, Mahfouz did not write. His publication of *Children of Gebelawi*, a work that defies a unilateral interpretation, invites a careful analysis of the relationship between Mahfouz's seven-year silence and his shift from the social realism of *The Trilogy* to the symbolic mode of *Children of Gebelawi.*

If *The Trilogy* can be read as a social history of Egypt between the two world wars, *Children of Gebelawi* can be read as a symbolic history of Egypt after the revolution. Whereas *The Trilogy* spans the recent historic period from the 1919 revolution to 1944 through a representation of three successive generations in a middle-class family, *Children of Gebelawi* transports us into a timeless, symbolic *hara* (alley), where the successive heroes (whose life histories parody those of the successive prophets)—all descendants of the imposing Gebelawi—reenact man's struggle for meaning, knowledge, and social justice.

Mahfouz has often remarked that literature should be more revolutionary than revolutions themselves, that writers must find the means to continue to be critical of the negative elements in the sociopolitical reality. One who agrees with this statement will have to accept Mahfouz's reading of his controversial novel: "In this novel [Gebelawi] he was addressing the leaders of the revolution who were ruling Egypt. In using the alley to symbolize Egypt, he was forced to use an inverted symbol. Normally one would write about Egypt and mean the world or the universe, not the inverse. But he had to do this in fear of censorship."[9]

Gebelawi first appeared in serialized form in the pages of *al-Ahram,* whose editor in chief at the time was Muhammad Hasanayn Haykal, the man responsible for transforming Egypt's leading daily newspaper into an intellectual fortress by inviting the country's leading writers and intellectuals to join its editorial staff. Even though Mahfouz offers us a political reading of *Children of Gebelawi,* the prevailing reading at the time was overwhelmingly religious. Before the complete serialized version of the novel had appeared in *al-Ahram,* trouble began. In Mahfouz's words, "Several petitions were sent to al-Azhar as soon as the novel appeared. For the first time the sheikhs of al-Azhar had to read a novel. And one must remember that the work was considered highly innovative even in the intellectual circles of the time. So the sheikhs cannot be blamed for their interpretation. The petitions had made reference to the prophet Muhammad, and accordingly the sheikhs condemned the work as blasphemous and demanded that it be banned."[10]

When I asked Mahfouz how he received this kind of blow, especially since *Children of Gebelawi* represented his return to the literary scene after seven silent years, he answered "Sabri al-Khuli [representative of President Nasser] said to me: 'We do not want a fight with al-Azhar. We will ban the book itself and anything written about it. But if you want to publish it outside Egypt you may do so.' I considered this a reasonable solution given the attack on the book."[11] The book was never published in Egypt, but it appeared in Beirut and continues to be sold underground in Cairo, with Mahfouz's knowledge. The serialized version of the novel was never discontinued. Haykal, who was a close friend of Nasser's, made sure that it continued, despite the protests by al-Azhar.

Mahfouz does not seem to have played a major part in this drama surrounding *Children of Gebelawi.* Haykal made the ultimate courageous decision in favor of Mahfouz. Patronage shielded Mahfouz, and in return he agreed to compromise rather than openly confront the religious authorities.

These strategies do work, but in this case not without a lesson for Mahfouz. One year before the publication of *Children of Gebelawi,* Mahfouz had been appointed chair of the Cinema Institute. This appointment, which Mahfouz speaks of as his favorite job, did not last long because of the attack on his "blasphemous" novel. "It was the first time I was ever appointed to a position that had to do with art. In addition I considered myself a friend of art rather than a censor. I used to defend it. I remained in this position for only a year or so, since the attack on *Awlad haratina* was already under way. The ministers took their complaints to Tharwat ʿUkasha [minister of culture], protesting my selection as the censor.[12]

But the turbulent history of *Children of Gebelawi* does not stop there; the whole issue came back to haunt Mahfouz thirty years later. When awarding Mahfouz the Nobel Prize, the Swedish Academy listed *Children of Gebelawi* as one of the milestones in Mahfouz's career that had earned him international recognition. The special attention paid to this banned book brought the fate of its publication in Egypt into question again. Some of Egypt's leading critics—including Ghali Shukri and Rajaʾ al-Naqqash—campaigned to obtain a green light from al-Azhar for publication, reiterating that there had been no legal action against the book. The Egyptian evening paper *al-Masaʾ* began to serialize the novel once more. The moment was indisputably a permissive one, but Mahfouz declined. He asked that *al-Masaʾ* stop publication with the excuse that his permission had not been obtained, and he refused to engage in the live debate that was taking place. Eventually, it died down.[13]

But this once forgotten episode of Mahfouz's life soon gained added significance with the appearance of the Salman Rushdie affair. With the publication of *The Satanic Verses* and the "deadly" debate that surrounded it, an association was established between *Children of Gebelawi* and Rushdie's novel. Indeed, Rushdie used Naguib Mahfouz as an example of the stifling situation for writers in Islamic societies. Concurrently, the foreign press bombarded Mahfouz with questions about his position on the Indian writer's predicament. The Nobel Prize winner spoke openly about freedom of speech and that of the writer, and he condemned Khomeini's *fatwa* [formal legal opinion] that Rushdie should receive the death sentence.

Mahfouz very quickly realized that he had made public statements that were being abused in the West and were definitely going to reflect on him in Egypt. Given the history of *Children of Gebelawi,* Mahfouz decided to issue a statement in *al-Ahram* in which he summarized his position on the Rushdie affair. Part of the text of that statement follows.

> I have condemned Khomeini's *fatwa* to kill [Salman Rushdie] as a breach of international relations and as an assault on Islam as we know it in the era of apostasy. I believe that the wrong done by Khomeini toward Islam and the Muslims is no less than that done by the author himself. As regards freedom of expression, I have said that it must be considered sacred and that thought can only be corrected by counter-thought. During the debate, I supported the boycott of the book as a means of maintaining social peace on condition that such a decision not be used as a pretext to constrain thought. Indeed, I even supported al-Azhar's request to ban *Gebelawi* so long as the Sheikhs have not changed their position concerning the book. I assured my interlocutor that my book contained nothing injurious to any religion or prophet and that to associate it with Rushdie's book is a grave mistake. I still have great hopes to convince those opposed to my book of its true signification.[14]

Nowhere in this statement does Mahfouz challenge *al-Azhar* regarding the fate of his banned book. In fact, he allies himself with the religious authorities against his own self-interest as a writer, even though in the very same statement he considers freedom of speech sacred.

Mahfouz may have thought that this compromise on his part would end the controversy, but the fate of *Children of Gebelawi* continues to take more dramatic turns. First, the whole issue was taken up by the fundamentalist groups. Even before the Rushdie affair, the Islamic newspaper *al-Nur* had started paving the way. When Mahfouz was awarded the Nobel Prize, *al-Nur* launched a major attack on the author of the "blasphemous" novel, accusing him of blasphemy, apostasy, and Freemasonry. This initial attack was followed by a decisive *fatwa* from Dr. ʿUmar ʿAbd al-Rahman, the mufti of the fundamentalist group al-Jihad, in which he decreed:

> Salman Rushdie has wronged Islam. He has wronged the wives of the prophet and has abused the Qur'an. In doing this he found appreciation in the West. From an Islamic point of view, Salman Rushdie, like Naguib Mahfouz, is an apostate. Anyone who wrongs Islam is an apostate and the religious jurisdiction in this case is that they repent. If they do not repent, they must be killed, since the prophet himself said "Kill him who changes his religion." Accordingly, Khomeini's *fatwa* is correct. Salman Rushdie must be killed. Had this sentence been passed on Naguib Mahfouz when he wrote *Awlad haratina,* it would have served as a lesson for Salman Rushdie to heed.[15]

From then on, Naguib Mahfouz received several threats on his life serious enough for the state to offer him personal security, which he declined. Ironically, al-Azhar, which had intervened to ban *Children of Gebelawi* thirty years earlier, came to Naguib Mahfouz's rescue. In an interview with the newspaper *al-Ahali,* the mufti of the republic, Dr. Muhammad Sayyid Tantawi, responded to the *fatwa* issued by Dr. ʿUmar ʿAbd al-Rahman "I am totally opposed to this *fatwa,* for it cannot have been decreed by a sane human being. . . . Mr. Naguib Mahfouz is an important literary figure. Should he do wrong, we must question him. But should he do right we must thank him."[16]

It is obvious from the mufti's response that Mahfouz's statement on Rushdie, in which he wooed al-Azhar to the detriment of his rights as an author, earned the great writer the authorities' "thanks" and protection. This ironic situation is produced without Mahfouz's direct intervention. More ironic, however, is that al-Azhar should suddenly support such liberal intellectuals as Naguib Mahfouz. The initiative taken by the mufti allowed Mahfouz to voice (obliquely) his opinion on Islam, liberalism, and freedom of speech and thought.

> Islam has been treated unjustly. For the real Islam is that which produced people like Taha Husayn, al-ʿAqqad, and Tawfiq al-Hakim with all their daring positions and opinions. The mufti of al-Azhar has responded to the *fatwa* of my death. This is the Islamic point of view. But the fundamentalists do not want to listen. And in the West they ignore what the mufti has said, and they use what has been said by the fundamentalists to abuse Islam.[17]

This carefully weighed position, which won Mahfouz the support of the same authorities that banned him in his confrontation with the fundamentalists, represents the fruit of the lessons he had learned over the years. When asked how he felt about the ban on *Children of Gebelawi,* he very calmly responded, "I had become used to these reactions to many things I have written. What I write triggers a lot of talk." [18]

Effectively, the postrevolutionary period opened with *Children of Gebelawi,* which triggered more than just talk; indeed, it cost Mahfouz his job. After *Children of Gebelawi,* the confrontations continued, this time with the political authorities. As with *Children of Gebelawi,* patronage rescued Mahfouz from danger. But this patronage gradually gave way, especially in the post-1967 period. The same regime that tolerated criticism during its early years became increasingly intolerant toward opposition in the aftermath of the defeat. During these years, the state tightened its grip on freedom of expression and imposed censorship on books and on the press.

The state's blatant intervention in cultural affairs is reflected in Mahfouz's literary production. Two contrasting examples come to mind in this regard: the story of the publication of *Tharthara fawq al-Nil* (Chatter on the Nile) in 1966, which shocked the Egyptian audience with its daring representation of defeatism and escapism in Egyptian society just before the 1967 defeat; and the example of *al-Karnak* (1974), the novel that exposed the dynamics of the police state during the Nasser period.

Tharthara fawq al-Nil brings Mahfouz into direct confrontation with the president himself. It is set in a houseboat on the Nile, where a group of men and women from various walks of life (a civil servant, a lawyer, a young female student, a housewife, an actor, and a journalist), intent on escaping a bleak outside reality, convene to indulge in hashish, sexual relations, and politically satiric hallucinations. Their recklessness and escapism culminate in the death of a peasant woman, whom, in their stupor, they run down with their car. They do not stop to see what happened to the woman; nor do they go to the police. Instead, they return to the houseboat.

When ʿAbd al-Hakim Amir, vice-president and commander in chief of Nasser's army, read the novel, the element of parody did not escape him.

> I was told after the publication of *Tharthara fawq al-Nil* that ʿAbd al-Hakim Amir had said, "This time he has gone beyond the limits, and he must be punished." I do not remember who it was who conveyed this to me, but I know it was not Haykal, because he did not like to scare me, and whenever he found out about something

> like this, he would not tell. What I do remember is that Tharwat ʿUkasha, who was preparing a trip to Europe was asked by Nasser, "Have you read *Tharthara fawq al-Nil*?" He answered, "No, not yet." Nasser said, "Read it and let me know what you think." So Tharwat ʿUkasha took it with him on his trip. After he read it, he understood the reason for Nasser's question. It had been an angry question. Tharwat feared that I might be in trouble, that I might be dismissed or transferred, so upon his return, he went to see the president. He said to him: "Mr. President, I tell you frankly, that if art is not allowed this kind of freedom, it will not be art." So Nasser said calmly, "Very well, consider the matter closed." [19]

Hence, this critical novel was published with Nasser's reluctant consent only because of Tharwat ʿUkasha's intervention. One might ask if *al-Karnak* would have ever seen the light of day had this kind of patronage not come to Mahfouz's rescue. In fact, soon after, during a visit to *al-Ahram* in 1969, Nasser made sure to challenge such patronage. During that visit, which Mahfouz recounts in more than one context, Nasser's threats were clear and unambiguous:

> "We haven't read anything by you for the past couple of weeks."
> "Tomorrow they're publishing a new story . . . "
> Haykal commented, "It is a story bound to send its author to jail."
> Nasser said, laughing, "Actually, it is bound to send you to jail."[20]

If the word *jail* looms large in the above conversation, it is only because jails were indeed part of a lived reality at a time when the regime cracked down heavily on any opposition or criticism. Mahfouz speaks about the difficulties of publication and about his fears of persecution and detention during the Nasser period, especially after the 1967 war, the defeat he had so brilliantly predicted in *Miramar* (1967) and later depicted in so many of his post-1967 short stories. "I used to write such stories that when the satiric writer Muhammad ʿAfifi read them, he would call me at home to make sure that I had not been detained. That was before 1967. After 1967 they imposed censorship on books."[21]

In order to escape censorship, Mahfouz resorted to symbolism so heavy that many of his critics accused him of having abandoned realism for the absurd. But he defends himself against such statements by reminding us that many of these "obscure" and "absurd" stories had been censored for political reasons: "Do you want clear evidence as to the nonabsurdity of my absurd works? They were all censored for political reasons. The publication of some was delayed; in other cases whole sections were deleted. Do you really think that the political censor would ban works that have no meaning?"[22]

Unlike the timely *Tharthara fawq al-Nil,* which could have cost Mahfouz his career, *al-Karnak* (1974) made a safe appearance. This novel, which exposes the torture in detention camps and the fate of political prisoners under Nasser, was published during the early Sadat period. The date and history of publication of *al-Karnak* instructively point to two new elements: Mahfouz no longer had intellectual patrons, yet the change of regime—which welcomed revisionism of the Nasser period—was enabling. Change of power therefore becomes a permissive moment, even if, as Mahfouz has implied, it introduces a crucial time-lag between the lived sociopolitical reality and its articulation in fiction. "During my evenings at the Riche coffee-house I used to listen to many things which people had repressed. Had I not written them they would have been lost. So I wrote. . . . But when I first wrote *al-Karnak,* it did not appear in *al-Ahram.* Ahmad Baha᾽ al-Din, who was then editor in chief, refused the manuscript, though at the same time he recommended it to Kamal Abu al-Majd, editor of *al-Shabab* magazine."[23] It is evident from the above incident that the patronage that Mahfouz had benefited from in the late 1950s and 1960s was no longer there, not so much because Mahfouz himself had changed, but because the political climate, which had tolerated such patronage during the early years of the revolution, had gradually been transformed.

If *al-Karnak* offers one example of such compromises, the *al-Hubb taht al-matar* (Love under the rain, 1973) offers another. Like *al-Karnak,* this work was serialized in *al-Shabab* and not in *al-Ahram.* When it came to its publication in book form, the compromise was even greater: a whole section was deleted from the book, with Mahfouz's knowledge and consent.

> They censored the entire section that had to do with the battlefront. I was tempted to withdraw my decision to publish the book. But the publisher threatened to charge me the cost of printing. And of course he would not have covered that. I would have had to cover it myself. That is why I agreed to having the book published, as censored, since I could not afford to pay the cost of

> printing. . . . The published novel was like a single-winged bird since we never saw the life of the draftee, in the novel, to justify the reason for the dissatisfaction and anger. [24]

Accepting censorship rather than militating against it, which curtails the very freedom Mahfouz has always advocated, has earned him substantial criticism, especially from the younger generation of writers who considered him the model. His response to his critics is always a variation on the same theme (one that ultimately refers to the opening passage of this chapter): "I was never the leader. But when the leadership figure, whether that be in the neighborhood or at school, called for a strike, I was among the first to strike and demonstrate."[25] Mahfouz assigns himself a passive, rather than an active, role; as a writer, he reacts rather than takes the initiative. If such are the strategies of nonconfrontation, then one must question their implications on Mahfouz's double existence: the writer/bureaucrat or the outsider/insider.

On a surface level Mahfouz may appear to have succeeded in leading two seemingly separate existences: that of the civil servant and that of the writer. From the start, Mahfouz imposed a rigorous system on his waking hours (newspapers and various readings in the early morning, the office, an afternoon nap, and an evening writing session) as a means of compartmentalizing his existence. But despite this regimentation, Mahfouz's literary history confounds and distorts the clear-cut distinctions that he makes between these two separate parts of his life.

After four decades of civil service, Mahfouz published his novel *Hadrat al-muhtaram* (*Respected Sir,* 1975), a satiric portrait of an aspiring government employee, ʿUthman Bayyuumi. No other work of his—and there are many populated with government bureaucrats—so successfully collapses the two components of his life that he tried to maintain apart. In this work Mahfouz provides us with his sarcastic views of civil service through his creative writing, so that *Respected Sir* embodies the intrusion of one existence on the other:

> He also told himself that "government official" was still a vague concept inadequately understood. In the history of Egypt, an official occupation was a sacred occupation like religion, and the Egyptian official was the oldest in the history of civilization. The ideal citizen of other nations might be a warrior, a politician, a merchant, a craftsman or a sailor, but in Egypt it was the government official. And the earliest moral instructions recorded in history were the exhortations of a retiring official to his son, a rising one.

> Even the Pharaohs themselves, he thought, were but officials appointed by the gods of heaven to rule the Nile Valley by means of religious rituals and of administrative, economic and organizational regulations. [26]

Furthermore, the position that Mahfouz adopts toward the protagonist in *Respected Sir* and his ironic use of language throughout the narrative make this work an important testimony. Indeed, this novel reveals Mahfouz's criticism of the function on which he remained begrudgingly dependent all his life. In *Respected Sir* Mahfouz adopts an omniscient point of view that probes the consciousness of the protagonist whose hopes, fears, ambitions, and disappointments in ascending the social ladder are rendered in an idiom that parodies the different stages of a mystical journey. The reader is made to follow the life history of a man who is "consumed" by the "sacred fires" of public service. ʿUthman Bayyumi lives the life of an ascetic, with one focal point for which all else must be sacrificed.

But if ʿUthman Bayyumi's life in *Respected Sir* is a gradual surrender to the "sacred fires" of the job, Mahfouz's life, in contrast, has been a constant, uneasy struggle against those very fires. The sarcasm, which elevates civil service to a historical, even divine necessity, is not altogether remote from lived reality. Mahfouz has always considered civil service part of an unwelcome fate from which he could be saved only through direct intervention from God. In an early personal correspondence with his friend Adham Rajab, published without their permission in Cairo's weekly *Uktubir* magazine, Mahfouz complains of this wearisome double existence: "I hope God will rescue me from my job . . . or that he will make me win a lottery."[27] Rather than make him win a lottery, God sent him the Nobel! But even that, according to him, came too late. When asked how he felt after receiving the prize, given the hectic schedule that he was forced to endure, he said ironically, "I feel like a civil servant for Nobel!" [28]

Civil service often invaded that other existence that Mahfouz worked so hard to keep separate: "There were several periods of interruption as I was writing *The Trilogy*, because of my position as parliamentary secretary to the minister of Waqf [1939–50]. Between planning and writing, I believe it took me four years to produce *The Trilogy*."[29] Mahfouz has told me:

> There were periods when the job by necessity took over the space allotted to literature. With time the importance of the job and its responsibilities increase in the life of a person. In my situation,

> after the revolution I was selected chair of the Cinema Institute [1960–1962] on the recommendation of a certain minister [Tharwat ʿUkasha] who was a friend of mine. I spent one and a half years in this position. And it was a most unproductive period as regards writing. [30]

Since his very early years in civil service, Naguib Mahfouz has never failed to complain, at every occasion possible, about the setbacks of being a government employee while at the same time aspiring to become a great writer. He never ceased to dream of becoming the man of letters who had no other commitments but writing. He expressed this conflict in several interviews before and after he received the Nobel Prize.

> Yes, I am very orderly. The reason is that I have lived the double life of civil servant and writer. Had I not been a civil servant, I would have never taken order into consideration. [31]

> The nature of my relationship with everything would have changed had I devoted my time exclusively to being a writer. [32]

> Had I received the Nobel prize earlier, it would have changed my life entirely. . . . It would have given me real incentive for writing. Had it come earlier, I would have had more time to enjoy it. [33]

Mahfouz's financial dependency on his earlier jobs is the subject of several of his letters to Adham Rajab. In the following letters, he compares his own financial situation to that of others, justifies his participation in writing competitions, and reassures his friend that scriptwriting—which became a means of supplementing his income for many years, and which he considered a compromise—was not about to take him away from literature.

> I must confess that when I compare my situation to that of other colleagues I am beset with black thoughts. But do not fear for your friend the scriptwriter, for he cannot live without art unless fish can live without water. I participated in the short story competition organized by the Academy of the Arabic Language (I know that this will upset you, but I was in dire need of the money). . . . The Academy awarded me 150 L.E. which were my consolation for the antiquated reports that I read about the novels.

> And since when has work in the cinema gratified a real artist? I do not want to compromise my pen. . . . And real literature can only be had through debts.[34]

He was in his thirties when he wrote this letter. By the time he celebrated his fiftieth birthday, his financial situation had not changed much: "As for money, let me confess to you that as we speak, I have not yet reached a salary that would guarantee me the basic needs in life. Every month I draw on outside sources to pay my bills . . . my royalties, grants from the T.V. and radio."[35]

Mahfouz has made similar confessions to me. When we talked about the various writing competitions that he had entered, he reiterated the same position he had presented to Adham Rajab in the letters, this time quite unapologetically.

> Financial need was absolutely basic. I started participating in these competitions even before I had started publishing. I was then a small employee. True, the cost of living was low, but literature is something we invest in. When you add it all up you will find that in the final count—what with book purchases, paper, etc.—what is outgoing surpasses what is incoming. . . . No one can ask you how much you make from writing. The real question is how much you spend on it. That is why when they first started these literary awards the most important objective was always the award itself.[36]

After many years of civil service, during which Mahfouz continuously mourned his curtailed freedom as a writer, it became increasingly difficult for him to think of himself as a writer without thinking of himself as a bureaucrat. In 1959 Mahfouz was asked to produce a formula that would allow writers to dedicate all their time to literary production. In Mahfouz's plan, "The realistic or pragmatic way for writers to dedicate all their time to writing is to affiliate all of them with a place like the Ministry of Culture or the Supreme Council for Arts and Letters. Two elements must be taken into consideration: first, they will write in exchange for a salary; second, their working hours will be from 9:00 A.M. to 2:00 P.M."[37] In this plan, Mahfouz transforms all writers into civil servants, whose freedom is not only curtailed but completely obliterated. Indeed, although in his younger days Mahfouz considered his relationship to his job an imposed dependency, that relationship gradually became an advocated necessity.

Mahfouz tried to make civil service a means to an end. But as he moved from the margins of civil service toward the center, he found himself at once within and without, a participant and an observer, a collaborator and a critic; in short, he came to occupy a tenuous position that was very difficult to maintain. To believe that civil service is but a means to an end is to oversimplify Mahfouz's relationship to his public function. If at certain moments the job acted as a limiting factor—given his consecutive appointments to relatively high-ranking positions, beginning with his chairship of the Cinema Institute and ending with his appointment, after retirement, as a member of the editorial staff of *al-Ahram*—the nature of his relationship with the job and, by implication, with the state changed.

When Mahfouz speaks about his hectic schedule after he received the Nobel Prize, he pays tribute to *al-Ahram,* its editor in chief, and to his colleagues who volunteered both their time and their energy to organizing his impossible daily schedule. One cannot overlook the change of tone that perhaps confuses the whole notion of ends and means and recognizes the important support system within the institution: "If any other Arab writer, with no public function, had been awarded this prize, it would have been a catastrophe. What saved me was my affiliation with *al-Ahram.* What would another writer have done when we, unlike Western writers, have no agents. "[38] It is no wonder then that Mahfouz's critics have something to say about his function as a civil servant. Yes, it may have had its negative effects on his life as a writer; however, civil service taught Mahfouz how to use the double-edged weapon of the job. As part of the system, he learned to do two things at once: internalize it, even in his attitude as a "free" writer, and attack it while shielding himself against it. His critics observe, "Bureaucracy has taught him to be disciplined, orderly, and to avoid problems";[39] "[Naguib Mahfouz] uses the job, subjugates it, and protects himself with it, all at the same time."[40]

There is no doubt that civil service has made a contribution to Mahfouz's literary biography. It helped him navigate inside the system so that he could participate and observe, collaborate and critique. These strategies have earned him an Arab League boycott for his position on the Camp David Accords. To defend himself against charges in the Arab press in the aftermath of his widely contested series of articles "October Lessons," in which he hailed the 1973 war, Mahfouz says: "Those who protested against these lessons were the same as those who grieved over our triumph [in the October war]. . . . I read in some of the Lebanese papers that in writing these articles, Naguib

Mahfouz has transformed himself into an employee in the service of the Egyptian Information Agency. . . . I laughed and said, 'I do not mind being an employee in the Information Agency at a time when my country is at war.' "[41] What others may have considered an unforgivable compromise, Mahfouz renames patriotism. Rather than shy away from the image of the man with a job, he manipulates the image to his own advantage. Hence, the separateness that he claims exists between being the civil servant and being the writer collapses, so that the one conditions and informs the other.

One of the most direct and striking examples of this collapse is Mahfouz's weekly column in *al-Ahram*. In fact, this short weekly column in *al-Ahram* acts as a counterpart to his fiction. These brief articles have recently been published in a three-volume collection of essays Mahfouz wrote over the past eighteen years.[42] The articles cover topics as wide-ranging as democracy, religion, youth, freedom, culture, and education; and they are an excellent example of the confounded dual role Mahfouz fulfills. In most instances, the articles represent the voice of the insider rather than that of the outsider, of the participant rather than of the observer. When contrasted with his fiction, which is predominantly critical, these pieces definitely serve a more conformist function—one that points to Mahfouz's role as a man of letters within the system, as one who is part of the establishment. In these articles he is careful not to take sides, and his pronouncements remain predominantly conservative. When confronted with criticism, he openly replies: "I am not a preacher, and I am not talented for political action in the sense of planning and leadership. . . . After the revolution, we all became members of the Arab Socialist Union, just like a new job."[43]

In his younger days, when he was still a small employee in the Ministry of Waqf, Mahfouz could afford to be critical of al-ʿAqqad's politics and his position on the 1936 Anglo-Egyptian treaty. After al-ʿAqqad was appointed senator, and writer-in-residence for *Akhbar al-Yawm*, Mahfouz wrote to a friend, "You ask me about al-ʿAqqad: . . . he is an (appointed) senator, a car-owner, and a writer-in-residence for *Akhbar al-Yawm* with L.E. 150 salary. I guess now you know his position on the [1936 Anglo-Egyptian] treaty."[44] Almost four decades later, Mahfouz ironically found himself in the very situation that he had criticised. His support of the Camp David Accords and his various statements on the Arab-Israeli conflict put him and ʿal-Aqqad in the same camp. Perhaps such is an inevitable end to being part of the establishment. But there is another edge to this problem: it reflects on Mahfouz's fiction itself.

Mahfouz has frequently been accused of being too detached, too neutral in his literary works. He is often seen as a writer with a pronounced position or voice, a writer without the vision of the future, who fails to create or clearly suggest a utopia. When pressed by Ghali Shukri to respond to this issue, Mahfouz said, "My sympathies for a certain character appear one way or the other within the novel. Whoever asks of me more than that is asking me to scream. And this is not Art. Do you not sense what I am for, or against, in both *The Trilogy* and *al-Harafish* despite my neutrality? . . . You know that there is no such thing as a neutral language. . . . I know only one thing: when I represent the world with neutrality, I do so without being neutral. "[45]

The culmination of this problem of neutrality is best exemplified in Mahfouz's more recent work *Amam al-ʿarsh* (Before the throne) published in 1983. Not a novel, this book bears the subtitle *A Dialogue with the Rulers of Egypt from Mina to Anwar al-Sadat.* It is set as a tribunal (*mahkama*) presided over by Osiris and Isis. Egyptian leaders file in, one by one, and are questioned on their deeds and misdeeds. Although *Amam al-ʿarsh* resembles a trial, no sentence is passed on any of the rulers who appear. The book remains faithful to its subtitle by being a dialogue throughout, and all leaders are asked to sit in the rows of the eternal until further judgment is passed. Even as the book exposes the critical areas under each leader's rule, it refrains from passing a sentence, and it insists on the neutrality so characteristic of Mahfouz. The trial of Anwar al-Sadat, the last leader to appear in the book, is a case in point:

> Nasser asked him, "How did you have the heart to take such a stance so disrespectful to my memory?"
>
> Anwar al-Sadat replied, "I had to, since the essence of my policies was founded on correcting the mistakes I had inherited from your rule."
>
> "But I knew you as a supporter and a friend."
>
> Mustafa al-Nahhas said, "I was surprised to hear that you advocated democracy. Then I discovered that you wanted a democracy through which you could exercise your dictatorial power."
>
> "I wanted a democracy that would protect the mores of the village, and the rights of paternity."
>
> So Saʿd Zaghlul replied, "That is correct. But real democracy is taken, and not given. So don't exaggerate in blaming him."
>
> Mustafa al-Nahhas continued, "The people were oppressed, and signs of civil war and extremism began to emerge. You let

> matters get worse, as if it were not your concern. Then suddenly you exploded and put everyone in jail, so that you angered Muslims, Christians, extremists, and modernists. And it all ended with the tragedy of your assassination."
>
> At this point Isis said, "Thanks to this son, the spirit of the country was revived, and Egypt regained its complete independence just like the days before the Persian invasion. He has done wrong, as others have, but he has done more right than many."
>
> So Osiris said, "I welcome you among the eternal sons of Egypt. You will later proceed to the next tribunal, with a high recommendation from us." [46]

In a perceptive lecture on the works of Mahfouz, Sonallah Ibrahim, a leading Arab writer who belongs to a generation younger than Mahfouz, provides an important distinction between Mahfouz and the post-Mahfouzian generation of writers. In his analysis, Ibrahim locates Mahfouz's neutrality, or his disengagement from politics, in the latter's continuous sense of double existence—of being at once the bureaucrat and the creative writer. For Ibrahim, this duality accounts for many of Mahfouz's positions on various urgent issues, including his position on the censorship of his own work. For Ibrahim, one important distinction between Mahfouz and those writers who succeeded him is the collapse of this duality in both life and creative writing. In speaking about his own generation, Ibrahim says:

> The majority of these were outsiders. They did not occupy any official position. Both in life and novels, they [were] revolting against the political experience of the country, its outdated social and moral traditions. What lay at the center of their perception was the need to fight against dualism, enforced by backwardness and dependency. They strove for a unification of form and content, commitment and creation, art and politics. [47]

Indeed, this sense of unification between commitment and creation, between art and politics, is the distinguishing mark here. But the real measure of freedom, according to Ibrahim, is to be and remain an outsider, to steer away from "any official position."

To this, Mahfouz would probably reply, "All I can say is that there are certain principles which saturate my very being. . . . That is why my works must defend them. The most important of these principles is social justice . . . and there are other, equally urgent needs, such as freedom, truth, and knowledge. I cannot imagine that any of my works fail to advocate such principles."[48] He would probably then add, as he did in Gamal al-Ghitani's *Najib Mahfuz yatadhakkar,* "Believe my literary works." [49]

8

EXISTENTIAL THEMES IN A TRADITIONAL CAIRO SETTING

MONA N. MIKHAIL

THE RELATIONSHIP between existentialism and Arab thought has been investigated by several Western and Arab philosophers. A summary of the findings of one of the foremost spokespersons of Arab existentialism, ʿAbd al-Rahman Badawi, will help us to understand its manifestation in contemporary literature in general and particularly the works of Naguib Mahfouz.

Badawi has discussed the striking affinities between traditional Islamic philosophy and modern existentialism.[1] He addresses himself to the complex question of whether a Muslim thinker can be an existentialist within his own cultural tradition. His brilliant study, *al-Insaniyya wa al-wujudiyya fi al-fikr al-ʿArabi* (Humanism and existentialism in Arab thought) traces deep-rooted links between existentialism and the philosophy of Sufism. "Between these two tendencies—existentialism and Sufism (mysticism)—there exist, in principle, deep affinities of method and ultimate goals. Sufism is based on a doctrine of subjectivity: by that we mean that it recognizes no true existence other than that of the individual."[2] Sufism and existentialism place humanity at the center of all things.

Badawi proceeds to demonstrate how the notion of the perfect human, (*al-insan al-kamil*) in Sufism corresponds to Kierkegaard's notion of the one and unique, a cornerstone of existential thought. "The idea of the perfect man makes manifest the union between Sufism and existentialism from a humanist tendency. Indeed we find the strongest assertion of this tendency here, as it amounts to a deification of man. Existentialism too substitutes human existence for divine existence" (328). The fiction of Mahfouz reflects this compound notion of existentialism and Sufism. Mahfouz's "Hikaya bi-la bidaya wa la nihaya" (Story without beginning and without end, 1971), from the collection of the same name, has as its hero a Sufi leader who is grappling with his existential surroundings and who finally realizes that his true Sufi beliefs are identical with those of his rebellious existential son.

Badawi's findings expose fascinating relationships between these two concepts. The similarity between the Sufi and existentialist definitions of *l'angoisse* (*qalaq,* "anguish") started him on his investigative course. "I found in Sufism a definition of anguish that resembled point-by-point that of Heidegger. We owe this definition to Shaykh Ahmad Dia᾿ al-Din al-Kamashkhanli al-Naqshabandi in his work *Jamiʿ al-usul fi al-awliya*" (328). In this definition, anguish experienced by an individual translates itself into a feeling of estrangement in the face of all that is not true and into a sense of alienation and isolation from the surrounding universe. Such was the essence of the thought of that Sufi philosopher several hundred years before the modern exponents of existentialism formulated their dogmas.

Badawi proceeds to show further parallelisms between Kierkegaard's modes of thinking and those of his Sufi predecessors. Both have used religious texts as myths to interpret their existential concepts. "It is exactly what Muslim Sufis have done, specifically al-Hallaj, al-Suhrawardi, and Ibn al-ʿArabi. Al-Hallaj in particular chose to relive, as it were, the life of the Messiah, attempting to experience it existentially, giving it comprehensive expression that would serve as a basis for existential analysis. This is precisely what Kierkegaard later attempted to do" (330).

It is therefore appropriate for existentialism to find a place in modern Arab thought and fiction. The attempt to find its sources in the Arab heritage is not a rejection of its modern European influence, for these affinities could not have become apparent in the absence of the Western model. Mahfouz reflects both of them in his fiction: "This literature, one of the youngest in the world, offers, by comparison with the West, the double interest of having been nurtured at the breasts of its art."[3] Therein lies the uniqueness and originality of contemporary Arabic literature: it is inspired by Western prototypes but retains its authenticity.

In his valuable preface to the 1964 edition of the *Anthologie,* Jacques Berque examined the disturbing effects of the West on the Arab soul.

> The term *qalaq* enjoys in Arabic a venerable and ancient history, and today it is used to describe what we term "anguish" [*l'angoisse*].

> By necessity it invites other nuances. It conjures up the unnerving image of the body breaking loose from its frame, the jarring noises such a state might produce. The Arabs understood this state of being long before Kierkegaard courted such notions. Nevertheless states of frustration (*hirman*) have taken on in modern times other added meanings that can be understood only in light of (non-Arab) foreign models. (16)

Mahfouz's works manifest those symptoms of "frustration" and "alienation" in forceful terms. Aside from their indigenous roots, Berque points out, those symptoms can be explained in terms of "modèles étrangers." It is a literary existentialism, rather than the purely philosophical one that will be examined here.

In *Taht al-mizalla* (Under the bus-stop shelter, 1969), a collection of stories written between October and December 1967, Mahfouz experiments with new approaches in both form and content. The title story is one of his most striking. It is in the vein of the absurd that students of European existentialism will recognize. The story represents a landmark of Mahfouz's development. The fabric of the narrative unravels before our eyes into a sequence of absurd, hair-raising episodes of dreamlike quality. The reader is twice removed from the scene of action to focus on a group of people standing under a bus-stop shelter, through whose eyes we take in their harrowing experience. This group of people may seem to be there merely as spectators, but in effect they are the collective protagonist of the story, and the reader is a reluctant participant.

An intermittent drizzle varies in intensity as a leitmotiv of the story, synchronizing with the events. The story begins with a number of people huddled together seeking shelter from the rain as they wait for the bus. This banal and commonplace opening is interrupted by the intrusion of someone who appears to be fleeing an angry crowd. The hot pursuit ends in the brutal beating of the man, who appears to be a thief. The onlookers watch and are astonished that a police officer is placidly observing the whole scene without intervening.

The most extraordinary things continue to happen, while the spectators under the bus-shelter continue to be amazed and the police officer watches nonchalantly, averting his gaze. The crowd realizes that something should be done about the situation, especially when two cars collide and the blood-soaked casualties are sprawled all over the scene. They decide among themselves that it may be wise to use a nearby phone to contact an ambulance, but no one budges. Meanwhile, the thief has succeeded in talking his way out of his dilemma and has stripped naked to the cheers of his onetime pursuers and persecutors. He dances to the tempo of their synchronized cheers, and the crowd watches in mounting amazement.

Attempting to ground this state of affairs in reality, the observers try to convince themselves that they must be witnessing scenes from a movie being shot on location. They keep expecting a director to appear and give orders to his actors or perhaps reshoot some of the scenes. Nothing of the sort happens, so they consider the possibility that they may be dreaming, or rather experiencing a nightmare. The height of absurdity occurs when an unidentified man and woman appear on the scene, strip naked, and begin making love over the dead body of one of those killed in the earlier car crash.

These tableaux culminate in the final scene, in which the police officer addresses, for the first time, two lingering spectators who seem a little bit more concerned than the others about these uncommon happenings and who demand that something be done about the situation. He responds by asking for their identification and then accuses them of unlawful assembly. Finally he takes out his pistol and murders them. This shocking conclusion seems an appropriate climax to the gory tale. What Mahfouz says here may be simply that apathy is alive in each of us and that not much can be done about it.

The author's clever manipulation of cinematic devices creates an element of artificiality that contrasts with the seemingly normal setting, as in the opening: "And the monotony of the scene almost froze the picture" (5). The episodes that break into the scene are narrated in the manner of a Godard film—in unrelated scenes of gore accumulated over time to have a deep effect on the reader. By sharing the bystanders' consternation and amazement at the developing events, the reader is also made to share their apathy and noninvolvement, which leads ultimately to their common destruction. Identification with hero or heroes extends in this story to sharing responsibility with the passive onlookers.

"Taht al-mizalla" bears a striking resemblance to Ionesco's "La photo du colonel" (1962) in both content and treatment. Both stories deal with the absurd in unassuming fashion, and both emphasize the themes of apathy and violence spreading into mundane, daily life. The events of Ionesco's story take place in an exclusive quarter of a modern city, presumably Paris. The outward beauty and harmony of the setting offset the subsequent ugliness of the killings that take place there. Here again a writer subtly weaves elements of the absurd and mysterious into seemingly commonplace events.

Both writers choose police officers as agents of law and order, as representatives of the establishment, and make them stand for apathy. The police officer in Ionesco's story is oversized, towering over the narrator, who tries in vain to seek help. The narrator pleads with the police officer to alert his superiors, saying that he has the incriminating evidence that could lead to the merciless murderer who has strangled and drowned his victims in the beautiful fountain of this rich area. The officer chides the narrator sternly, asking him to mind his own business, and warns him not to disturb the peace. The narrator's response is natural but, in context, comically naïve: "The attitude of the police officer shocked me. He had the duty of being polite in public. It must be written in the rules." [4]

Ionesco presents the sequel as inevitable. And when the narrator levels his pistol and is about to shoot the murderer, he is suddenly seized by a feeling of helplessness in the face of that personification of evil: "I felt helpless, in total despair, for what can bullets do, or my feeble force in the face of cold hatred and obstinacy, against the infinite energy of this absolute, merciless, mindless cruelty?" (52).

Mahfouz and Ionesco end these two stories on a pessimistic note: helplessness in the face of uncalled-for cruelty. Thus both stories may seem statements of despair. But remember Camus's dictum that a literature of despair is a contradiction in terms. "The important fact of existentialist living and dying is that each is given in naturalistic and psychological depth, and that style, in the best of works at least, is within and a part of the process of self-awareness." [5]

"Hikaya bi-la bidaya wa la nihaya" (Story without beginning and without end), from the 1971 collection of that title, is a more complex and elaborate treatment of the interrelated themes of religion and politics. The nine-part story draws heavily on dialogue to carry the action forward. The philosophical speculation and spiritual ambiance form the story's background, on which the political overtones are superimposed. Without directly tracing the history of a whole family, that of al-Akram the central figure, the story delves into the psyches of three representatives of three successive generations. Mahfouz's intimate familiarity with his subject matter enables him to conjure up those characters and trace each one's development or moral deterioration or both in a highly intricate design.

The enigmatic central figure, the *wali* (holy man) Mahmud al-Akram, exercises absolute influence on his followers in a Rasputin fashion. He is the indisputable dictator over the minds and hearts of his people; he is a living legend as far as they are concerned. The symbol of his influence is centered in his Big House (*al-bayt al-kabir*), the general headquarters of his despotism. The Big House is the spiritual center that diffuses light and guidance to followers not only in Egypt but in far-off lands from Morocco to Iran, where the house represents the beating heart of a whole spiritual movement.

As al-Akram, an aspirant lover of Sufi philosophy, reaches by degrees the object of his love, the reader gradually unravels the entangled circles of this story. Circular patterns prevail throughout, bringing both content and form into focus. The central figure goes full circle and undergoes a fundamental change in personality, embracing spiritual purity and rejecting his other wicked self. The discovery of a father-son relationship long kept secret by the betrayed mother falls within those converging circles. The title itself, "Story without beginning and without end," is the graphic equivalent of those unending circles.

The first lines set the tone and mood of the story. We are in the midst of a *dhikr* gathering of al-Akram's *tariqa*.[6] The chant is accentuated by the choral response of the adept, and it gradually heightens in intensity. Mahfouz subtly uses this framework of the chant to impart the history of the founding of al-Akram's brotherhood. We also learn that the ritual of the ecstatic order is under a cloud that day: the elders and sheikhs are disturbed by the rumors that some strange happenings are going on in their *hayy* (quarter). The young men of the quarter have banded together and seem to be concocting some trouble. The younger generation is said to have mocked and derided the order and even to have dared to attack Mahmud al-Akram. So that day's mystic contemplations are set aside for more pressing matters that seem to question and endanger their very existence.

The name of ʿAli ʿUways is soon associated with this trouble, and the holy man recognizes him as the brother of Zaynab, the school teacher who was known for sacrificing her whole life to the upbringing of the orphan ʿUways and who now seems to be leading the rebellion. Indeed, ʿUways came as the spokesperson for those angry young men seeking clarifications and demanding accounts from the venerated leader. They came to tell him that they could no longer accept the contradictions that surrounded them: on the one hand, the opulence and luxury al-Akram enjoyed; on the other hand the dire poverty the rest of the quarter was experiencing. They have learned in their universities that progress is inevitable and that it is their duty as individuals to do something about the inequities of their society. At that point, al-Akram, having had a secular as well as a theological education, thinks he can win them over to his side by agreeing to talk to them as equals and colleagues. Thus, at the end of this first part, al-Akram faces the dilemma of how to handle that critical situation—how to appease the growing wrath and discontent of the rising generation while at the same time maintaining his authority and prestige.

The second part of the story is devoted to a brief encounter between al-Akram and Zaynab, who—more threatening than begging—asks al-Akram to release ʿUways and the others who have been arrested. For al-Akram, this face-to-face confrontation with Zaynab suddenly unleashes repressed memories that momentarily surge to the surface. He remembers how beautiful she used to be and tells her she still is. We thus learn that he has had a brief affair with Zaynab, and that she has kept her shame a secret and carried on with courage and endurance all these years, pretending that ʿUways was her younger brother.

The events that follow lead to the inevitable finale—a confrontation between the two conflicting forces in the story. The young disgruntled men come out with tracts denouncing and exposing the atrocities committed by the "great master" and his ancestors. Al-Akram feels the grip of his authority loosening, and in his hour of trial he seeks the support of a venerated dervish who has broken away from his brotherhood in protest of his life-style.

Most of the scandalous information about his immediate family comes as a shattering shock to al-Akram. Tortured and humiliated, he seeks no mercy when he forces his aging governess to verify all the shame and guilt he deserves. His fury is expressed in his outburst at the end of part 5.

> "O Shaykh ʿAmmar, do not talk to me in the language of the wise, for I am no wise one. I am a criminal in whose blood crime has flowed since time immemorial. . . . We are in the midst of a struggle that involves life and death; we need cunning, ruthlessness, violence, and not beautiful slogans. You are a cunning fox, and I need every drop of cunning from your heart. Do not bother about appearances, for the stench is out. Summon all the demons that live in this house, and get whoever you can from the quarter—enough cheating with false virtues . . . draw out from the graves of your heart the beautiful vices originally born for struggle and triumph." (58)

We see al-Akram's mask falling, revealing a merciless fiend bent on annihilating his opponents at any price. Al-Akram has come full circle, unveiling his other self after having succeeded in camouflaging it for so long. This aspect is further accentuated in his ensuing encounters with ʿUways and, after ʿUways is arrested once more, with Zaynab, who as a last resort, reluctantly unveils to him her long-kept secret that he—al-Akram—is the father of ʿUways.

Thus ends part 6 of the story, which brings us full circle to that long-forgotten beginning of intentionally repressed memories. Mahfouz makes us all relive this scene through a short dialogue between Zaynab and Mahmud and a flashback to the time of her discovery that she was with child. Al-Akram's cowardice and irresponsibility at that point are revealingly in character.

This turn adds new dimensions to the story. Here the archetypal father-son relationship with its Freudian overtones inevitably comes to mind. Mahfouz employs the archetypes of the rebellion of the son against the father and of the desire to oust the ruler and lord of the tribe, and he adds the irony of the mistaken identities of father and son. Al-Akram's words corroborate this primeval, inevitable state of things: "The struggle going on today is beyond and stronger than any personal relationship." Again indicating the devastating effect of this revelation, al-Akram sums up by saying to Zaynab, "Believe me, everything is out of balance: the stars have gone out of their orbits, words are denuded of their logic, the cupolas of the shrines have brought forth idols" (74). Thus the sense of doom that often surrounds myths is clearly present in the story. Scattered throughout are utterances that underline the mythical implications of the father-son conflict ("What is the use of debating when we are on the verge of fighting? When the father may kill the son or the son his father? . . . but they are ousting a usurping king from his fake throne" [81]). This sets the scene for the final confrontation that concludes part 8 and that puts the conflict on another level, averting disaster when al-Akram tells ʿUways that he is his father.

At this juncture the story bifurcates. The revelation momentarily paralyzes the father and son. The forces that had been operating all along within al-Akram surface, and his complex character undergoes a harrowing internal conflict. His mystical teachings and ascetic heritage—in short his Sufi affiliations—are at war with his more worldly, avidly criminal nature. For since the crisis developed, he has not ceased to ruminate about his life, its meaning, and its direction. To the old sheikh, he hints that he yearned for a simple, pure mode of living. "I had to choose either prostitution or sainthood. And I have chosen my way, from my heart came stubborn and unexpected decisions, like a hammer beating on my head, which swept away the viscous sliminess of prostitution. I refused defeat and disdained easily won happiness. It seems that my faith in the essence of what my grandfather was is greater than my belief in his miracles. (97)

In these terms, al-Akram sums up his crisis to ʿUways, who has come to accept these realities. ʿUways and his father and mother are ready to face life in the quarter in spite of its expected hardships. They are all aware that the internal commotion that has pitted father against son, wife against husband, and brother against brother is far from being appeased. Yet ʿUways, armed with his newly acquired self-knowledge, al-Akram with his undaunted drive, and Zaynab, who had finally shared her secret with her son and his father, are all ready to start anew. They consider that they have lived their season in hell and have emerged purified.

As the old sheikh had formulated it earlier:

> "Life is seething before your eyes: its corners collapse, illusions evaporate, truths come tottering like bombs, elements disintegrate demanding new components, new voices destroy the deaf walls and rise, species amalgamate, forces are set free from their hiding places, and the conscience asks the individual to take a stand. Hold on . . . escape . . . live . . . die . . . complicate . . . renew . . . but there is no way except to immerse oneself in the sea of darkness and to swim to the shore of light." (85)

This apocalyptic vision of things before a possible redemption seems to have been a favorite formula from Dante to Conrad to Mahfouz. The inferno, the heart of darkness, or the waves of darkness seem an inevitable phase for humankind to pass through in our eternal pursuit of truth. Like Conrad's Marlowe, al-Akram has to descend into his heart of darkness and cry out "the horror, the horror" before he can emerge with a clearer vision of his role in life or of the meaning of life in general.

Mahfouz's story traces the emergence of the revolt in humankind. ʿAli ʿUways is the Prometheus who dares to defy the gods. He is not, however, depicted as an abstract personification. He is very much the existential man because he translates his revolt into action and achieves the change he desired. In the Sartrean sense, he participates in history, pursuing the eternal and discovering universal values in concrete action, which he shapes with a particular goal in view.[7] ʿUways plunges into concrete action to change a state of affairs imposed upon him. His uprising is also directed against the notion of the godhead and results in the "god's" defeat and surrender to human recriminations. Al-Akram, that deposed "god," is like Sartre's Jupiter in *The Flies*, a god who bargains and compromises with his creations. There is nothing divine or godly about al-Akram; indeed, he is conceived strictly in human terms.

"Ruh tabib al-qulub" (Spirit of the doctor of hearts), from Mahfouz's 1971 collection, *Shahr al-ʿasal* (Honeymoon), is an intriguing quest for truth. As usual, Mahfouz feels more at ease among types he knows best: he puts together a motley crowd of the underworld of his beloved city. His heroes are a wali, a street girl, a guardian of a cemetery, and a police officer. The action of the story is delivered largely through dialogue. The effect of the short and at times cryptic questions and answers of the dialogues between the different characters is most striking. Throughout the story, those one-word answers and questions carry the action to its zenith in a most impressive fashion. Particularly in this collection, Mahfouz seems to be experimenting with this innovative use of language in prose fiction, a development that may prefigure his subsequent experimentation with drama.

To set in motion this strange conglomeration of characters, and to have them act and interact in quasi isolation from the rest of the world, Mahfouz chooses as a site the shrine of a man who seems to have recently acquired his sainthood. Tabib al-Qulub, or the doctor of hearts, has been rising in importance and becoming the most venerated holy man in the area. So it is appropriate for the wali to seek his shrine for shelter. The manner in which the characters happen to fall into each other's company is reminiscent of Samuel Beckett's *Waiting for Godot*. Like Estragon and Vladimir, the wali and the girl are stranded in this deserted spot and engage in repartee that is equally profound and moving. Beckett's world is flat, sterile, and lonely—doomed from the very start. Mahfouz is more interested in tracing a certain degeneration from innocence, in exposing corruption lurking in the folds of false saintliness. He wishes to show how decay spreads because of long periods of stagnation, how the social fiber of people wears out because of the putrefaction of their ideals.

The opening encounter between the wali and the girl sets the tone for the action. From the very beginning, one is struck by the allegorical nature of the characters. The girl is nameless, almost ageless, because she ignores everything about herself. She has no place to call home and seems to have sprung out of the earth like an unwanted weed. She is totally unaware of the significance of such vague concepts as honor, conscience and religion, and the wali consequently brands her a demon when she cannot recognize him as being a man of God. Her spontaneous, unequivocal, earthy answers contrast her real humanity with the calculated, bigoted, empty rhetoric of the covetous wali. His pretended unworldliness is only a façade, behind which he nurtures vile and vicious feelings.

The guardian of the cemetery can see through the wali best. It is as if the guardian's lifetime occupation and his proximity to death have paradoxically left him more aware of the things of this life. And so he merely articulates the intentions of the wali when he suggests that they seize the gold and jewelry the girl wears. Their greed is only whetted by the thought that they may have to share their booty with the police officer if they consult him about her fate. Once the police officer is introduced to the scene (as a final resort), he too is shown to be an empty, corrupt representative of law and order; and the three begin disputing their lawful rights, after having shut up the girl within the walls of the shrine.

In the midst of their haggling, an old blind man and the young blind man who leads him arrive, presumably seeking the shrine of "the comforter of broken hearts." The appearance of these two uninvited intruders creates much embarrassment for the three criminals. Their embarrassment turns to irritation, then to fear when the young man suddenly, as if in a state of trance, cries out that he has heard some mysterious voice. He unhesitatingly decides it must be the voice of "the comforter of broken hearts," the champion of lost causes. His insistence draws some lingerers who have converged on the shrine. In their blue *gallabiyyas* (long cotton robes) and naked feet, they stand bewildered at the developments that ensue. No sooner has our young man forced his way into the shrine than he can be heard shouting hysterically that a miracle has taken place and that he can actually see. The crowd in the courtyard of the shrine chant in unison the mercy of the Creator and demand to see a miracle happen.

In mounting mass hysteria, the crowd, also acting as a chorus, becomes the protagonist of the story. It takes over and initiates what follows. The seeing young man begins representing the "spirit" to the crowd. The story then takes a turn hardly expected by either party, for obviously the imprisoned girl in the shrine has been mistaken for a curing spirit, though she remains totally unaware of it. The three miscreants are caught in a critical situation and have to find a way out, while the cured young man thinks of himself, and in effect appoints himself, as the intercessor for this "holy spirit."

The girl's initial request is for the return of her stolen jewels. Understandably, her request causes endless speculations on philosophical meanings of "real jewels" and an instant acceptance that their appearance is a sign from above corroborating the saintliness of the girl. The sudden appearance of the real owner of the jewels, who insists on claiming them as stolen property, is met with angry denials and threats of a lynching. From this point on, the crowd is totally under the sway of the girl, "the spirit of the doctor of hearts." She orders them to tie up the three criminals, who at different points in the story have tried to indict her, and to throw them into the mausoleum. The money and jewels are distributed to the masses, who then disperse them according to their will. The acclaimed saint is then left alone with her intercessor, who is totally under her spell.

Meanwhile, the imprisoned group decide to reenact the whole drama and force the girl to play their game once more so that they can expose her. The following morning, imposters of the old blind man and the young blind man approach the mausoleum and reenact the scene from the day before. Finally, the "spirit" emerges in shackles and asks the crowd to return the jewels and money. Reluctantly, they listen to her exhortations; and when the incredulous young man who only the day before had confirmed her sainthood bursts out denouncing her, the masses are again ready to believe him. "A warm, approving wave surged from the hearts of the masses. They believed him from the depths of their tortured souls. Their view changed and the object of their vision changed. Shouts of anger and rebellion followed" (148–49).

Denounced, forsaken, and accused, the girl suddenly turns to the masses and throws her lot in with them. She cries out for help and denounces the criminals who had forced her to delude the masses into returning their newly found fortune. She declares that she is merely a poor, destitute girl—neither angel nor spirit—and that she was threatened either to go along with their farce or die. A bloody fight between factions follows—"a fight where the hands and the feet and the sticks and stones and teeth were used. Each side fought with perseverance and anger. The young man of the day before saw the girl fighting like a man, and it occurred to him that she must be his promised girl, and this filled him with added strength and heroism. . . . and the fight continued to grow in violence and brutality" (150).

Mahfouz's story ends on this ambiguous note. The enigma of the personality of the girl, "the spirit of the doctor of hearts," is never really comprehended either by the young man who was instrumental in creating her aura or by the credulous masses who bestowed her with immediate recognition. Even if Mahfouz is intentionally cryptic and the nature of his subject is meant to remain on that level of ambiguity, he certainly succeeds in again proposing layered levels of interpretation.

One cannot disregard the political and social overtones of this story. Mahfouz's sensitive analysis of the behavior of the masses—their conditioned responses, reactions, and interactions, and their readiness to engage in mass hysteria on the spur of the moment—aside from being of immediate importance to the development of the story, certainly demonstrates well-studied personal observations on the part of the author. One can discuss these political overtones at greater length or even name possible historical counterparts for the fictional characters. But this exercise would be of little consequence to the evaluation of this work as art. This story should be classified among Mahfouz's recent attempts to experiment with new subjects and new modes of expression.

Mahfouz draws heavily on dialogue to carry the action forward and to delineate character. His heroes are nameless and faceless. They are theatrical, because they are designated by their functions rather than by their names and separate, observable identities. The girl, the police officer, the wali, the two blind men, the guardian, the crowd, and the man whose fortune was stolen are summoned and dismissed according to methods of stage direction. One could conceivably, and without great difficulty, stage this story and achieve dramatic effect. Traditional stage directions are actually incorporated in the story. Examples abound: "And while the gentleman claps one hand over the other, his sight falls on the girl. He looks at her amazed and shouts . . . " (137); "The girl pointed to the gentleman, the servant of the mausoleum, and the wali and said . . . " (139). The movements of the masses, and therefore the action, are directed through these brief "stage directions": "The crowd pounced on the four men and tied them and led them inside the mausoleum, and the girl handed the key to the young man, saying . . . " (140). We can thus deduce Mahfouz's intentions to make this piece of literature as dramatic as he could, both literally and figuratively.

Mahfouz indicts decayed religious practices both explicitly and implicitly. Religion as an institution is exposed. And Mahfouz goes even further by questioning the very existence of any supreme being or providence. By choosing officers of established religion to be his criminals and picking a ragged street girl to embody the spirit that exercises its influence on the minds and hearts of the masses, Mahfouz makes an ironic commentary that cannot go unnoticed.

The interplay between appearance and reality is also significant within the framework of the story. The mistaken identity of the girl as a spirit and the attempt of the crooked men of religion to use this coincidence to their own vicious ends underlines this interplay. Confusion, however, always rests with the masses, thus emphasizing Mahfouz's lack of trust in the sense of judgment and the lucidity of vision among the fickle, swaying masses. Thus we get an intermingling of levels, the sociopolitical with the religiospiritual. Mahfouz presents us with a many-layered, suggestive story in a new mold. Indeed, it is a successful attempt to exploit dramatic effects within the framework of the short story. And it extends the dialogic framework of "Story with no beginning or end" into a social setting where the community itself is given a definite, if ironic, voice.

9

THE MAHFOUZIAN SUBLIME

MICHAEL BEARD

There are years when the Nobel Prize for literature is an event that honors its recipient, when the prestige of the grant-giving institution is of greater significance than that of the writer. There are also years when the honor flows the other way. (The 1982 award, for instance, to Gabriel García-Márquez, did less to increase the fame of the recipient than it did to enhance the reputation of the award.) The 1988 award to Naguib Mahfouz was a recognition of the latter kind. With it the Nobel committee has made a selection that validated its own relevance to world letters.

On a fundamental level, the committee called our attention to a part of the world whose culture is regularly left invisible to us. And the writer in this case is concerned particularly with people away from scenes of power: his paradigmatic setting is the *hara,* the *zuqaq,* the alley, the district, the neighborhood, the urban equivalent of a village, the home of people ordinarily outside the reach of official history, unnoticed and voiceless. Representing the voiceless is always a commendable project, but it is valuable only when the writer can do so in a way that the potential audience can hear; a hack who dealt with important issues awkwardly, without vision, would do those themes a disservice.

But if it is Mahfouz's style which validates his project (the particulars of expression which weave the fabric of his vision), the Nobel Committee and the Western reader would seem to be at a disadvantage. Everything depends on translations. Between us and those districts of Cairo stand not only Mahfouz's writing but the version of it available to us as western readers. So I claim for my subject not Mahfouz as he appears at home but the international Mahfouz, who consists of a series of fragments, the particular series of books that have become available in the West. Indeed, Mahfouz is, for me, the particular selection of books that have, by one accident or another, fallen into my hands. This is not an apology but a claim for a particular subject matter. The minute we take world literature seriously, we are committed to the intermediary of translation. Books emigrate piecemeal, in fragments and haphazard choices, finding their fortunes according to another set of accidents.

In a recent work, I am on record with a potentially disparaging comment about the Middle Eastern novel as an institution: "The non-western novel, with its occasional deviation from patterns western readers anticipate, its hesitation to stray from the thematically obvious, an occasionally audible creakiness in the mechanism, a sense of absence somewhere in the discursive structure, often strikes western readers as unworthy of their attention—irrelevant to our indigenous novelistic tradition."[1] I had Mahfouz in mind when I wrote those lines, specifically the Mahfouz of *Midaq Alley,* which is the only work of his I had read. I could spend time on an apology here, explaining away my insensitivity by citing the tentative nature of my criticism, the fact that I suppressed his name, or the fact that I suspect I am describing the experience of a lot of Western readers. But in any case, the strangeness of Mahfouz is, for us, the irreducible fact with which we have to come to terms.

We could think through this problem historically. The novel offers us the vista of two parallel streams of literary history. One is the European novel, the style that defines realism for us, whose major innovations we can trace back to Balzac—the emphasis on the relation of character and setting, the fascination with appearances and social roles, and the self-conscious manipulation of point of view—a tradition whose reversals in this century are founded on those patterns. The other stream is the more recent series of novelistic traditions that have grown up outside Europe or the United States—usually as part of the process of an awakening national identity—which conceive the novel as a tool for defining a national character and articulating national problems.

The dilemma, perhaps too obvious for us to focus on immediately, has to do with the neutral, transparent appearance of the novel as a form. In the acceptance speech Mahfouz wrote to be read in his absence in Stockholm, he speaks of himself as the son of two civilizations—Islam and the Egypt of the pharaohs, which seems to me a valid statement that leaves out something important—that the project of becoming a novelist is itself a career determined by Western modes of vision. The novel evolved as a response to nineteenth-century social changes in Europe. It is designed to focus on the particular problems of the industrialized world, and the possibility exists that the novel is a distorting lens outside the European community. Without entering the debate, we can at least acknowledge that two powerful views of the novel coexist among us. One reads it as a culture-specific form, a mode of storytelling that matches the concerns and ways of seeing of industrialized society. The other reads it as a neutral, flexible vision, nondistorting and infinitely exportable. For this reason I want to start with a quality of Mahfouz's writing that strikes the Western reader as unfamiliar, eccentric, and, well, strange.

A particular passage in Mahfouz's 1972 novel *al-Maraya* (*Mirrors*) exemplifies a peculiarity of his style, something irreducible and strange no matter how thoroughly it is rendered smooth and idiomatic in translation. The narrator has been visited in his office by the husband of a woman with whom he has been having an affair: " 'I've come to see you as Amani Muhammad's husband.' " The narrator recalls: "A second went by without my registering what he meant, but then it burst inside my head [*infajara ma'nahu fi wa'yi*] like a rocket. To tell the truth, I lost consciousness in a certain kind of way. Place and time disintegrated; all I could see was Abduh al-Basyuni's brown, circular face. It looked like someone else's face, a statue standing in front of my desk since time immemorial."[2] For me, as a Western reader, this passage can be read as an example of bad form, an attempt to produce an intensity of emotion through telling instead of showing. It is not the way Western novelists are expected to show interiority. Yet that right-angle turn into timelessness is a striking trope, and it demonstrates a narrative habit that plays a thematic role in Mahfouz's work—a fascination with language that concretizes consciousness (moods, metaphysical states), that objectifies and stands outside emotion. Thus the surprise becomes an explosion, the source of the explosion a statue; and between motion and stillness the passage finds its poles.

The passage from *Mirrors* stuck in my mind as something noteworthy but unclassifiable, an effect without a category, until much later, when I happened upon a similar concretion of an interior state in the opening pages of *Respected Sir* (1975). Novice clerk 'Uthman Bayyumi is on a tour of the government office where he will work and has a vision of his possible success rising through the bureaucracy. "I am on fire, O God. Flames were devouring his soul from top to bottom as it soared upwards into a world of dreams. In a single moment of revelation he perceived the world as a surge of dazzling light which he pressed to his bosom and held on to like one demented. He had always dreamed and desired and yearned, but this time he was really ablaze, and in the light of this sacred fire he glimpsed the meaning of life."[3]

Again, a moment of emotion seems too intense for its cause. Again, the word *meaning* has a cardinal function. In part, the excess of the description can be ascribed to irony—the ambition of a clerk transcribed into hyperbolic theological terms. At the end of the scene, however, readers are given a very realistic assessment of ʿUthman's ambition, and it leads in a different direction: "There was a happy path which began at the eighth grade in the government service and ended at the splendid position of His Excellency the Director-General. This was the highest ideal available to the common people, beyond which they could not aspire." ʿUthman lists the grades in turn, concluding: "The miracle could be brought about in thirty-two years. Or perhaps rather more" (*Respected Sir,* 6). ʿUthman is looking at something oversize, an institution so wide that it takes a whole life to cross, and the rest of the book simply documents his crossing of it. In a way, the subject of the book is ʿUthman's tangible contact with the infinite—or with the idea of the infinite—and in this we may take him as an emblem for Mahfouz as a writer, a restless observer fascinated constantly by what is beyond the available limits and by discrepancies of scale.

Something of the Piranesian sublime[4] lurks in Mahfouz's writing at every step in his career. The very project of a pharaonic novel—he wrote three out of a projected thirty-seven—is always in some way a dizzying perspective, a vista of unimaginable tracts of history. And as Mattithayu Peled has argued, Mahfouz handles them through characterizations that are themselves peculiar for a Western reader, because they depend so entirely on the relation of individual to society. One could in fact conclude (and Peled does work out a variation of this)[5] that in them our notion of literary character as a site of interiority does not exist, that the constitutive features of identity are elsewhere.

In his famous and influential article "The Metaphoric and Metonymic Poles" (1956), Roman Jakobson suggests two modes or processes by which information is stored in memory, paradigms that become visible when one or the other dominates in cases of aphasia. One he dubs metaphor, a relation of resemblance; the other metonymy, a relation of congruity or contingency.[6] He adduces the case of the

Russian novelist Gleb Ivanovich Uspenskij, who suffered a progressively worsening aphasia that resulted in an inability to store analogies, that is, in a loss of his metaphor-making power. In Uspenskij's novels, Jakobson finds an ultrarealism in which (to quote one critic) "the reader is crushed by the multiplicity of detail unloaded on him in a limited verbal space, and is physically unable to grasp the whole, so that the portrait is often lost."[7]

I recently went directly to Jakobson's essay when rereading the Trevor Le Gassick translation of Mahfouz's 1947 novel *Midaq Alley*, because it became clear that metonymy governs the structure of that book in a remarkable way—it gives the reader a sense of the infinite. The alley is not large, but the distinctive narrative rhythm Mahfouz develops to move us from one scene to the next generates a circling, decentered, disorienting series of points of view. And the alley is repeatedly set against a threatening larger world (modern Cairo, and beyond that against an outside Western world represented by the Allied troops) whose scope never really materializes, because the alley is too inconsequential to use as a measure. The narrator's role is ambiguous. He typically speaks as a local voice, submerged in the day-to-day perceptions of one or another character; but there are striking forays into omniscience (e.g., when Hamida's passage into prostitution is judged in absolute terms: "From the very beginning Hamida chose her path of her own free will"),[8] which seem to remind us how much more he could tell us if there were room.

By the end of the novel, a widening range of scenes circles outward from the neighborhood (into the house of prostitution, into the Cairo boulevards, and into the graveyard) and makes that voice begin to seem an agent of the outside world. As our attention moves us to identify with one character after another, our eyes sweep across the tableau as they might sweep across the figures in a mural. In fact, I suggest for the aesthetic of Mahfouz's realistic novels a painterly analogy that refers not to the centered realism of Vermeer or Courbet but to Orozco or Diego Rivera, whose flatness and broad, lateral scale make the overall design more telling than the individual character. (We could consider the Mexican interest in pre-Columbian design as a formative influence parallel to Mahfouz's fascination with pharaonic history.)

For American undergraduates, I like to imagine a course on Mahfouz that would be put together from available translations and would sum up his career not from a distance, as I am doing here, but through his own voice—in its English guise. I would suggest, before exposing students to Mahfouz's realism, opening with another novelist of the Cairo cityscape, Sonallah Ibrahim for instance, or even the francophone Albert Cossery, whose *Men God Forgot* (*Hommes oubliés de Dieu,* 1946) had some notoriety as a City Lights paperback—anything to avoid the tiresome oversimplification that makes Mahfouz synonymous with Cairo. The project is to see how the same city opens up different views inside the imaginations of different observers.

The traditional threat posed by courses with reading lists of such formidable size is that the first few books tend to crowd the syllabus. Among the most important aspects of Mahfouz are his restlessness and persistence. Edward Said has written an appreciation of Mahfouz in Arabic in the Saudi magazine *al-Majalla* (16–22 Nov. 1988: 22–23) in which he says that Mahfouz, during the thirty-year span of his own career, has lived two hundred years of the development of the novel. We find novels in a style reminiscent of Defoe, Smollett, Dickens and Hugo, and after *The Trilogy* novels that sound like Galsworthy or Thomas Mann, followed eventually by a series of experimental styles reminiscent of surrealism or of Kafka.

For the centerpiece of our imaginary course on Mahfouz I would suggest not *Midaq Alley* or *The Trilogy* but the inventive and monumental novel which was his response to the new Egypt after a seven-year retirement from writing, *Awlad haratina,* translated as *Children of Gebelawi* by Philip Stewart. My imaginary American students would have an advantage over Egyptian readers, who are still not officially allowed to read it—an act of censorship that Mahfouz has famously not contested, no doubt on the grounds that acts of censorship are always temporary. We could make the case that *Children of Gebelawi,* rather than the realistic novels, establishes his greatness. It deserves a central position in my Mahfouz syllabus because it marks the beginning of that period of experimentation when he began to pursue possibilities beyond the constraints of his realism. The spectacle of a productive novelist at the top of his powers, with a recognizable, established style, who retires from writing for six years and returns to the scene with a radically different kind of narrative, is interesting in itself. But the important elements may be those that remain the same: the variation allows him to discover the possibilities already implicit in his old style.

The obstacle to overcome in our reading of *Children of Gebelawi* is that we have a category to put it in prematurely. We see that it is an allegory—that Rifaʿa seems to represent Jesus and that Qasim seems to represent Muhammad—and having seen that, we often feel we can short-circuit the reading process. I like to imagine tracing an evolution of forms that would show the consistency of vision. Despite the foreshortening of history that allows Mahfouz to talk about the history of the Middle East—that is, the history of its three religions—the action is still played out in a single urban neighborhood, a stripped-down structural transformation of the scenes we are already used to from *Midaq Alley* or *Khan al-Khalili.* The scene is still a variation of a Cairo neighborhood, but the infinite, which we always sensed there, has been imported physically into the setting—in the person of Gebelawi and his paradisiacal mansion, and in a style of narration itself.

The opening scenes when Gebelawi calls his children together convey a feeling of intensity, of being present at a noumenal moment in the history of the world, a world of radiant forms—our world before the film of mundanity had settled over it. (We might compare the scenes of the originary Earwicker family in *Finnegans Wake* or the Egyptian mythology sequence in part 2 of Norman Mailer's *Ancient Evenings.*) We sense not so much abstract ideas looming behind the physical scene but some intermediate state of being in which a mundane narrative, a father assembling his sons, has taken on, intermittently, random characteristics of the story of the fall of Iblis.

> One day the master of the house summoned his sons to the downstairs drawing room, which opened on the terrace. All his sons came, Idris, Abbas, Radwaan, Gelil and Adham, wearing silk smocks. . . . he stood up and went over to the great door on to the terrace and gazed out at the huge garden, crowded with mulberry and fig and palm trees, up which climbed henna and jasmine whose branches thronged with singing birds. The garden was full of life and song, but in the room was silence. It seemed to the brothers that the chief of the desert had forgotten them. With his great height and breadth he seemed superhuman, a being from another world.[9]

Even in translation I can feel a rhythmic precision that shows Mahfouz's narrative control—the control of a writer who has imagined a total universe of details and held back, transcribing it sparingly, in minimal gestures. The mundanity of the architecture—the drawing room and the terrace whose silence is made more noticeable in comparison with the garden outside—provides just sufficient backdrop. In front of that screen, our attention drifts to the brief moments that separate father from sons, seen in a sequence of austere details: he looks out the window (anchoring us momentarily in his review of the garden), and directly, without warning, we have begun to watch the scene filtered through the eyes of the sons.

As we begin to see the story of Iblis and Adam strangely altered from its Qur'anic form (Gebelawi entrusts the garden for unfathomed reasons to his youngest son), the split between points of view becomes wider still. And over the course of the narrative, as the action of the story moves outside Gebelawi's mansion into the neighborhood outside and Gebelawi fades into the background, we recall the opening scenes of the novel as privileged moments, until finally the silences or absences that surround Gebelawi are more important than any positive defining characteristic.

Sasson Somekh has argued that the characters of *Children of Gebelawi* have limited interiority, like the animal characters of Aesop's fables or Orwell's *Animal Farm*.[10] This observation is true, but I think that Mahfouz has developed a style of narration where this limited interiority matters less and less, one in which the constituent units are defined by rhythm as much as by theme. The unit of narrative here is the transition, the edge between one scene and the next, and the abrupt shifts suggest narrative potency, warning that at any moment we could turn in any direction. The sense of overwhelming scale has been transposed from the style of narration to the theme of the novel, lodged in the character of Gebelawi and his monumental house. But this theme frees Mahfouz to experiment with a narrative speed utterly unlike the narrative pace in his earlier novels.

Those experimentations may be easier to visualize against a backdrop that may seem inappropriate on an occasion like this—the attack on Mahfouz by the Palestinian writer Anton Shammas in the *New York Review of Books* (2 Feb. 1989; 19–21). His counterpart to our celebratory tone is a bemused pity, apparent when he describes the most recent works of Mahfouz: "sketchy texts that sound as if they were written at random, desperately in need of a meticulous, compassionate editor" (19–20). I do not cite this to refute it. The strangeness Shammas finds in Mahfouz's writing is perhaps not unconnected with the quality I have been trying to articulate. His figure for what I have called the strangeness of Mahfouz is musical. He defines the full-voiced novel through the analogy of a piano piece for two hands, where the melody works against bass accompaniment (or, in painterly terms, where figure works against ground), and his figurative term for a proper Western novel is a storyteller with two hands. Shammas's discussion is in some ways elegant, perhaps most of all as a distillation of Western taste and a fine circumscription of what our intellectual world looks for and is willing to accept into its canon. The obstacles that prevent us from seeing Mahfouz as part of our literary dialogue are important to discern, and we should be thankful for the voices that make them clear. There are moments when Shammas seems rather ambivalent about Mahfouz: "Most of what has been translated from Mahfouz (except for *Midaq Alley* perhaps) are works limited to the 'figure.' It takes a great deal of charity on the part of the reader to enjoy these superb, albeit unaccompanied, melodies." An "unaccompanied melody" is a plot whose social background has been reduced to a sketch. It is a figure we can accept, though it is harder to accept the implication that there is only one kind of music, particularly when the maddening, inexplicable gap between individual and collective is the theme.

Shammas is perhaps most eloquent when his embarrassment shows through his project of representing Mahfouz to the *New York Review of Books's* readership. It is in part the embarrassment of having a subject whose style is outside the networks of power, of not wishing to be mistaken for another outsider; and of course it is embarrassment over the strangeness we have been discussing all along. Mahfouz's acceptance speech is one of the primary sources of Shammas's embarrassment. He reads it as enigmatic and rambling, superficially Borgesian (i.e., cryptic), and ultimately without a point—as the voice of a sphinx without a secret.

In the play of voices that makes up that curious, tortured, undelivered speech, there is a double bind that Shammas does not want to acknowledge because it may sum up the constraints on other novelists outside the West. Mahfouz, a writer who is the epic chronicler of his culture and for many readers a paradigmatic indigenous voice, at the same time has come to represent compromise with European values and is even a kind of outsider (accused of blasphemy for *Children of Gebelawi* and of political betrayal because of his support of the Camp David Accords). It is no wonder that Mahfouz relies so heavily in his acceptance speech on a trope that makes the Arabic language, rather than him, the recipient of the prize—a trope that dissolves him in his cultural identity—or that he lists pharaonic Egypt and the Arab world as his two parent cultures and portrays Europe as a place infinitely inaccessible and far away. (His defense of the powerless and abandoned in the Third World, though eloquent, may seem to Western readers unconnected; in this context, it is central to the speech, a way of showing that he is a spokesperson for his culture.) It is as if the receipt of the award were both an honor and a reproach, a demand for a loud, public voice from a person whose persona has always been elusive, in a society whose cultural values pull him in two contrary directions. The Nobel Prize makes visible crosscurrents in Egyptian culture that leave Mahfouz a perilously narrowing space from which to speak. And if those crosscurrents are also at work in his fiction, his project is to transcend them in imagination, by creating a world so wide and all-inclusive that one can never quite see them entire.

Even in the shorter novels of the post-Gebelawi period, we can find the same sense of lateral vertigo that has marked the Mahfouzian vision all along. In *The Thief and the Dogs* (1961) and its companion piece, *The Beggar* (1965), Mahfouz presents an explicit political scenario that opens out its vistas just to the edge of the canvas. *The Beggar* presents us with what at first seems the personal, typically bourgeois theme of a midlife crisis: ʿUmar has a series of affairs in response to his wife's pregnancy. The affairs take up what seems to be the foreground of the narrative, but we learn only toward the end that ʿUthman, a friend from ʿUmar's revolutionary youth, has been in prison during ʿUmar's entire career. ʿUthman's release (a variation on Said Mahran's in *The Thief and the Dogs*) coincides with the moment when ʿUmar's crisis reaches a peak, so that we see a whole other alternate narrative running parallel to ʿUmar's. Meanwhile, we learn that ʿUmar is also a former poet, and it is suggested that his crisis is a result of suppressed art. Thus still another vista opens out on the other side of the action, also emphasized, equally vast, as we see in ʿUmar's complaint, "What we consider real art is only the light coming from a star which died millions of years ago." [11]

In *Miramar* (1967) and *Wedding Song* (*Afrah al-qubbah,* 1981), Mahfouz develops a *Rashomon* pattern that fragments the narrative through monologues that emphasize the gaps between the perceptions of various observers. But the ambiguously related vignettes in his fictionalized autobiography, *Mirrors* (1972), are evidence that narrative can be just as fragmented when it is seen through the eyes of a single observer.

In this context, I want to single out the eminently teachable book *Hikayat haratina* (1975). Translated twice (once as *Fountain and Tomb,* once as *Neighborhood Story*), it is perhaps the shortest novel I know in which the reader can truly get lost. It comprises a series of seventy-eight barely connected vignettes about neighborhood life. Each is like a dehydrated novel and could indeed be expanded to a novel. To leaf through *Fountain and Tomb* is to feel Mahfouz's uncanny narrative potency. He employs narratives with the abandon and assurance of a writer possessed of formidable reserves, a sense of power that must be intimidating to a fellow novelist. You can feel the justice of the bon mot. "Before any younger writer sits down to write anything, he must make sure that Mahfouz has not already written that novel. And if he is lucky and Mahfouz hasn't done it already, that is still no guarantee that he will not have done so before the younger writer gets around to writing his."[12]

Hikayat haratina is exactly what the Arabic title, "Tales of our neighborhood," promises. Readers might think of it as *Midaq Alley* turned inside out, though one does not feel that the artistry dwells in the stories so much as in the spaces between. Mahfouz develops a logic that seems at first chronological—a series about the narrator's childhood, after which a series of stories explore themes of sexual initiation and initiation into political life. These stories resolve into a series that we might call musical, where the sequence of mininarratives follows an order that is easier to intuit than describe—a series of love stories followed by stories about beggars. The opening episode, the memory of a childhood encounter with the imposing sheikh who lives in the Sufi center (*takiya* or *khanqah*) located at one boundary of the neighborhood, centers on an enigmatic moment: the sheikh's only words are a verse, cited in Persian, of the Persian poet Hafez.[13] The episodes digress and turn in such a way that when the opening theme of the childhood encounter returns, it is as if some mysterious pivot—a hidden mechanism, the hand of the puppeteer—had suddenly come into view.

Since Balzac, the novel has been a tool for grasping the elusive shape of history, for personalizing the vast, often inexplicable forces in which we find ourselves immersed. Peled's book opens with a discussion of Mahfouz as a historiographer (a *mu'arrikh*). I concur that the imperative to understand history is stronger and nearer the surface in Mahfouz than it is with us, which in turn creates a different set of demands on his style. It is as if the recalcitrant and forbidding precipice of history had left a mark on his imagination in the form of something too big, something outsize and formidable that he had to attempt again and again to assimilate. What the Western reader hears as an emptiness in Mahfouz is perhaps the opposite, the sound of an excess of history.

10

MEN CONSTRUCTED IN THE MIRROR OF PROSTITUTION

MIRIAM COOKE

If you would like to know what men are, then you should be a woman. If you would like to know what women are, then you should ask God.

—*Jacob Lorenz*

Any discourse which fails to take account of the problem of sexual difference in its own enunciation and address will be, within a patriarchal order, precisely indifferent, a reflection of male dominance.

—*Steven Heath*

As Arthur Brittan has written, masculinity and femininity are not givens but power-based constructions that are in a state of perpetual negotiation both in everyday life and in literature. I shall therefore examine some of the early novels of Naguib Mahfouz to uncover the dynamics of gender construction.

At a time when metanarratives are coming under scrutiny and criticism, it is appropriate to examine some in modern Arabic literature as well. I am particularly concerned with the notion of neopatriarchy, for example. In his innovative theorization of modern Arab society, Hisham Sharabi has described the dichotomization of emergent classes as neopatriarchy.[1] At the top is the newly empowered, traditionally patriarchal, yet spiritually bankrupt, bourgeois man, schooled in ways of the European former potentate. At the bottom is the ever-poorer and ever-weaker subaltern. Naguib Mahfouz's novels and short stories may be considered multiple, Egyptian elaborations of such a totalizing discourse.[2] His men are either obsessed by an empty striving for advancement within a circumscribed, deified[3] bureaucracy, or they are alienated, disillusioned, revolutionary intellectuals who search—often aided by drugs or drink—for the meaning of existence in a modernizing, amoral, Godless world. A subplot of this master narrative is the psychological and sexual victimization of women by selfish, greedy men. In her full-length study of Mahfouz's women, Fawzia al-Ashmawi-Abouzeid describes Mahfouz's oeuvre as yet another kind of metanarrative: "the struggle between tradition and modernity as well as the evolution of customs and relations between men and women in contemporary Egyptian society."[4]

To read Mahfouz's fiction as metanarrative is to approach his work from only one of many possible directions. Perhaps part of the problem, for a Western reader at least, is that literature from the Arab world and from all parts of Asia and Africa—those dark continents of which Westerners know little—is read as allegory. Allegory is one of a text's subtexts for which the protagonists are vehicles. For the literary detective, these novels wear their plots as coats. Once this coat has been peeled off, all are relieved to find the reassuring meaning. Whatever does not fit the broad strokes of the allegory is artifice that should not interfere with the social or political message. The sleuth's work has been accomplished, and the reader can proclaim the coat to have been well tailored or cut with an axe.

For this study, I have tried to read Mahfouz without expectations of allegory derived from mandates for sociopolitical commitment. Liberating the text from its immediate subtext opens up semiological depths that would otherwise remain masked by that seemingly impermeable level. The text is now susceptible to different readings that uncover new facts and foci. Mahfouz's protagonists can be read not merely as messengers but as textual constructions that construct the text. If they are not credible, nothing else will be.

Mahfouz has pluralized the actors on his urban Egyptian stage to portray men and women from the rich, the petit bourgeois and the destitute classes. The heterosexual relations he portrays are paradigmatic of relationships of power pertaining throughout Egyptian society. In their relationships with others, Mahfouz's male characters are constructed according to the binary model of master/slave. Men who cannot control their own lives, or the lives of insubordinate men, turn to women as objects over which they can have dominion. The relationships Mahfouz's men initiate with women are always explicitly grounded in asymmetric power. Women's insubordination—any hint of autonomy—threatens these men's fragile identities and represents the final stage in their alienation. They cannot confront, and therefore they escape, women's challenge, thereby stunting any possibility of growth. Their conception of masculinity is too rigid to accommodate interaction with women on the basis of equality. The women, however, enter into relationships for a variety of reasons. Because they are less programmed in their needs and desires, they are more difficult to fathom. Women's lack of clear definition, despite apparently self-evident categorization, emblematizes the incomprehensibility of forces confronting Mahfouz's men.

Yet Mahfouz seems to be saying something else. He told Salwa el-Naimi: "Our world is `masculine,' and one cannot imagine it otherwise. . . . Women continue to struggle to become part of social life. But I could not describe a world in which women play the same roles as men."[5] But is this the point? A world in which women play the same roles as men does not yet exist, nor is it perhaps desirable that it should. Sameness implies mimicry and therefore a replication of a system of asymmetric power. Because domination is inherent to these same roles, a world in which women played the same roles as men would look the same and would be as unjust and patriarchal as one in which men were the sole players.

What matters is equal access to power, defined as audibility and effectiveness of voice. Reading with the protocols of the text, though apparently against the author's intention, I argue that Mahfouz's fiction echoes with women's voices as they act out their lives in society, whether it be in the home or with the men in the "public sphere." Yet I do not claim that he has concentrated on them at the expense of his male protagonists. His fiction often betrays the delicate balance of power maintained in real-life relations among men, among women,[6] and between the genders.

Mahfouz's women are not images—not flat symbols of good or evil in Egyptian society. Yet most critics have asserted that they are. Fawzia al-Ashmawi-Abouzeid concludes her study of Mahfouz's women with a taxonomy of what female protagonists represent: (1) social situations; (2) a whole class; (3) a type of daily life; and (4) the evolution of customs over three generations. She adds, "The role of the female character consists in making this social evolution more concrete and clarifying the nature of male/female relations in contemporary society" (161). Her study focuses on three protagonists. Nafisa of *The Beginning and the End* is the incarnation of the "middle class Egyptian woman of the between-the-wars period who is living through a harsh economic crisis and of a struggle between tradition and modernity." Her quest is "passive" (161). Nur of *The Thief and the Dogs* is another incarnation, this time of the "proletarian woman [*fatat al-tabaqa al-sha'biyya*] whom misery and social ill-fortune have turned into a prostitute" (162). Finally, Zahra of *Miramar* is the incarnation of "the Egyptian fallaha [peasant] after the 1952 revolution. . . . [She] is a symbol of the myth of Woman/Egypt" (163–65).

George Tarabishi has analyzed Mahfouz's portrayal of women in *Respected Sir* and *Miramar,* although he is more interested in 'Uthman Bayyumi's mystical quest and in the development of the four male characters in *Miramar* than he is in Mahfouz's women, the avowed subject of his inquiry.[7] Tarabishi calls 'Uthman's struggle with women "not so much a struggle between the sacred and the profane as between depravity and life, between selfishness and life. . . . 'Uthman escapes women because they are the mirror in which he sees reflected the barrenness of his soul. . . . His relationship with Qadriyya is not with her but with himself" (91–92). This is also true for the four men in *Miramar,* who use Zahra as a reflection of themselves (120). Zahra is a symbol, but she is a "living symbol" who is skillfully drawn despite her symbolic role. Tarabishi concludes that Zahra's future is in her hands (124), but he does not consider that fact significant enough to warrant revision of the mirror/symbol role. In the interests of uncovering political allegory, Menahem Milson has reduced characters to symbols to further his detective work.

> Na'ima in "al-Khawf" (Fear) and Saniyya in "Hanzal wa al-'askari" (Hanzal and the policeman) represent the idea of Egypt, the motherland and the people. This is a most important icon which appears in quite a number of allegorical stories of Mahfouz: Zahra in *Miramar,* the young women in "Yumit wa yuhyi" (The Lord giveth death and life), the woman in labor in "Walid al-'ana" (The child of pain), Qaranfula in *al-Karnak,* Saniyya al-Mahdi in *al-Baqi min al-zaman sa'a* (There only remains one hour), Randa in *Yawm qutil al-za'im* (The day the leader was killed). . . . The outstanding qualities of . . . secondary female characters are charm, endurance, fortitude in adversity and hope."[8]

For Mona Mikhail, Mahfouz's women are symbols who "tend to embody ideas and ideals. . . . Mahfouz's classic 'putain respectueuse' of *The Beginning and the End* or that of *Miramar* represents an always illusory truth."[9]

Perhaps the symbolization of Mahfouz's women persists because, until recently, the study of women's roles in men's literature has been confined to the discussion of images in isolation from their impact on the evolution of the male characters. If a woman made only brief appearances, critics did not feel she warranted much of their discursive space. But Mahfouz's women are much more than symbols. They are as critical to the development of the plot as are male protagonists. Indeed, they are often critical to the development of the male characters. While Mahfouz's men need women, his women would like to—and quite often do—escape their need for men. His female protagonists are much more than Luce Irigaray's masquerading woman whose desire exists only as a mirror to masculine desire. Mahfouz's women have ambitions and desires that propel the narrative in ways that masquerade would not allow.

To understand the significance of Mahfouz's female characters, we must strip away the sexist bias that has informed canonical readings and instead view his works through a feminist optic. Such a reading resembles the Western tourist's first visit to the Arab world. This tourist, filled with prejudices and stereotypes, ventures into the streets of Casablanca, Tunis, Cairo, and Baghdad and suddenly realizes that the women are not all veiled. When we read Mahfouz's novels, we are like that tourist, preconditioned by the often repeated and apparently axiomatic commentary that his female protagonists are flat symbols of one thing or another. When we come across a woman with a complex personality who is motivated by individual goals that have nothing to do with men except as instruments of her advancement, we label her amoral. We gloss over the intricacies of her evolution in the plot, all the while commending Mahfouz for having drawn a credible woman among a panoply of paper dolls.

Because of the profusion of characters in a majority of Mahfouz's novels and short stories, it is not always possible, or indeed desirable, for each character to be rounded. Mahfouz has said that "from a minor real detail, I manage to create a whole life" (Salwa El-Naimi, 28). The reader should be sensitive to the fact that this is just as true for the women as it is for the men. Yet when critics have described sketchiness, or flatness, in Mahfouz's character portrayal, they have often singled out women for attention.

Mahfouz has provided his readers with a wide tapestry in which women's experience is elaborated and valorized. He does not allow the reader any one image, because for him no group, however apparently homogeneous, behaves in uniform fashion. We must read Mahfouz's *œuvre* as a whole so the resonance from one novel to the next can be felt—so echoes of a simply delineated woman in one story can be read in the thoughts and actions of a woman in another story.

Fully aware of the sexist preoccupations and prejudices of his fellow men, Mahfouz has depicted among his vast cast of women strong moral individuals who have been able to survive despite male opprobrium at their trespassing on "men's turf." But he has also portrayed weaker women who have not been able to overcome the obstacles. He has satirized men who respond in stereotypical fashion to women's new, unexpected roles. He has painted the canvas of Egyptian society, always striving to get the whole picture, either by proliferating characters or by embedding a single character in a vivid social context. Mahfouz's women do not live in a world apart where they suffer independently; his men and women are part of the same universe. They are locked into mutually dependent relationships in which one's behavior influences the other.

In fact, Mahfouz's men are often flatter than his women. The women cannot be reduced to a few types. What draws many of the women characters together is terminology: beautiful or ugly daughters, piously self-sacrificing or assertive mothers, virtuous or adulterous wives, fading or alluring spinsters, and, above all, prostitutes. The simplicity of these designations is deceptive, for Mahfouz creates memorable women whom readers grow to love or hate as though they knew them personally. Some are educated, some illiterate, some kind and some mean, some chaste and some loose.

Mahfouz creates vivacity by introducting the unexpected into a mundane character. For example, in *Bidaya wa nihaya* (*The Beginning and the End*), the reader learns that the tender-hearted, recently bereaved widow has never kissed her children (203). This piece of information explains the previous and later behavior not only of the widow but of all who come into contact with her. Then, as though he were wont to stereotype, Mahfouz writes of this same woman that "unlike many of her sex, Samira was not a chatterbox" (231). Samira has been eased out of any possible pigeonhole, and although she is only a secondary character, we feel that we know her as an individual distinct from the others we have met and will meet in Mahfouz's literature.

Mahfouz's most interesting and creative women characters, however, are the prostitutes, those literary figures whom Simone de Beauvoir has described as projections of male fantasy.[10] What does the word *prostitute* mean to Mahfouz? In his 1946 novel *Khan al-Khalili,* he wrote that "the real woman is the prostitute who has rejected the mask of hypocrisy and who does not have to pretend to love and to be modest and loyal" (39–40). Twenty-seven years later, he takes this definition further. In *al-Hubb taht al-matar* (Love under the rain), Mahfouz has Husni Hijazi say, "But `prostitute' no longer means anything" (87). Does this mean that throughout his considerable oeuvre Mahfouz is using a signifier whose signified is other than expected? I suggest that this is indeed the case and that this is why so many readers have misread Mahfouz's women. They have viewed them from a single vantage point that—like the assessment of plot in relation to allegory noted above, allows only for praise or regret of in-depth characterization.

The *Concise Oxford Dictionary* (1984) defines a prostitute as one "who offers her body to promiscuous sexual intercourse esp. for payment or as a religious rite." Does this exchange adequately express the motivations and actions of Hamida of *Midaq Alley* (1947); Nafisa of *The Beginning and the End* (1949); Yasmin of *Children of Gebelawi* (1959); Nur of *The Thief and the Dogs* (1961); Riri of *Autumn Quail* (1962); Basima of *al-Tariq* (The path, 1964); Warda of *The Beggar* (1965), and Qadriyya of *Respected Sir* (1975)? If we deconstruct this word in the context of all of Mahfouz's works that contain prostitutes as main or subsidiary characters, we see that they have in common not so much a commodification of body for survival but an urge for independence.

This subsuming of Mahfouz's prostitutes under a single rubric of revolt is meant not to essentialize but to open new possibilities of analysis. Seen through the lens of revolt, the behavior of Mahfouz's prostitutes acquires a level of activism absent from the creation of prostitutes in conventional male writing. Amy Kaminsky has written: "Even among male writers who are sympathetic toward prostitutes, the tendency is to create the character from without, to rely on the role of 'prostitute' in defining the character, rather than to single out the individual in that role. . . . [Their men] see the women's actions in terms of themselves and are blind to their meaning for [the women].[11] Reading acts of revolt in the behavior of Mahfouz's prostitutes allows us to understand their literary roles also.

Mahfouz's depiction of prostitutes makes explicit what remains implicit in his other women—that men reify all women to avoid dealing with the reality of their lives and experiences. This objectification protects men against their own weakness and allows them to weave fragile delusions of power and control. One of the best-known examples can be found in the first volume of *The Trilogy, Palace Walk* (1956). Sayyid Ahmad ʿAbd al-Jawad is a stern patriarch who rules his household with unrelenting rigidity. During one of his rare absences, his secluded wife Amina is urged by her children to visit the Husayn Mosque. While she is out, a car knocks her over and injures her slightly. The affair comes out into the open. To her surprise, the stern patriarch does not punish her at once: he waits until she has recovered from her accident and then throws her out. The moment of independence that she stole forces him briefly to view her as an individual, and as one whom he loves. His love frightens him because it makes him vulnerable, so he has to close her out. Mahfouz's men are safe only as long as the women with whom they consort are subsumed in their roles. A measure of Mahfouz's control in characterization is that it remains allusive.[12] Amina is not unrealistically transformed by her experience; she is merely shown to have become wiser. The Amina of *al-Sukkariyya,* the third volume of *The Trilogy,* is a gloomy, inflexible woman, a far cry from the bright innocent of *Palace Walk.* ʿAbd al-Jawad's Achilles heel has been glimpsed. Time takes care of the rest.

Each of Mahfouz's prostitutes is a self-willed, strong individual who, for the space of the novel or for part of the novel, finds herself linked to a man—as his source of paid pleasure, as lover, wife or mother—whose need for her is greater than her need for him. In *Children of Gebelawi* (1959), Rifaa tries to save Yasmin from her pimp, the alley strongman. Rifaa marries her. But Yasmin is disappointed that Rifaa is more interested in her soul than in her body, in what she represents than in who she is. She rejects this spiritual commodification and returns to her pimp. Her indignation is so great that she becomes instrumental in Rifaa's execution. In contrast with this Judas-like figure, Mahfouz creates a completely different prostitute two years later in *The Thief and the Dogs* (1961). Nur, meaning light, is the only enlightenment that the alienated protagonist can find. She is more honest, more patriotic, and closer to God than is the God-fearing sheikh. Yet like many other women in Mahfouz's fiction, Nur is a resource Said Mahran is unable to tap because all he wants is to control her.

Mahfouz often portrays prostitutes as stronger and more intelligent than the generality of womankind. Basima in *al-Tariq* (The path) tells her son: "Your mother is far more honorable than their mothers. I mean it. They do not know it, but if it were not for their mothers, my business would have floundered" (5). Sabriyya al-Hishma, whose name suggests "the patience of modesty,"[14] uses her profession to achieve the kind of respectability and security of which she had always dreamed. She collects enough money to be able to leave her brothel, at the age of fifty she marries a young man, and she lives happily ever after. These women are aware of the social opprobrium attached to their label, but it does not keep them from accomplishing their goals. For them, prostitution is not a problem. But for the men who choose to interact with them, it is.

The men who choose to interact with these prostitutes do so with the understanding that they are quite simply prostitutes—women who sell their bodies and who in that transaction temporarily lose possession of those same bodies. Mahfouz demonstrates again and again that this is not the case. The woman who sells her body retains control not only of that body but of its surplus value. She is doubly empowered: she is in control of the illusion that she is surrendering, and she is in control of the man's desire and burgeoning need for her body and not that of any other woman.

Mahfouz uses prostitutes to demonstrate his male characters' inability to deal with women except as masks and symbols. In *Respected Sir,* ʿUthman Bayyumi, the son of a cart driver, is promoted again and again until he becomes director-general. Throughout his journey to the top, ʿUthman feels he might be aided by marriages to daughters of influential superiors, yet the time never seems quite right. For example, the eligible woman he fancies when he is at a particular civil-service grade is no longer a social superior and is therefore no longer helpful, when he has moved up.

While he waits, this respected civil servant virtually lives with Qadriyya, the somewhat unattractive, "half black" prostitute he has frequented since youth. From time to time he resorts to the local matchmaker, only to be disgusted with her suggestions. One candidate is an aging, though attractive, never-married headmistress, whom he finally manages to seduce, and in whom he then promptly loses interest. At another time, he courts one of his office personnel. But as always when the woman seems to want marriage, ʿUthman escapes. He is afraid that marriage, at least with someone of her station, will not help but hinder his plans (85). Marriage must bring advantages, not responsibilities. He can think of only one escape from this fear engendered by connection with women who need him: marry a prostitute, the emblem of passivity and confirmation of his masculine power. Surely Qadriyya will not threaten his control over his own life and affairs.

Marriage is not for the autistic, however. It compels recognition of another as a human being. ʿUthman comes to realize that Qadriyya the prostitute is above all a woman with a will and a way of life of her own that she is not willing to sacrifice because of a change in her institutional status. When she spoke to him earlier of her political concerns and commitments, he dismissed them as irrelevant (42). He had never felt the need to keep himself politically informed, much less to sympathize with the political activities of a prostitute. Anything she had done that did not relate directly to pleasure he gained from her body was of no interest to him, and it presented no threat. But then he marries her—this unattractive woman with her political passions and her drink and drug addictions. Marriage makes them both miserable: Qadriyya, because she has to contend with a man who has never taken women seriously as individuals, Uthman, because he has never taken women seriously as individuals, lest they threaten his smug sense of self.[15]

Indeed, *Respected Sir* exemplifies the problematic relations all Mahfouz's men have with women. To them, middle- and upper-class women represent their class and nothing more. They are prizes to be coveted because of the social prestige that association with them promises. Prostitutes are symbols of pleasure. Mahfouz's men cannot imagine that a woman's function masks an individual, and that once they have stripped away her function—by marriage, for example—the individual remains.

As long as ʿUthman keeps Qadriyya on the side and does not have to deal with her on a level of equality, he does not have to try to understand who she is. He continues to preoccupy himself with other women, but as always at the level of function: Who are their parents? Will they help him fulfill his grandiose ambitions? Would they make attractive wives? These are flat questions, and because our point of view is ʿUthman's, we get flat answers going little beyond yes or no. Whenever these women start to encroach on his life, start to make demands (however undemanding), he immediately backs away, afraid of losing part of himself in a relationship he will not always control. Losing his life's companion—the "half black," fat prostitute—to his wife deprives him of the only relationship role it was possible for him to have with anyone, that of taker. The novel ends with ʿUthman ruminating the only satisfaction he can wrest out of life: a splendid tomb.

Many of Mahfouz's male protagonists are torn between attraction to and fear of women. ʿUmar in *The Beggar* and ʿIsa in *Autumn Quail* hope to reconcile desire and disgust through association with a prostitute. ʿUmar cannot keep away from women, yet he rejects all who need him—the greater the need, the more violent the rejection. First he abandons his pregnant wife, who had cut all ties with her Christian family by marrying a Muslim. He turns to the prostitute Warda, assuming that she will demand nothing beyond financial recompense. But Warda has feelings, and ʿUmar turns from her when she begins to love and, he fears, need him. He grows to hate women, his hatred exemplified by his relentless chasing after anonymous women.

Warda perspicaciously observes: "Men don't believe in love unless we disbelieve in it" (85).

After the revolution, ʿIsa, a high-ranking civil servant in the pre-1952 government, loses his position and his hope for an advantageous marriage. Like other of Mahfouz's men who have despaired of life, ʿIsa takes up with a prostitute, Riri. His relationship with her is not real but symbolic. It concretizes for him his own degradation. She was "a symbol of the utter humiliation into which he had sunk" (80). Yet even at his most abject, ʿIsa clutches at the shabby remains of his masculinity to protect himself against any weakness. When Riri announces to him that she is pregnant—establishing herself in the role of wife and therefore representing possible demand—he rejects her summarily. He even ignores her when they run into each other in a café. Years later, he sees her in her husband's café with "his" daughter. By that time he has come to need her and the stability she offers in the new role she has assumed. But she no longer needs him. This incongruence of needs in time and kind is one of the topoi of Mahfouz's writings.

What is the motivation for these women into whose minds we are not allowed to enter? How did Qadriyya, Warda, and Riri become prostitutes? Were they victims of terrible circumstances? That is the usual literary explanation proffered for the fall to prostitution, often with the added flourish that this victim's virtue exceeds that of those whose business is virtue. Yet if we turn to two of Mahfouz's earlier novels, we read of two prostitutes, Hamida in *Midaq Alley* and Nafisa in *The Beginning and the End,* whose destinies elaborate another story. These are not so much stories of a fall as of a rebellion couched in terms of a fall.

In *Midaq Alley*—his best known novel in the West because of its early translation into English—Mahfouz creates one of his most convincing women characters. Hamida, the beautiful orphan adopted by the alley matchmaker, is the evil product of socialization by vicious women. She is so strong and determined that Mahfouz can ironically describe her as "most unfeminine" (21). Here he sets up the norm of femininity: weakness, passivity, and vacillation. Hamida knows this norm, and she eschews the feminine condition. She has to break out of a world that expects her to be other than she wants to be, a world that condones older women's oppression of young women. She will break that particular cycle only if she can escape the constrictions of her space. We get to know Hamida through her conversations with the alley inhabitants. We sympathize with her claustrophobia and are ultimately relieved that she escapes its stranglehold, even though the agent of her release is a pimp ironically named Ibrahim Faraj, or Abraham the Liberator.

Hamida is one of the few women characters in Arab men's literature who makes a real choice. She makes her decision as an individual with complex interests and goals. She chooses prostitution because her choices are limited, not because she is forced. Mahfouz does not present society as uncomplicatedly oppressive. Hamida has rejected her destiny as a traditional Egyptian woman for whom marriage is the sine qua non for social acceptability. She is not condemned by her circumstances to sell her body—she is engaged to a respectable young man and has a secure, if poor and unexciting, future in the alley. She chooses to emulate the Jewish factory girls whose economic freedom gives them the means to dress well and the appearance of control over their lives and their bodies. Hamida craves this freedom, despite the pain she inflicts on all who care for her. Freedom from the alley means more, much more, than security in an oppressive world.

Hamida thinks carefully of her options and chooses outside what was offered. Certainly, Hamida's fate can be explained as an allegory for the way in which the invasiveness and corruption of Western values leads to the fragmentation of traditional society. The use of a female protagonist as the vehicle for this allegory indicates how this form of imperialism is perpetrated through women, the vessels of honor and culture. Moreover, the fact that her decision mirrors and participates in a stage of Egyptian feminism does not mean that we should reduce Hamida to yet another kind of symbol.[16] This symbol would be of the morally reprehensible influence of Western notions of equality and women's rights at the expense of community. Hamida emerges out of a milieu in which there is almost as little freedom for men to act out new patterns as there is for women.

Had she been upper class, Hamida's decision might have led to an exemplary path, such as that trod by Huda Shaʿrawi, the pioneer of Arab feminist activism. Under such social and economic circumstances, her courage and anger at her limited horizons as a woman could have helped others, as did Shaʿrawi's. But Hamida is not upper class. She is from the lowest echelons of society, and worse, she is an orphan. She has no status and no resources other than her beauty and intelligence. She uses the one to exploit the other so that she can effect the break. Mahfouz does not indicate whether Hamida is happy. Here we have an example of his intuition of a twentieth-century Egyptian woman's dilemma: rejection of socially sanctioned norms of behavior had become for some women an imperative for which the cost could not be counted.

Why does Hamida choose not to work in the factory like the Jewish girls and opt instead for the most compromising of all women's occupations? Is it because the rewards are more immediate and less strenuous? Or is working in a factory—or even only as a seamstress, as does Nafisa in *The Beginning and the End*—no more valued and no less shameful than earning an honest wage as a prostitute? The issue is women's independence. This independence is at the core of men's fear of women, disguised as indignation at the threat directed at family honor.

In *The Beginning and the End,* Mahfouz traces the "fall" of another woman. In this case, however, the woman is from the petit bourgeois, and far from being beautiful, she is plagued by her ugliness. More than most of his women characters, Nafisa demonstrates Mahfouz's ability to create not only a woman but a prostitute from within. Nafisa is not universal woman but a unique individual. Nafisa and her three brothers are introduced just after their father has died suddenly, without leaving provision for his family. General consternation reigns because none of them has a skill or training. But Nafisa has been sewing for friends and neighbors gratis, and the family realizes that her dressmaking skills are their only immediate resource. Although her three brothers—a drug addict and two schoolboys—are at first shocked that they have sunk low enough to have a seamstress in the family, their attitude does not outweigh their satisfaction with her earnings. Very soon none can imagine life without the fruits of Nafisa's labor.

Mahfouz allows the reader to enter Nafisa's confusion as the certainties of class and status are undermined. The previously inconceivable is now possible, particularly in her relations with people outside the family. She no longer has to play the game by the rules of the class into which she was born. No man of her class has ever expressed the slightest interest in her. The only man who has paid her attention is the grocer's ugly son, Sulayman. While Nafisa was securely fixed in the ranks of the lower middle classes, Sulayman was beneath contempt, a worm whose lechery she shunned with horror. Yet with the destabilizing of her social situation, she begins to humanize the worm. She sees in him the possibility to rebel against the limitations of her physical handicap. She can break out of the prison of her petit bourgeois upbringing and of her ugliness; she can initiate contact with a man. She no longer flees but seeks Sulayman's previously unwelcome admiration.

Sulayman is delighted with this turn of events. Before her father's death, Nafisa had been a social superior and therefore his hope for improvement in status. He had dared to hope, because she was so ugly, that she repelled peer suitors. Now that she has sunk to the lower classes, however, she represents something else: satisfaction of lust. He is soon able to make this desperate woman do what she knows she should not do and what she never would have done before: walk hand in hand with him in a disreputable part of town. He finally lures her into his family apartment while everyone is out. This is not a scene of easy seduction presented from the male or the outsider's perspective. Mahfouz articulates Nafisa's experience as though seen through her eyes. Nafisa's monologues, which combine admonitions to herself with desperate justifications, guide the reader through each tiny decision that leads to her submission. When Sulayman has his way, the moment is evoked in her mood, "a mixture of anxiety, pleasure, and despair" (104). She knows that she is losing control, but the hope of realizing her goal as a woman, which was to attract a man and to get married, makes her act in ways she would never have anticipated.

But Sulayman is a man like all the others. To him women will always be one-dimensional, reducible to icons and epithets, such as *respectable* or *shameful.* He has had his pleasure, and now he despises this shameful creature. The courting pretense is over. He has proven his virility at no cost at all—he even asks her to lend him money that she knows he will not return. Another monologue takes the reader into Nafisa's confusion: "How can I squander money like this . . . when our home needs every millieme I earn. . . . He is not a man. . . . But I love and want him. . . . I have no one else in the world" (116). He has not acted as he should have, and therefore Nafisa declares him not to be a man. Yet much to her dismay and confusion, she thinks she loves and needs him. For him this circumstance is a victory. For her it is shocking because she realizes that she has no one else to care for her. Moreover, she has now become a prostitute—though without the assurance that she is indeed a prostitute, for the usual exchange has not happened, except in reverse.

Confirmation of Nafisa's ignominy and doom comes soon with the announcement of Sulayman's engagement. Ironically, she is asked to sew the bridal gown. Betrayal gives her the courage to confront the scoundrel, to mock his unmanly—the ultimate insult—subjugation to his father and, finally, in a farcical scene, to beat him in public. Sulayman begs her to stop, and when she will not, he threatens to call the police. Although he acts like a woman, he can paradoxically invoke male prerogative, saying, "You have no claims on me" (131). As a man, he has socially sanctioned rights that allow him to escape what a woman could not escape: answerability for amoral behavior. Even at her bravest and most rebellious, Nafisa's actions serve only to consolidate an unmanly man's manliness.

Nafisa has encouraged the advances of a social inferior whom she despises but has come to need because he is her only hope for affection. Here Mahfouz indicts Nafisa's family, who use her, in fact need her, to earn their living as a seamstress, but who condemn her for what they have driven her to do. Her brothers, despite their radically different characters, are chips off the same block. Their equivalence is nominally marked. Each of their names—Hasan, Hasanayn, and Husayn—is derived from the same root, HSN, which means good. Hasan is good, Hasanayn is in the dual form and means doubly good, and Husayn is in the diminutive form and means quite good.

Husayn is the most virtuous in his manner and is therefore the most sinister and hypocritical. Nafisa gives him money that allows him to start his career as a teacher in Tanta. Piously mouthing concern at the need to take dirty money, he starts his new life full of good intentions toward his family. Now he is going to be the breadwinner, and this bread will be clean. For the first few months, he sends home a substantial share of his salary. With time, however, he is less happy to part with so much. One month he tells them that he is sick. He keeps the money to buy himself a suit. His mother is worried and comes to Tanta to make sure her son can cope. He lies without flinching. His defense of this purchase out of the allowance he should have sent to his family is heinous. He has acted against the interests of his family, yet he has convinced himself that he has done no wrong. He continues to bemoan his misfortune at having the siblings he has and longs for the return of the soul to the family when it has been cured of its evil ways (200). Mahfouz's intertextual reference to Tawfiq al-Hakim's patriotic novel *'Awdat al-ruh* (Return of the soul, 1933), which extols the woman as a symbol of purity and Egypt, is ironic. Nafisa is a symbol of shame; all family members know that their honorable and successful futures depend on Nafisa's dishonorable employment. Without her dishonor, there can be no honor for them.

Hasanayn represents lust. Lust for his chaste fiancée prefigures the lust for power and social standing that allows him to betray his family. He sees in Bahiyya, the daughter of the esteemed Ahmad Bey Yusri, the satisfaction of carnal desire and the hope for social advancement: "Mount her and you'll mount a whole class" (246, cf. 276, 287). Throughout his three-year engagement, he can only talk to Bahiyya of his desire, knowing that her honorability mandates modesty. Yet as soon as Hasanayn's illustrious colleagues at the War College pronounce Bahiyya unsophisticated, he loses interest. His disinterest grows with her growing interest and reaches crisis when she offers herself to him (298, 315–16). In the meantime, he is fashioning a respectable façade. He moves the family out of their neighborhood and tries to keep Nafisa at home and out of the sight of their new neighbors. Like Husayn, he hopes that papering over the past will assure another future. Yet, like Husayn he continues to use the money that Nafisa earns from her prostitution and that Hasan earns from pimping to establish his highly respectable career.[17]

Hasan does not have the pretensions of his brothers. He knows he has failed, and in some ways his marginality mirrors that of Nafisa. Yet he, too, despises and ignores Nafisa. Before establishing himself as a pimp and alley bully, he tries singing for a living. When he hears of Sulayman's wedding, he rushes over to offer his services. No one is more surprised or gratified than Sulayman, who had expected Hasan's visit to be one of revenge for his sister's disgrace. Hasan's offer to sing at Sulayman's wedding implies condonement—even if only through ignorance—of Sulayman's dishonorable behavior and of Nafisa's betrayal. Patriarchal forces regroup and close out space for women, except in their routinized roles.

As her world collapses, Nafisa turns against her mother (126). This turn is as powerful as it is unexpected. With the death of the father, her mother has become the primary authority figure. In some ways, she has assumed the male role and in the mimicry has become male. This female father figure incarnates Nafisa's shame.

Shame is incurred when Nafisa leaves home to earn her family's living. The transition from seamstress to prostitute is easy and almost irrelevant. After rejecting the lewd advances of a mechanic, she gives in. She is hurt by his roughness after he has had his way, yet she eventually picks up the ten-piaster piece that he has thrown at her. She knows that the decision to take the money is part of a continuum that began with her family's launching her into the outside world to sell her services on their behalf and that will end with her determination to sell her body on her own behalf.

Mahfouz repeats throughout that Nafisa gains pleasure from her sexual encounters. Thus though Nafisa may not be happy, through this vocation she finds a level of satisfaction of which she would otherwise have been deprived. In a society that values women for their physical charms, an ugly woman has no place, no right to happiness, and certainly no right to physical pleasure. With the loss of Sulayman, Nafisa knows that she has no hope of marriage. By offering her body, she can attract the attention of men who would be repelled by her face.[18] Unlike the beautiful Hamida, who became the prostitute Titi to gain autonomy and independence, the ugly Nafisa used her body to glean seconds of pleasure and tenderness, even if they were then turned into the coldness of cash and cruelty.

To her two younger brothers, Nafisa's work as seamstress and her unmarriageability epitomize the family's degradation. The irony underlying the novel is that the anxiety all feel about Nafisa's job and status is simultaneous with their ignorance not only of her prostitution but above all of her independence of them and of social convention. The family's blindness to the reality of Nafisa's life reflects Mahfouz's awareness of the shallowness, selfishness, and insensitivity of men and their surrogates with respect to women.

Nafisa's suicide reveals the chasm dividing the world of men from that of women. When the ruthlessly ambitious young officer Hasanayn is summoned to the police station to identify his sister, who has been caught with a man, he is horrified. He does not and never will know that this is not the first incident. His outrage is so great that he feels honor-bound to kill her to safeguard the family reputation. But he cannot do the deed. Nafisa senses his anguish and offers to kill herself. For Hasanayn her offer is the ideal solution. He has been instrumental in this result, yet he does not have to compromise his situation further by soiling his hands with shameful blood, and he will not have to render an account to the world of the reasons for this murder.

When Nafisa throws herself into the Nile, Hasanayn feels a slight twinge. Yet when the body is dragged out onto the bank, he is just one of the curious onlookers. His decision in the last lines of the novel to throw himself into the Nile from the same spot Nafisa has chosen does not mitigate his crime but suggests at best that he has been inspired by his sister's courage, at worst that he cannot face a life that his family has tarnished beyond repair. Mahfouz's depiction of this blindness, terminal selfishness, and cowardice parodies patriarchal obsessions with honor, which he presents through men's objectifying perceptions of women. No act that Nafisa can commit, however depraved or noble, will make her real to the men with whom she deals. To them she is as flat as a mirror. Yet like a mirror, she reflects and thereby creates their image.

Mahfouz's prostitutes are not fallen women but rather modern women who have been exposed to new options and values and who have rebelled against traditional social expectations. They are forging a different future during a period of transition. Despite the gravity of this challenge, men continue to be preoccupied with themselves and with existential issues. They are blind to reality, particularly to that of the women with whom they absentmindedly consort. When these women assert themselves, the men withdraw.[19] This inability to relate to women except as fantasy or stereotype replicates or perhaps constitutes their alienation.[20] Mahfouz mocks his men, whose delusions of power and knowledge women expose.

From his first publication, a collection of short stories entitled *Hams al-junun* (Whisper of madness, 1939), to his most recent, classically intertextual novels, such as *Layali alf layla* (The nights of the thousand nights, 1982) and *Rihlat ibn Fattuma* (The travels of ibn Fattuma, 1985), Mahfouz has created a cast of men and women whose actions and beliefs affect each other. In the longer works, Mahfouz explores heterosexual relationships in depth. In the shorter fiction, he relies more heavily on allusion. The intensity of women's relationships with men rather than their symbolization of larger forces makes Mahfouz's portrayal of women exceptional.

Considering his vast and varied oeuvre, can we argue that Mahfouz writes as a feminist? If the criterion is attention to the multiplicity and evolving nature of urban Egyptian women's experience, then perhaps we can. Mahfouz has opened up the deprived and angry lives of women in the poor and not-so-poor areas of Cairo. He has written of the first women students at the Egyptian University, where he was matriculated only two years after women were first admitted. He has written of the changing reaction to women's education in the course of half a century. He has focused on changing marriage customs; he proceeds from a time when neither men nor women could see their prospective partners, to a time when they were introduced through a photograph,[21] to a still more recent time when women propositioned men.[22] He has concentrated on the workplace and shown how time has changed men's attitudes.[23] He recognizes that this new economic freedom also entails emotional freedom—that women have earned the right to choose whom to love and especially whom not to love (e.g. *al-Maraya,* 112). He has written about powerful women who were part of what he calls the women's renaissance or who were members of the Women's Wafdist Committee (e.g., *al-Maraya,* 9, 55, 87)—women who did not have to bow to society's conventions. Above all, he has entered the Cairene and Alexandrian underworlds and has fully fleshed out the lives of prostitutes who are not merely symbols or projections of fantasy but often complex personalities who use their humiliation against their humiliators.

But is Mahfouz a feminist? His depiction of women has changed during the past fifty years. In his sociorealist novels of the 1940s and 1950s, he displayed a sensitivity to women's issues and particularly to prostitution as a form of rebellion that may be dubbed feminist. In his existential novels of the 1960s that revolve around a single male, many of the women seem flat and transparent. Young women during this period represent the extremes of emotion latent in the men who are so self-absorbed that they can only see and interact with these women as aspects of themselves. In the 1970s, Mahfouz's attitude changes once again. By constantly proffering the male perspective and reiterating the strangeness of women's new visibility, Mahfouz emphasizes the importance of caution. Like Camelia Zahran, these women had to "bear in mind the eastern complexes that their male colleagues inherited from their forefathers at home" (*al-Maraya,* 294). If women did not remain constantly on their guard, men would be vindicated in their fearful preconceptions.

During the latter half of Mahfouz's career, we read of men's fear of phallic mothers, "the real killers" (*al-Tariq,* 78). *In Wedding Song,* Sabir says, "She is my foremost enemy: Father is insane, an addict, but mother is the engineer of all the evil in the world" (80). The man who is intoxicated with one woman will be like the son under the control of his mother; he will lose his reason because he will need the object of his obsession no matter how vicious and adulterous she may be. The only solution for the man is to control this woman with an iron fist, to refuse her any freedom, and to refuse himself feelings. The woman who is not controlled will surely control. Mahfouz tries to overcome this negative attitude toward women that is prevalent in twentieth-century Egypt, but he is increasingly trapped in a web of prevailing notions and fears.

When he wrote *Midaq Alley, The Beginning and the End,* and *The Trilogy* more than thirty years ago, Mahfouz must have felt free to create specific, complex women characters who gradually attained a measure of autonomy. Subsequently, his portrayals of women have become flatter, the characters more sketchily delineated. We can only speculate about the reasons, but it could be that women have become more threatening as they have attained greater acceptance in society. It is not so easy to be a male feminist in a world full of women.

11

MAHFOUZ'S DREAMS

FEDWA MALTI-DOUGLAS

"THE BALZAC OF EGYPT." "a Dickens of the Cairo cafés"—thus was the Egyptian Naguib Mahfouz, 1988 Nobel laureate in literature, described to non-Arab audiences.[1] But circumscribing Mahfouz's enormous and decades-long literary corpus with comparisons like these is at best misleading. Mahfouz is far more than simply a novelist in the European realist or even naturalist tradition. And the Arabism of his discourse transcends his locales and the society he describes. Through the analysis of a recent short-story cycle, itself a set of dream narratives, I will examine some new trends in Mahfouz's recent fiction, trends that are part of a larger movement transforming the face of contemporary Arabic literature.

During the last decade, Mahfouz has played a significant role in what may be the most important new development in modern Arabic prose since the adoption of the Western forms of the novel and short story more than half a century ago. At stake was (and is) the redefinition of modern Arabic prose and its relationship with its centuries-long textual ancestry. After a brief neoclassical phase associated with the names of Muhammad al-Muwaylihi, Ahmad Shawqi, and Hafiz Ibrahim came the alignment of modern Arabic prose on European models, which has meant (despite a few partial exceptions) a dramatic break with traditional Arabic prose and narrative forms.[2] The resulting situation was in sharp contrast to that of poetry, where greater formal and thematic links have been preserved with the highly prized premodern corpus. The literary distances between the twentieth-century novel launched by Haykal's *Zaynab*[3] and the entirety of the Arabic textual tradition are being crossed in various and ingenious ways.

Critics can no longer speak of the late-twentieth-century Arabic novel as simply an imitation of its Western cousin.

The name most clearly associated with this indigenous wave in the novel is that of Egyptian Gamal al-Ghitani. Al-Ghitani is an internationally recognized novelist with numerous works to his name. In his literary experiments, he exploits the classical Arabic textual tradition—be it the mystical, biographical, or historical—by combining the classical idiom with a modern vision. Al-Ghitani's great innovation has been to associate with Mamluk and other premodern settings the appropriate prose styles, language, and formal compositional features of the texts of the period in question to tell essentially modern stories.[4]

Sometimes the anachronism goes deeper. The famous Mamluk historian al-Maqrizi penned an indispensable description of Egypt, known as the *Khitat*.[5] Closer to our own time, ʿAli Basha Mubarak used the same title for his own description of Egypt.[6] The twentieth-century literary descendant of both has unabashedly titled one of his works *Khitat al-Ghitani*.[7] Set in modern Egypt, this work combines formal properties of its Mamluk predecessor with archaic stylistic and narrative features.

Al-Ghitani's manipulation of the classical textual tradition is perhaps the most visible in modern Arabic literature—both the best known and, from a certain point of view, the most evident. His intertextual games can hence be said to differ to some degree from those of other contemporary authors. The Egyptian Muhammad Mustajab, for example, winner of the State Prize in literature, mocks the entire classical Arabic lexicographical and onomastic tradition (it is hardly a coincidence that he works for the Arab Academy) when he carefully indicates to the reader how the name of his character should be pronounced but does so in dialect.[8]

Nor is the intertextual exploitation of traditional materials geographically restricted. The brilliant Palestinian writer Emile Habibi sets his novel, *Ikhtayyi*, in a completely different context by preceding it with a text from the historical and literary compendium, the *Muruj al-dhahab* (Prairies of gold), by the tenth-century polymath al-Masʿudi.[9] On the other end of the Mediterranean, the Tunisian Mahmud al-Misʿadi performs a literary tour de force in his novel *Haddatha Abu Hurayra qal* (Abu Hurayra related, saying). Abu Hurayra was one of the famous companions of the prophet Muhammad and a *hadith* transmitter. Even the title of al-Misʿadi's novel exploits the narrative structure of the *hadith*.[10]

This intertextually laden fiction has been existing alongside, and sometimes in combination with, a metafictional wave in contemporary Arabic writing. This wave involves, among other techniques, a consciousness of the narrative process, a destruction of traditional narrative structures, an ability to play with onomastic data, and so forth.[11] Some texts, like Yusuf al-Qaʿid's trilogy, *Shakawa al-Misri al-fasih* (The complaints of the eloquent Egyptian), exploit both phenomena simultaneously.[12] Al-Qaʿid's three-volume work is a masterful narrative that ties together the pharaonic subtext (known as "The Eloquent Peasant"), rather than a traditional Islamic one, with the heightened metafictional sensibility and burning sense of social justice characteristic of that author's fiction.[13]

One could argue that many of these trends are universal literary ones of largely Western origin. After all, did not the French Alain Robbe-Grillet shed a completely different light on the Oedipus legend in his *Les gommes* (Erasers)?[14] And what is the American Donald Barthelme doing in his novel *Snow White,* if not rewriting and recasting the traditional folktale?[15] Other examples are Italo Calvino's pseudomedieval narrative *The Castle of Crossed Destinies* and John Gardner's *Grendel,* named after the monster from the *Beowulf* legend who takes on the task of narrating his own story.[16]

But Arabic literature deals with many of these issues in a unique and non-Western way. The ludic aspect that dominates Western metafiction[17] is less common in Arabic fiction and is replaced by a far greater social and political consciousness. In contemporary Arabic literature, the breakdown of narrative is often a searing commentary on current social and political problems in the Middle East.

More importantly, the gap at once cultural and especially formal between the Western-inspired modern Arabic novel and short story and the traditional, premodern Arabic prose text is far greater than that between modern European literature and its premodern or folkloric antecedents. As a result, the blending of traditional and modern in contemporary archaizing postmodern Arabic literature produces a more radical formal alterity and hence a greater break with the canons of modern narrative as they have been developed in both the West and the Middle East.

Where does Naguib Mahfouz stand vis-à-vis these contemporary Arabic narrative trends? His *Layali alf layla* (The nights of a thousand nights) is a recasting of *The Thousand and One Nights.*[18] His *Rihlat ibn Fattuma* (The travels of ibn Fattuma) is a pseudoclassical travel narrative, a contemporary echo of the famous travel text of the fourteenth-century North African ibn Battuta (*Rihlat ibn Battuta*). The two titles are a near match as are the name patterns of the respective heroes (ibn Fattuma/ibn Battuta).[19]

Curiously enough, Mahfouz's relation to this Arabic archaizing postmodernism combines both the filial and the paternal. Al-Ghitani has always looked up to the older Mahfouz as master and guide in the world of modern Arabic prose. His sophisticated *Najib Mahfuz yatadhakkar* (Najib Mahfuz remembers) exudes a filial respect.[20] But the younger man pioneered the archaistic style that Mahfouz echoed in his later *Layali alf layla* and *Rihlat ibn Fattuma*. The master, one might say, has imitated the disciple.

Yet in at least one of his works, Mahfouz has created a discourse whose formal properties and whose sense of the dialogue between the modern and the traditional show a unique subtlety and complexity. This work, which may prove to be seminal in the redefinition of contemporary Arabic literature, is a set of dream narratives. "Raʾaytu fima yara al-naʾim" (loosely translated, "I dreamt")—published in a collection of short stories bearing that same title—is composed of seventeen dreams, labeled as Dream (*al-hulm*) Number 1, Dream Number 2, Dream Number 3, and so forth. These seemingly independent dream sequences are all narrated in the first person, and each is introduced by the phrase "raʾaytu fima yara al-naʾim" (literally, "I saw as the sleeper sees.").[21]

This phrase is a highly unusual (if not unrecognizable) way in modern Arabic for expressing the idea of dreaming. The word normally used to express the dream state is *halama* (*yahlumu*), "to dream." And the noun used in the Mahfouzian text to label each of the dream narratives (*hulm*) is, of course, derived from this verb. Why did the narrator of the Mahfouzian dream narratives not use the appropriate form of that verb (*halamtu*)? After all, this is not an unfamiliar form for Mahfouz. We see it, for example, in his masterful story "Zaʿbalawi," where another first-person narrator recounts a dream.[22]

Whence comes this unusual phrase? Its source is the classical Arabo-Islamic tradition itself. Dreams were extremely important in this tradition. Of the various forms of divination of non-Islamic origin, oneiromancy was the only one fully accepted by Orthodoxy. A glance at the *hadith* material will show, without doubt, the level of integration.[23] And in the Islamic Middle Ages, an important Greco-Islamic oneirocritical tradition blended the Greek science with its Islamic counterpart, much as was done with Greco-Islamic medicine.[24] This oneirocritical tradition, with some important adaptations, has continued to be a vigorous form of popular culture down to the present.[25]

"Raʾaytu fi al-manam" (I saw in a dream) or "raʾaytu fi al-nawm" (I saw in sleep), with a clear stress on the idea of seeing from the verb *raʾaytu,* were the classical writers' favored ways of signaling to a reader that an oneiric narrative was in the process of unfolding.[26] Mahfouz's "Raʾaytu fima yara al-naʾim" ("I saw as the sleeper sees") has hybrid qualities. Although it evokes the classical formulas for dream narration, it is not a direct borrowing. The juxtaposition of the word *hulm* effects a shift in registers between the modern and the quasi-classical. A further tension results because the act of seeing (from the verb *raʾaytu*) is linked to the concept of vision, *ruʾya,* derived from the same root. *Ruʾya* implies, in an Islamic context, a privileged means of communication with the supernatural or the supramundane.[27] The opening of each of the dream narratives (repeated seventeen times) sets *hulm* alongside *ruʾya* in a potentially problematic relationship. The Prophet Muhammad is quoted in the *hadith* literature dealing with dream interpretation (in the "Kitab al-Taʿbir" of al-Bukhari's *al-Sahih,* for example) as saying, "*al-ruʾya* is from God and *al-hulm* from the devil."[28]

This evocation of the classical tradition in Mahfouz's dream narratives is certainly not accidental. The interplay and even the dialogue between the classical and the modern are among the most significant components in this cycle of narratives. Nearly half the cycle (in page length) is centered on characters derived from the rich Islamic heritage.

This repeated refrain composed of the dream number and the phrase "I saw as the sleeper sees" does more than signal a change in register. It reminds us that we are dealing with independent literary units, each formed of an individual dream account. The episodic nature of the narrative and its seeming absence of unity brings it close to the metafictional. In addition, the first-person narrator of the different episodes is never identified. In fact, one can refer to this narrative voice as the dreamer. Is the same dreamer responsible for all the dream accounts? The reader assumes so, although there is no reason why this must be the case. Is the dreamer male or female? The gender in the majority of the episodes is undefined. In one case, the dreamer notes that "I took my seat like a student" (of the male gender), and in another, he is welcomed as "Sir."[29] The reader tends to assume the subject of all the oneiric experiences is a male (because the writer is a male?), and in one dream episode (discussed in detail below), the dreamer is given a male name. The social situations in which the dreamer appears would normally be associated in the Middle East with the masculine estate, but such association need not apply to dreams. These narrative uncertainties are modern not only in an artistic sense but in a cultural one, since they represent a departure from the Islamic oneiric tradition.

This Mahfouzian story cycle is by no means a direct imitation or even a pseudoimitation of a medieval oneiric narrative. In this way, it distinguishes itself from Mahfouz's other pseudomedieval texts, such as the *Rihlat ibn Fattuma.* Medieval Arabic dreams were divided into two types: those that were relatively clear and those that needed interpretation. Dreams fulfilled a number of functions, including the prediction of political events, the solution of crimes or controversies, and the cure of disease. The dream narrative in the classical literary corpus generally entailed not only the recounting of the dream but its interpretation when needed and sometimes even the fulfillment of the dream prediction. In these accounts, the dreamer invariably awoke, so the dream state remained a transitory phase.[30] In an example cited by the Mamluk polymath Khalil ibn Aybak al-Safadi, ʿAli ibn Ahmad al-Hanbali al-Amidi had some silk stolen from him. He dreamed that he saw his sheikh (teacher), al-Imam Majd al-Din ʿAbd al-Samad, who told him who had stolen the silk, where it was, and that he should go and get it. When he awoke, ʿAli observed that because his sheikh had always been truthful in life he should be after his death, and ʿAli proceeded to recover his silk.[31]

By contrast, the structure of the Mahfouzian dream episodes is, in a certain sense, simple. The phrase introducing the dream state ("raʾyatu fima yara al-naʾim") is followed directly by the dream account, most often introduced by *anna* (that), "I dreamt that. . . ." In fourteen of the seventeen accounts, no allusion is made to a waking state. One dream state follows another, broken only by the opening material composed of the dream number and the ubiquitous phrase. The three exceptions involve, in the first case, a rooster crowing and announcing the arrival of dawn; in the second, the dreamer knocking his head against the wall to awaken himself; and in the third, the dreamer realizing that only awakening will get him out of the nightmarish situation in which he finds himself. The last two examples involve life-threatening situations for the dreamer, and they are the only two cases in which the word *kabus* (nightmare) appears. In one

(Dream 15), he is awaiting his execution; in the other (Dream 16), he falls into the hands of pursuers. In none of the accounts is interpretation provided for the dream material.

For the purposes of discussion, the dreams in this corpus can be divided into three groups:

1. Storylike narratives that evolve along reasonably logical lines. These can be more or less complicated.

2. Dreamlike and surrealist narratives that are characterized by uncertainties in narrative changes. The dreamer here seems to move from one state or setting to another without knowing quite how this transition took place.

3. The oneiric narratives that have direct reference to the classical tradition. These can be either reasonably straightforward or more complex.

The first type of narrative comprises four of the seventeen episodes. A good example is Dream 7. The dreamer is in a garden of lemon trees. People crowd around the trees filling baskets with the fruit. Buying, selling, and haggling occurs. The competition even causes the police to intervene and blood to be spilled. The dreamer is walking around without a basket, and the broker sarcastically says, "A crazy man has come to the market without a basket." The dreamer tells us that the aroma of the trees drew him to the market. He praises the trees, their greenness, and their branches. Then he grabs a branch and escapes from the broker. Time passes while he sways with the breeze and drinks in a freedom fragrant with the aroma of lemons.

The storyline in this dream presents no problems of coherence. There is no shift in locus; the major action transpires in a garden/ market. But coherence in the story line does not imply a simplistic interpretation. This dream functions as an allegory. The garden with which the narrative begins turns into a market, a place of commerce, which even becomes dangerous to those involved in it. The dreamer is uninterested in this commercial setting, having been drawn to it by the aroma of the trees, itself an elusive element. A clash is present between the semimystical desires of the dreamer and the crass materialistic desires of the other individuals. The dreamer is even considered crazy for not wishing to participate in this commercial existence. What better way to portray today's material world and the attempt to escape it?

The second type of dream narrative is surrealistic. Events seem to take hold of the dreamer, who then moves about in a dreamlike existence. In Dream 15, the dreamer is walking down a long, narrow street. He is preoccupied and does not pay attention to the passers-by. At the end of the street, a building somewhat like a temple, a mosque, and a house faces him. He enters it, sure of an invitation, although he does not know when or how he received it. He then crosses a foyer and enters through a door. The dreamer sees nothing of the place but a man sitting in the front of the space. He is old but healthy, with a dignified bearing and a white beard, and he emanates a perfume that reminds one of olden times. The dreamer kisses the old man's hand and says that he has come in answer to the invitation. The old man answers that he is late, but that that is no problem. The dreamer sits in front of the old man, his eyes drawn to the older man's eyes, which he imagines to be two burning pieces of crystal. The world and existence disappear. Then the dreamer returns to consciousness when the old man touches him, and he hears the old man commenting on the nature of the conversation. The dreamer intended to say that he remembered nothing, but the old man sent him off.

The dreamer returns from the long, narrow street, feeling that he is attached to the old man with invisible strings and that he is his eternal prisoner. Wishing to return to his familiar life, he starts out on his favorite promenade, but the hidden strings control him. He resolves that he will do what the old man wishes, not what he himself wants. The old man drives him to do various things, and he is no longer able to use either his intellectual or his sensory faculties. The dreamer hears people talking about what is happening and about the "unknown agent." They are following the dreamer, and the circle is getting narrower, but they are unable to agree. Some want his neck, others his good health. The dreamer tells us that the old man has not inspired any hatred in him; he only wishes to liberate himself. He does not know how luck drives him to the Bureau of Investigation, but he sees himself in front of the investigator, who says to him: "Confess. It will be better for you." The dreamer replies that he is innocent and that he could only do what the old man dictated to him. But the investigator replies mockingly that the old man denied the story and that the dreamer was legally free and competent. The dreamer answers as though he were addressing the old man: "You know the truth, so save me." The dreamer remains in jail awaiting the day of execution. He is extremely uncomfortable. Then he senses that it is all nothing but a nightmare. At that point, he decides to awaken no matter what the cost. He begins beating his head continuously, persistently seeking the hoped-for wakefulness.

This particular dream must be read in a nonrealist fashion. The events do not succeed one another in a clear, logical manner, and the dreamer himself seems to be the passive recipient of the actions, when not of the objects—the building faces him, not the reverse. His main assertive act is beating his head to awaken from his nightmare. More significant, the entire experience is bathed initially in a mystical aura, which is then destroyed by the bureaucratic system, which is even ready to execute the dreamer himself. The episode recalls Mahfouz's mystical masterpiece "Zaʿbalawi." There the speaker (also a first-person narrator), who has been searching for the sheikh Zaʿbalawi, likens the regaining of consciousness after a semimystical dream state to "a policeman's grip." [32]

Similarities exist between this dream and the earlier one about the lemon garden. Both evoke mystical allegory, though on different registers. But the second does so far more directly, and its mystical experience almost immediately begins to become threatening, ending in a modern bureaucratic nightmare. Philosophicotheological speculations on free will and divine causation appear in both dreams. And both oneiric narratives portray the dreamer's attempt to escape his dilemma.

The content of the third group of dream accounts in this Mahfouzian cycle is overtly related to the classical Arabo-Islamic tradition. There are four such dreams in the cycle, varying in their degree of complexity and in their mode of interaction with the tradition.

In the first narrative with classical overtones (Dream 5), the dreamer is in a film studio. A fat man approaches him, and the dreamer becomes aware that the man is the producer and that he himself is the representative of a magazine of the arts. During the dream, he watches the filming of two scenes, both set in the desert with a palm tree. In the first, two men, an Arab and a Persian, approach a sleeper, and the Arab addresses the sleeper as Amir al-muʾminin" ("commander of the faithful," the caliphal title). It turns out the sleeper is ʿUmar (context suggests the famous ʿUmar ibn al-Khattab) and that permission from the censors to film only came through the intercession of President Reagan. The second scene to which the dreamer is privy involves Juha, the wise fool of Islamic civilization. When the dreamer asks the producer why Juha shows up in a film on ʿUmar, he is told that the producer is working on two films simultaneously, one on each of the characters, and that he wished to benefit from the common decor to save money and effort. He is using the same actor for both films because he is a box office star who excels at both drama and comedy.

The dreamer then sees himself running extremely quickly but he does not know whether he is running after some specific goal or because someone is pursuing him in an attempt to apprehend him.

This, the first classically inspired oneiric narrative to appear in the text, in a way sets the stage for the later ones. The appearance of the characters derived from the Arabo-Islamic tradition is mediated through a cinematic experience. The cinematic context calls attention to the make-believe nature of the material. It is as though the Islamic tradition was, on one level, only an illusion. More important is the element of disguise and role playing so essential to cinema. Even the actor's cinematic identity is in question, since he plays two roles. The dreamer here is merely a passive watcher, distant from the tradition played out in front of him. His role in the dream is that of a modern character watching other modern characters who play classical roles.

More insolent is the intertextual juxtaposition of Juha and ʿUmar ibn al-Khattab. Juha, the ubiquitous wise fool of Islamic civilization in all its manifestations (is it a wonder that his name changes from Arabic to Persian to Turkish?), is placed alongside the revered second caliph.[33] ʿUmar was known as the paragon of justice. His whip became proverbial, vying in its frightening nature with the sword of al-Hajjaj, the governor famous for his cruelty.[34] In the dream, the ruler is told, "you were just,"[35] reviving ʿUmar's image and placing it in a modern context. Juha and ʿUmar redefine one another in this intricate cinematic onomastic game. Yet standing outside this juxtaposition and recasting it is the modern Western political system personified in the American president Reagan, without whose intervention, we are made to understand, the film could not have been made. Not only is the tradition a fleeting, undefined entity, but it must be mediated through the West.

This oneiric experience foregrounds the idea of disguise. And this element, with classical reverberations, is vital in the Mahfouzian dreams. Perhaps the most important oneiric narrative, in size and in content, is Dream 8. Composed of five consecutive episodes, this minidream cycle is rich in literary allusion. Only the first of the five episodes has the key phrase "raʾaytu fima yara al-naʾim." The other four simply indicate a change of space and locale. The five episodes have much the same structure. The dreamer finds himself usually in an unknown time and place. In the first episode he is simply there; in the other four, he is transported to a new location on the back of animals that differ from episode to episode. He is invariably in the midst of a crowd, be it a demonstration or a gathering. He hears someone preaching political messages to the audience, gets close to him, and identifies him as Abu al-Fath. The latter responds with some poetry, heralding the end of the episode. The speaker's clothing changes from episode to episode: he wears Azhari garb in the first, a Western suit in the next, and pants and a shirt in the third. In the fourth, he is speaking from a car and using a loud speaker. And in the last episode, he is an old man.

In the opening lines, the dreamer identifies himself: "I am ʿIsa ibn Hisham, the hero of the *Maqamat* of al-Hamadhani and the disciple of Abu al-Fath al-Iskandari."[36] The *maqama*, created by Badiʿ al-Zaman al-Hamadhani (d. 1008), was a totally new and yet lasting genre in classical Arabic prose. The *Maqamat* of al-Hamadhani are a set of adventures narrated in rhymed prose and also including poetry. They revolve around a rogue hero, Abu al-Fath al-Iskandari, and a narrator, ʿIsa ibn Hisham. In the most common (though by no means the only) structural pattern in the *Maqamat*, ʿIsa finds himself in one of the cities of the Islamic world and happens upon a swindler who is invariably cheating his audience. After much verbal display, usually on the part of the rogue hero, ʿIsa discovers that he has indeed been witnessing a disguised Abu al-Fath in action. After this process of recognition, the two bid each other adieu, until the next *maqama*. The literary role of ʿIsa ibn Hisham in al-Hamadhani's *Maqamat* is not restricted to that of narrator. He at times performs tricks of his own.[37]

The Mahfouzian dreamer's self-identification is hence not free of pitfalls. ʿIsa ibn Hisham is not the hero of the Hamadhanian narratives (as Mahfouz's dreamer/narrator suggests) but merely their narrator. And is he Abu al-Fath's disciple (*murid*)? Although al-Hamadhani's text certainly portrays a teacher/student relationship between the narrator and the rogue hero,[38] this association does not have the mystical implications of the word *murid*. Our modern text is, to say the least, redefining the classical progenitor to which it links itself explicitly. The reverse is also true, as we shall see, since the classical text intertextually reshapes its modern descendant.

Another ʿIsa ibn Hisham lurks in the Mahfouzian oneiric sequence, and we should not let the overt reference to al-Hamadhani hide him from us. This second ʿIsa, also interestingly enough a narrator, stems from the pen of the turn-of-the-century neoclassical author Muhammad al-Muwaylihi. His *Hadith ʿIsa ibn Hisham* forms part of the neoclassical experiment in modern Arabic literature that also gave birth to Ahmad Shawqi's *Shaytan Bintaʾur* (The devil of Bintaʾur) and Hafiz Ibrahim's *Layali Satih* (The nights of Satih). Naguib Mahfouz is fond of saying that the only literary work that he saw in his father's house was that of al-Muwaylihi. The latter was a friend of Mahfouz's father and had given him a copy of the book.[39] More important, the neoclassical text is also cast in the form of a dream, although its dynamics are different.[40]

Hence, the intertextual parentage of this Mahfouzian sequence is quite complex. The overt reference to al-Hamadhani is coupled with a latent one to al-Muwaylihi. Both al-Hamadhani and al-Muwaylihi constructed narratives in which structural repetition plays an essential role, and this factor is equally important in Mahfouz's text. Were there not five encounters between the contemporary ʿIsa and his equally contemporary Abu al-Fath, the force the reader encounters in Dream 8 of "Raʾaytu fima yara al-naʾim" would not exist. More to the point, by composing his text of a series of potentially independent (yet nevertheless interrelated) narratives—eschewing thereby the extended linear narrative of modern Western literature—Mahfouz has returned to the dominant procedures of classical Arabic prose. The evocation of the neoclassical moment associated with al-Muwaylihi functions as a temporal bridge or way station on the pilgrimage back to the shrine of classical Arabic narrative.

The medieval Abu al-Fath shied away from political criticism, but his twentieth-century descendant finds himself in the thick of it, perhaps as a result of the narrative's hybrid parentage. Al-Muwaylihi's narrative is rich in social criticism.[41] The dreamer in Mahfouz's contemporary composition listens to the character subsequently identified as Abu al-Fath discourse on Egyptian politics. Beginning in the first episode with the British occupation and the need for a revolution, the orator then moves on to the necessity of following the king. In the third episode, praise is given to a leader who eliminates the monarchy; then that leader is pushed out by an even greater leader, who subsequently becomes the object of acclaim in the fourth episode. In the fifth and last episode, the by-now familiar voice of our orator is addressing throngs of mourners, comforting them and enjoining them to begin life anew. The rule of the last leader, he assures them, was one of torture, bankruptcy, and defeat. The political allusions are obvious, the episodes of Egyptian history to which they refer clear. Beginning with the British, continuing through Faruq and Najib, and ending with Nasser and his funeral, our master of words is there. ʿIsa confronts him as he hears him first praising one and then the other of the changing leaders. Abu al-Fath has, in fact, echoed the changing positions of Egypt's governing elite—supporting nationalism and the king, then praising Najib, then praising Nasser, then criticizing the rule of Nasser after his death.

The political discourse in this dream sequence operates on different levels. On one level, there is the nationalist political discourse associated with the actual events themselves. Politicians are praised in a given period and others are not, which is the normal flow of politics. On another level, placing the words in the mouth of a modern Abu al-Fath who changes with the political winds turns the nationalist discourse into a set of cynical apologies for a given period of rule. It is, however, when the last ingredient, the Hamadhanian Abu al-Fath, is added, that the coloration changes. Abu al-Fath al-Iskandari, the rogue hero of the medieval *maqama,* was a character whose scruples were few. His eloquence was the means to his existence, and his verbal skills were put to advantage in his eternal search for trickery. To liken a modern political orator to Abu al-Fath is subversive to say the least.

Mahfouz merges the two Abu al-Faths, and in the process redefines his narrative through a masterful literary tour de force. He merges the two through a skillful intertextual device in which verses uttered by the medieval Abu al-Fath al-Iskandari are put in the mouth of his twentieth-century descendant. Each of the five episodes in the dream sequence ends, much like the overwhelming majority of al-Hamadhani's *Maqamat,* with verses of poetry uttered by the Mahfouzian Abu al-Fath. But his contemporary voice is a far cry from the medieval versifier's. Instead of composing his own poetry (as did al-Hamadhani's rogue hero), this modern preacher borrows the words of his ancestor, without intermediary or attribution. Hence, the modern dream sequences end with medieval verse.

The medieval verses in the modern text can be examined from different perspectives. What do the verses themselves express, since they are a literary entity with an existence outside the Mahfouzian text? Which Hamadhanian *maqama* is the source of each set of verses, and how do these *maqamat* illuminate our contemporary text?

Each set of verses uttered by the Mahfouzian Abu al-Fath comes from a different Hamadhanian *maqama.* Because the last dream episode contains two sets of verses, the number of *maqamat* exploited is six. In one, "al-Hirziyya," Abu al-Fath sells amulets to a group of passengers who find themselves on a boat during a storm and at risk of losing their lives (al-Hamadhani, 118-20). In another, "al-Qirdiyya," our medieval rogue hero is a monkey trainer entertaining a crowd with a dancing monkey (al-Hamadhani, 96–97). The third *maqama* exploited is "al-Maristaniyya." Here, Abu al-Fath plays the role of a lunatic in an asylum, who demonstrates his eloquence and philosophical knowledge by discoursing on free will and justice (al-Hamadhani, 121–26). In "al-Maqama al-ʿIraqiyya" the rogue exhibits his poetic skills, whereas in "al-Sasaniyya" he is the leader of a group of beggars (al-Hamadhani, 92–95, 142–50). Last, "al-Maqama al-ʿIlmiyya" treats the reader to a soliloquy on knowledge and how one acquires it (al-Hamadhani, 202–3).

In these six *maqamat,* Abu al-Fath shows his skills at role playing. He is at once the master of eloquence and of disguise. But his supposed occupations (monkey trainer, chief of beggars, lunatic, etc.) are all less than dignified. He does play other roles in al-Hamadhani's literary masterpieces: we even see him as an imam in a mosque (e.g., in "al-Maqama al-Asfahaniyya," al-Hamadhani, 51–54). The roles that the contemporary author chose to emphasize further define his own political orator, Abu al-Fath. The latter takes on the undignified and socially questionable attributes of his ancestor. He wears disguises and is also a swindler, duping his public. His characterization is quite a commentary on political orators.

Is our modern rogue hero to blame for his behavior? When ʿIsa, the dreamer, confronts the twentieth-century Abu al-Fath, the latter replies with the verses his literary ancestor created. These poetic interludes justify the shifts in the rogue's behavior. Not only are the vicissitudes of time to blame, but so are the stupidity of the age and its hostility to culture. Anyway, can this Abu al-Fath do otherwise? He is the source of wondrous acts. He is a priest in a monastery and an ascetic in a mosque, and he is geographically unsettled as well, experiencing his night in Syria and his day in Iraq. The fluidity and the versatility of the medieval character becomes a model for the instability and insincerity of modern political discourse.

In Dream 9 our dreamer finds himself in a verdant and nature-rich city. He walks around in it without encountering any other being. Then he sees a lion reading. He asks the lion what he is reading, to which the lion replies, "*Kalila wa Dimna.*" When the dreamer inquires why, the lion answers, "From it we have learned how to live happily." When the dreamer notes that the city is empty, the lion tells him that he must learn how to look. He then inquires as to the dreamer's occupation. When he learns that the latter is a singer, the lion remarks that they only receive singers, and he asks the dreamer to demonstrate his skills. The latter does so. What difference does it make to him, he sings, whether night is long or short because neither in daytime nor in nighttime does he have any freedom from adversity. The lion welcomes him to the city, urging him to remind its inhabitants of their old misery so they will be increasingly grateful for their blessings. The king of beasts then calls for an eagle to take the new guest to the Hotel of Contentment.

In this dream, the dreamer once again has an encounter with a character from the classical Arabic literary tradition. *Kalila wa Dimna* is the title of an Indian work that falls within the mirror-of-princes genre. It was translated from Pahlavi into Arabic by one of the earliest prose writers, Ibn al-Muqaffaʿ (d. 757). The text is a set of enframed animal fables designed for didactic (and entertaining) purposes.[42] The lion (symbolizing the king) is a major character in the work, and in the Mahfouzian narrative a lion is benefiting from the perusal of the work.

Perhaps most distinctive about this dream narrative is that it is one of the few in which the dreamer ends with contentment. This ending is an interesting commentary given the cynical, essentially Machiavellian nature of the political wisdom distilled by *Kalila wa Dimna.*

In Dream 10 the dreamer is in a limitless desert that is uninhabited except for a kite overhead. He is in the process of setting up a tent in which to spend his weekend. Suddenly a man wearing a red outergarment (*ʿabaʾa*) appears. The two exchange looks and greetings, then the dreamer asks the newcomer if he is on a break like himself. The other, as though not hearing, asks the dreamer who he is. "My name is Nadim," answered the dreamer. "Whose companion (*nadim*)?" retorts the newcomer, to which the dreamer replies that this is a name and not a descriptive. The newcomer then expresses surprise at the dreamer's clothing and begins to identify buildings that stood on that location, including a palace. The dreamer, doubting the newcomer's sanity, asks him when he last visited the location, to which the newcomer replies: "Five thousand years ago." Another lost place is identified, and the dreamer, acting as if he believes the man, asks him who he is. "I am al-Khidr," he answers calmly. "Sayyiduna (Our Lord) al-Khidr?" replies the dreamer. "Sayyiduna?" questions al-Khidr. The dreamer replies, "You have attained eternal life, for you are the master of humanity." Al-Khidr retorts that he is the prisoner of loneliness. And when the dreamer wishes to keep him company for a while, he answers that he will not be able to keep up with him. Then he moves away with the speed of lightning.

This dream is quite complex in its message about the Arabo-Islamic tradition. This time, the dreamer, still a modern individual, has a direct and unmediated experience with a character from the tradition, the legendary religious figure of al-Khidr. The latter, according to his biographers, can fly through the air, appear in many different locations, and speak the languages of all peoples. But it is his immortality that is always emphasized.[43]

This Mahfouzian narrative recasts al-Khidr in modern terms and creates a dialogue between tradition (represented by the legendary figure) and modernity (represented by the dreamer). This dialogue is indeed potent. First set in the context of superficial and external differences, such as clothing and destroyed buildings, it soon begins to demonstrate the futility of an encounter between the representatives of these respective periods. This futility is centered on the identity of the two individuals, the very definition of their being.

When al-Khidr asks the dreamer who he is, he answers, "My name is Nadim," a seemingly reasonable answer under the circumstances. But al-Khidr responds as a medieval Arab might have responded: "Whose *nadim*?" A *nadim*, a boon companion, was part of classical Arabo-Islamic civilization, an individual chosen for his wit and good company. The dreamer's response that *Nadim* is a name and not a descriptive goes to the heart of the anachronism. One of the striking characteristics of the classical Arabic onomastic system, largely missing in the modern period, is the tendency of name elements (with the general exception of the *ism*, or first name, and partial exception of the *kunya*, or patronymic) to exist in a constant tension between name (whose referent is the individual) and descriptive (whose referent is a characteristic).[44] Further, since a name normally defines an individual, the dreamer's identity is questionable, at least as far as al-Khidr is concerned. And the latter fares no better. After identifying himself, he questions the label "Sayyiduna." Even more eloquent, when he is told about his immortality, he redefines it as the prison of loneliness. The distinguishing mark of al-Khidr has been turned from a positive force into a negative one.

The dialogue between tradition and modernity goes further than the conversation, however. The oneiric narrative begins with the dreamer setting up a tent in a desert environment—in effect, making an encampment like the Arabs' bedouin ancestors. When al-Khidr appears, he bemoans the disappeared sites of times gone by. The entire episode echoes the classical Arabic poetic tradition. The revered traditional *qasida* began with a bittersweet evocation of an abandoned campsite. And the ruins of abandoned cities were a frequent topos in ʿAbbasid poetry.[45]

But by its situational bisociation, the oneiric experience questions the appropriateness of the traditional in a modern context. The dreamer is setting up his tent for the weekend, a modern concept and, in the Arabic, a modern phrase. This anachronistic bisociation brings about the encounter with al-Khidr. Thus it is another commentary on the enormity of the breach between the traditional and the modern.

Perhaps the ending of the dream narrative is most eloquent in this regard. The modern dreamer attempts to keep company with al-Khidr, only to be put off and to have the latter disappear with the speed of lightning. Before departing, however, al-Khidr replies with a Qurʿanic verse that his own namesake used during his encounter with Moses in the Surat al-Kahf.[46] The intertextuality from the most sacred of Islamic texts merges the identity of the two Khidrs, in much the same way that the modern Abu al-Fath's borrowed verse put him in collusion with his literary ancestor.

If we consider the dreams containing classical material to be one literary unit, this encounter with al-Khidr provides the closure to the set. It is a grim closure, indeed, in which tradition escapes the modern individual. One can play at being a character in a classical text (as with the *Maqamat*), or one can attempt to escape into the fabled animal world of *Kalila wa Dimna,* but the true encounter with the Arabo-Islamic tradition is doomed to failure.

Despite this pessimistic commentary on the dialogue between the traditional and the modern, the oneiric encounters with the characters from the Arabo-Islamic tradition are salutory in a certain sense. They call attention to the supremacy of narrating/writing. An underlying optimism exists because the hero of the *Maqamat* is not the rogue but the narrator. Singing proves a positive element in the run-in with the lion. It also saves the dreamer and other individuals from a near disaster in Dream 2. The singer is hence one of the major guises of the dreamer and an obvious reference to the writer.

This theory assumes that the dreamer/first-person narrator is the same individual in all the oneiric narratives. Important thematic elements do recur in the seventeen episodes. The most potent of these is without doubt the desire to escape. The dreamer in the majority of cases finds himself fleeing a pursuer or pursuers, who are sometimes unknown to him. A sense of claustrophobia, sometimes of paranoia, pervades the collection. Finally, in the last dream episode, the hero makes good his escape.

Dream 17, the last dream narrative, is strangely premonitory. The dreamer, seeing the periods of history parade before him, gets an overwhelming desire to go to the moon. He is surrounded, however, by much lavish furniture that covers the walls and blocks the windows. Because his body is weighed down by prizes and expensive gifts, he is unable to move and begins to sink into the ground. He feels that he is awaiting an important visitor but wonders where he will seat him. He moves the prizes off him and throws the furniture right and left until he makes a path for himself. He breathes deeply and is surprised by the lightness of his body. The visitor is arriving, but the dreamer is unable to wait for him because he begins rising from the ground. He then realizes that he is flying in the air and that as he rises, he is going progressively faster. He is flooded with a feeling of escape, which promises him happiness that words cannot describe.

As a closure to the cycle of seventeen oneiric narratives, this dream is most appropriate. The dreamer's physical escape, which has been finally effected, is symbolic of other escapes. The literary form of Mahfouz's cycle also represents a narrative freedom, but this time from the conventions of normal prose, both classical and modern. It permits anachronism while commenting on the whole archaizing (and by implication, neotraditionalist) trend in contemporary Arabic letters. Perhaps it is all a dream. Or perhaps as Abu al-Fath put it in "al-Maqama al-ʿIlmiyya," knowledge cannot be seen in dreams (al-Hamadhani, 202).

The dreamer's escape is, in its own strange way, a premonitory wish fulfillment. The Nobel Prize has certainly brought Mahfouz much glory, but it has also been a burden on his failing health. He is constantly accosted (dare we say pursued?) by crowds. And he is bothered by the lights of television cameras. Is the prize weighing him down physically, as happened to the dreamer, who wished to escape to the heavens but was weighed down by the signs of earthly success? This dream narrative is a strange prediction indeed, but it would not have surprised Mahfouz's literary ancestors.

12

FROM "NAGUIB MAHFOUZ'S CRITICS"

GABER ASFOUR

Translated by Ayman A. el-Desouky

No contemporary Arab man of letters has managed to preoccupy our literary mentality as much as Naguib Mahfouz. His multilayered fictional world, with its complex set of relations and its elusive symbols, provokes unending arguments, lays the groundwork for interminable problems, and stimulates ongoing critical efforts aimed at discovering that world's constituent elements. As long as this fictional world remains a bearer of meaning, a generator of signification, it produces seemingly inexhaustible analytical activity, commentary, and interpretation. On their performative level, these activities may be identical, or they may be in conflict—they may differ or agree in terms of their goal or perspective, yet in the end they present us with a complex posture of commentaries and interpretations. In other words, they present a posture characterized by complexity, variety, and richness as much as by discordance, opposition, and contradiction.

Luwis ʿAwad has spoken of a "chorus of critics" that rings out with hymns of praise whenever Naguib Mahfouz publishes a new work; rivers of interviews and articles flood the newspapers, the magazines, and the radio waves. "I have never known a writer," he said,

> who has remained, throughout a good part of his literary career, so submerged, so undermined and neglected, for no obvious reason—and before whom all the avenues of glory have, again for no obvious reason, opened up all at once in the past five years—none except Naguib Mahfouz. Nor have I ever known a writer so well

> received by the right, the center, and the left—whose works are appreciated by traditionalists and modernists, and by those in between. Naguib Mahfouz has become in our country an established literary or artistic institution, like those many lofty institutions we read about without really knowing what goes on inside. Tourists may come, or be brought over, to view this institution along with the hallmarks of our modern civilization; yet even more wondrous, this institution, which is Naguib Mahfouz, is not only a government institution, drawing sustenance from official recognition, but a popular institution that people talk about spontaneously in cafés, at home, and in ordinary literary gatherings.[1]

Luwis ʿAwad said this in March 1962, more than twenty years ago. What can be said now, after all these years? Mahfouz's writing has gone on, and the admiration he receives has never flagged. Even when admiration for him was contested by opposing voices, we find its intensity has increased with the passing of the years. Thus, we now find before us more than twelve books in Arabic on Naguib Mahfouz and a huge number of books that discuss the Arabic novel or Arabic literature in general. We also find many special issues on Mahfouz in widely distributed periodicals and a noticeable collection of M.A. and Ph.D. theses on him, as well as innumerable articles not yet compiled in books. Add to all this a collection of plays, radio and television serials based on his novels or short stories—presenting us with more than one perspective on the interpretation of the same author—and two books by Hashim al-Nahhas, *Najib Mahfuz ʿala al-shasha* (Naguib Mahfouz on the screen) and *Yawmiyyat film* (The diary of a film), based on *al-Qahira al-jadida* (The New Cairo). Were we to focus our study on Arabic criticism only, leaving aside criticism in or translated from foreign languages—and there is much of it (really worth a separate study)—we would encounter a unique quantitative and qualitative critical posture that has never been accorded to any other Arab novelist in our modern age.

In this unique situation the result of that single-minded vision that sees no one but Naguib Mahfouz in the novel, Tawfiq al-Hakim in theater, and Yusuf Idris in the short story? Single-mindedness may be a reason, but a partial one. The amount of writing on Tawfiq al-Hakim or Yusuf Idris or both has never approached either in quality or quantity that vast body of writing on Naguib Mahfouz. The increasing amount of writing, however, does not necessarily mean increased clarity; it may, on the contrary, render ambiguous what is normally considered clear and self-evident. As much as each new writing, or new reading, dispels ambiguities in the text and unfolds the intricacies of its codes, it draws attention to more ambiguities and hints at various other obscurities. It also stimulates more and more writing. The world of Naguib Mahfouz thus remains, in spite of all that has been written about it, in need of yet more disclosure and consequently of more writing and reading. Indeed, it may be said that the reason behind the unique status of Naguib Mahfouz's fiction is its inherent ambiguity. But what about the poetry of, say, Adonis (ʿAli Ahmad Saʿid)? Is not his long poem *Mufrad bi-sighat al-jamʿ* (Singular in plural form) more ambiguous than the most ambiguous of Mahfouz's stories, those stories that were described once as mere "riddles and mysteries"? Yet does the available commentary on Adonis amount to even one-tenth of what has been written on Naguib Mahfouz?

The fictional world of Naguib Mahfouz is so complex, encompassing historical and realistic narrative, containing the partially symbolic that may infiltrate the dominant tone of a realistic work and the general symbol whose manifold meanings lead to more than one interpretation or become unified and revert to allegory. His fiction contains within itself different schools and trends, ranging from critical realism to existential realism to socialist realism, and including naturalism, surrealism, and the absurd. It is as if the fictional world of Naguib Mahfouz were a museum exhibiting all the doctrines and trends the novel has known or a laboratory containing all the theories and methodologies known to criticism, starting with historicism and ending with structuralism.

Leaving aside the comprehensive aspects of Mahfouz's world, it may also be said that his various heroes and heroines represent different sectors and character types of Egyptian society in their development and maturation from the 1919 coup d'état up to the *infitah* [literally, "openness" to the West]. Indeed, those protagonists exhibit a search for something better, a desire for redemption from the past. Their heated and enthusiastic protests, often sharp and relentless, reflect an audacity in attempting to reach at roots and a sincerity in unveiling the real cause behind the tragedy of Egyptian society. It is as though those protagonists, gathered in one fictional world, presented a well-polished mirror in which society could see its real reflection—"the auspicious future behind the restless present and the speedily waning past."[2]

The world of Naguib Mahfouz reflects contradictory and complex circumstances—the social factors and historical traditions that worked hand in hand in defining the psychology of the sons of the petite bourgeoisie.[3] Mahfouz depicts the identity crisis of those characters and the consequent indecisiveness and contradiction in their attempts at solving the problems of freedom and justice without forsaking their dream of the "eternal revolution." How often they quote, in this respect, Kamal ʿAbd al-Jawad's remark in *al-Sukkariyya.* "I believe in life and people. I find myself obliged to follow their ideals as long as I believe that they are true, for to shrink from this is cowardice and escapism, just as I find myself obliged to revolt against their ideals when I believe that they are false; for to shrink from this is treachery. This is the meaning of eternal revolution."[4] And how often they identify Kamal ʿAbd al-Jawad with Naguib Mahfouz, an identification that leads to the notion that Naguib Mahfouz has excelled over his peers by virtue of his "awareness of the reality of cultural and historical circumstances, the nature of the social forces and their conflicts, and evolutionary movements in Egyptian society."[5]

As for renovating intellectual content, the fiction of Naguib Mahfouz achieves a middle vision—and we are a nation of the middle—and in this respect it achieves an intellectual blend to which all the contending intellectual factions in the Arab world may be drawn. It is useful, in this context, to recall what Jaʿfar, the storyteller, says in *Qalb al-layl* (The heart of the night) about his intellectual project: that it is based on a philosophical stance, a social ideology, and a style of government. This project then becomes the basis for a political order that is "the legal heir of Islam, of the French Revolution, and of the Communist Revolution."[6] But if Naguib Mahfouz's fiction refers to this political order, it could indeed make him a writer "well received by the right, the center, and the left, by traditionalists and modernists, and by those in between," as Luwis ʿAwad said. Such a project provides each faction with a portion of what pleases it and lures it into accepting this fictional world in the hope of gradually winning it over. Such an interpretation would lay a foundation for conflicting motives behind critical approaches to the world of Naguib Mahfouz. It would also bring to light those repeated attempts, on the part of some critics, to exert control over this world or to capture it in place within a certain intellectual system or systems. No matter how enticing this interpretation may be, it still circumscribes Mahfouz's world, transforming it into an "intellectual document," while it raises doubts concerning the validity of such unanimous admiration among the various factions.

The critics' responses to the world of Naguib Mahfouz are widely discordant and chaotic. Luwis ʿAwad writes: "Naguib Mahfouz to me is one of those few writers in the literary histories of the East and the West who makes my blood boil whenever I read him, and I wish I could beat him soundly. And yet, at the same time, whenever I read Mahfouz, he makes me live for some time among the glories of man, and I say to myself, 'There is no art above this art, no summit higher than this highest of all summits.' "[7] The critic's response, in this context, is clearly contradictory because it vouchsafes the positive and the negative, both admiration and rejection.

Such a multitude of critics, however, can never form a "chorus," to use Luwis ʿAwad's term. A "chorus of critics," if it really existed, would have to adhere to a unified orchestration to guide its performance and to make their voices agree. The critics of Naguib Mahfouz lack such harmony. The voice of Muhammad Mandur, for example, will not harmonize with the voice of ʿAbd al-ʿAzim Anis, even though both speak about a petite bourgeoisie. Mandur's sympathies are with a class that "still clings to many of the highest virtues of humanity, particularly the sanctification of the family and the readiness to sacrifice for its sake,"[8] while ʿAbd al-ʿAzim Anis's position demonstrates suspicion, restlessness, and a belief in the absence of leadership. While Mandur draws on the pronouncements of Gustave Lanson, ʿAbd al-ʿAzim Anis draws on various other pronouncements, mixing Christopher Caudwell with Roger Garaudy.[9] Moreover, the voice of Mandur can never harmonize with that of Luwis ʿAwad, even when it comes close. And neither voice will harmonize easily with the voice of Yahya Haqqi, who follows the trail of the man in the artist, and who attempts to interpret his own feelings toward the artist he discovers. Those voices will not harmonize with Mahmud Amin al-ʿAlim (whose voice differs considerably in tone from his *Fi al-thaqafa al-Misriyya* [On Egyptian culture, 1955; with ʿAbd al-ʿAzim Anis] and his introduction to *al-Anfar* [Individuals] or *Qisas waqiʿiyya* [Realistic stories, 1956], and which differs in degree in *Ta'ammulat fi ʿalam Najib Mahfuz* [Meditations on the world of Naguib Mahfouz, 1970]).

What a distance there is between all those voices put together and that of Sayyid Qutb (the first critic to discuss Naguib Mahfouz, who initiated a debate about him with Salah Dhuhni over *Kifah Tiba* [The struggle of Thebes], in *al-Risala* 44 and 45, 1944) or that of Ahmad ʿAbbas Salih (in his writings on *al-Sarab* [The mirage] in *al-Adib al-Misri,* 1950, and on Naguib Mahfouz in general in *al-Shaʿb*, 1959, and *al-Katib,* 1966). Further, the notion of Anwar al-Maʿaddawi (the second critic to allot to Naguib Mahfouz a considerable introduction), whose readings stress "psychological performance," differs from Rashad Rushdi's conception of Eliot's "objective correlative." And Rashad Rushdi is, in turn, far from Latifa al-Zayyat. (Among the unmistakable paradoxes are her translation and analysis of the first complete collection in Arabic of T. S. Eliot's essays, which discordantly, adopt Lukács's pronouncements, and Rushdi's incessant talk of "the objective correlative," which he forgets all about when it comes to application.

It is possible to add even more names of Egyptian critics to this list, yet the names are so many that one is apt to imagine that there has never been a critic in Egypt who has not written on Naguib Mahfouz.[10] If we broadened the circle to include the rest of the Arab world, the voices would become even less harmonious, and the "chorus" would disappear altogether: the "road" to the world of Naguib Mahfouz would be transformed and Mahfouz's creations metamorphosed into a "tale without a beginning or an end."

Considering its complexity and contradictions, the criticism of Naguib Mahfouz is an exemplary case for literary hermeneutics and metacriticism. This is a critical tradition that acknowledges both conflicting interpretations and internal inconsistencies in its critical pronouncements, giving rise to a need for further revision. The fictional works of Naguib Mahfouz say, in their own way, something about a world from which they are derived and to which they return. Then critics come along: one group relates these texts to a particular world; another group to a second world; and a third may make them transcend any particular world, thus shutting them up and denying them immanent reference to whatever is external to them. All such critics make different pronouncements about how the texts "speak." Once we step into such a framework of diversity, difference, and discord among pronouncements on how the texts "speak," the need for revision arises.

Revision here is founded on that kind of meditation that may discover some underlying systems to harmonize this discord. Revision is also based on a consideration of the internal relations of each system and on the recognition of its elements, just as it considers its compatibility with systems other than itself. Again, revision is based on the careful observation of how close, or how alien, such systems are to the texts of Naguib Mahfouz. This last revisionary activity, however, cannot take place unless we consider the texts of Naguib Mahfouz as constituting another system, independent of the critical systems. Such a revisionary process may imply, at first sight, that one word in the critical vocabulary can have two totally different meanings, neither of which can be grasped in itself without first referring it to its context. Consequently, one term may signify two conflicting elements, one in each system.

A critic may come along, Edward al-Kharrat for example, and tell us that "the art of Naguib Mahfouz is not fundamentally a realistic art" and that his characters—especially grandparents and parents—are "fixed major types that belong to the greater human types" because they "surmount all the spheres of reality."[11] Another critic, such as Mahmud Amin al-ʿAlim, may equally assert the contrary, that the art of Naguib Mahfouz is drawn to those realistic spheres more than we can imagine and that his characters represent "mature social types" in whom individual psychological features blend into intellectual and social evolutionary processes.[12] We thus find ourselves confronted with a situation in which critical pronouncements about the same literary utterance contradict each other, and so we must compare the critics' use of terminology.

The two critics use the term *type* to mean two totally different things. (It is also important to notice that both use the same term synonymously with *archetype* in more than one place.) *Type* (*namat*), according to Mahmud Amin al-ʿAlim, is a fundamental concept in the discourse of "realistic" criticism.[13] According to Edward al-Kharrat, however, *type* is a concept in discourse on myth, where the term *archetype* plays a vital role in the quest for the different manifestations of universal human images, something close to the submerged symbols in the human collective unconscious.[14] It is possible to relate the opposition between the two meanings of the term to the conflict between two systems, in which the same term plays different roles. It is also possible to explain the opposition in terms of a certain inaccuracy in employing the term—that is, by saying that the two critics unfortunately use the same Arabic word for different foreign terms. In either case, we are bound to realize the need for a revisionary circle, so lacking in our critical activity, the circle of metacriticism and hermeneutics.

If we bypass terminology and move to the motivating value judgment behind the formation of *type,* we might be able to pose a group of questions about the way Naguib Mahfouz's art, according to al-Kharrat, transcends "the spheres of reality," and about the way this same art, according to al-ʿAlim, is bound by those very spheres. Al-ʿAlim, who incorporates Marxist aesthetics, will not accept an art that indulges in the symbols of the ritualistic collective unconscious, apart from the spheres of reality, for this would mean an estrangement of reality and a falling away from realism. Al-Kharrat would cast angry looks at any art that indulges in realism without appeasing his craving for metarealism.

Such questions would naturally lead us to the constituent elements of two opposed systems of critical discourse and thereby afford us the opportunity to examine these two systems at the level of application. This opportunity would further lead us to review the evidence the two critics use to vindicate their opposed views of the relation between that same art and the spheres of reality. In the same vein, an examination of the two critics' logical structure would require us to examine the integrity of their principles, their ability to enable a system to explain most or all of the elements in the texts of Naguib Mahfouz.

We may examine al-Kharrat's concept of *type* based on statements of Jung, Frazer, and Northrop Frye, and that of al-ʿAlim, in whose understanding of *type* many ideas are assembled, starting with Engels and ending with George Lukács on "reflection." This step will enable us to determine how precise each concept is and how far it can function as a decisive critical tactic. Then we can pose other questions. Does *type* function as a general critical tactic, or does it succeed only with some texts and not with others? Why should the presence of *type* be the condition for a value judgment in the first place? Does it have to be *type* alone or should the other elements that constitute the critic's system also be taken into account? We can also question why al-Kharrat saw—in the same passage—something other than what al-ʿAlim was able to see. And if both critics draw on Western critical discourse, why did al-ʿAlim choose to adhere to the concepts of "realistic" criticism while al-Kharrat chose those of myth? Is it because of a difference in temperament or cultural mold, or is it because of a difference in social perspective and, subsequently, class position and affiliation between the two critics? Furthermore, if we leave aside the critics and shift to the relationship of their critical discourse to the texts of Mahfouz we may also ask whether the opposition between the two concepts of *type*—as a constituent element—originate in the critics' systems, or if the literary utterance itself—Mahfouz's text —invites and indeed encourages such opposition in critical discourse. Which of the two critical discourses is closer to the literary discourse, or text?

If Edward al-Kharrat considers discourse [*qawl*] to be a mute voice, semiunified, as it came to be defined in the 1960s, we should look for the reasons why the voice of al-Kharrat's discourse, despite his persistence and constant modification, is indeed mute. Then we find ourselves on the fringes of a struggle between ideologies—with both its deeper and its more superficial forms—reflected in the struggle of the critical discourse over the literary discourses. The struggle of the critical discourse, furthermore, corresponds to and reflects internal struggles at the various levels of Mahfouz's texts. These texts are undoubtedly not unilayered; nor are their relationships fixed. They have multiple centers and conflicting levels.

Critics are bound to ask such questions, explicitly or implicitly, before formulating their discourses on a literary work. But once critics have spoken out and their discourses are found to contradict, oppose, parallel, agree with, or even complement the discourse of colleagues, the entire critical discourse must undergo revision.

No other critical discourse is more persistent in its need for revision than the critical discourse on Naguib Mahfouz. Every time Mahfouz publishes a work, a torrent of studies and commentaries begin to flow, and as soon as he creates a symbol, such a variety of interpretations begin to cluster around it that both work and symbol turn into disputed territory over which critics fight like the Karamazov brothers. The revisionist's job in Mahfouz's case is not an easy one. They should not play the role of father Yanaros in Kazantzakis's *The Fratricides* and attempt a reconciliation between Marx and Christ;[15] nor should they array themselves in judicial garments and start issuing convictions and acquittals. They should, in effect, search out any constituent elements, the relationships among which would create systems out of the apparent chaos of accumulated critical discourses. (Even though such a revision would normally claim to be unprejudiced, it must, of course, stake out a position toward its subject of study, or it would dissolve behind the illusion of pure objectivity or false practicality.)

Whatever the consequence of this revision, it should help reorganize the processes of reading a literary text. Just as this revision helps to deepen the reading processes and to enhance their development, it unveils—through the study of a particular case—the underlying conflicting systems, the totality of which forms what we call contemporary Arabic criticism. Such revision also discovers those basic spheres in which the contemporary Arab critic orbits, and which define his discourse, and guide his exposition of the literary discourse, and thereby govern his interpretation of the literary text.

The world of Naguib Mahfouz consists, on an empirical level, of a group of texts: his novels and short stories. No matter how numerous these texts may be, they form a meaningful context, a set of relations between constituent elements that permeate all the texts to such a degree that they become one major text. This one major text is characterized by a kind of internal regularity that does not undermine the variety represented by the multiple levels of the individual texts themselves. This internal regularity does not prevent the existence of conflicting elements in the totality; nor does it contradict the obvious manifestations of any particular text.

From this perspective, *The Thief and The Dogs* is compatible with *al-Karnak*, just as both are compatible with *al-Qahira al-jadida* (The New Cairo) or *ʿAbath al-aqdar* (The absurdity of the fates). All these texts, furthermore, fit into one major net of relations that connects them with other texts, such as *The Trilogy, Kifah Tiba* (The struggle of Thebes), or *The Children of Gebelawi.* The distinctions among these texts are not so radical that they would shift us from one kind of totality to a contradictory one. The distinctions are typical of those differences that would exist among the various manifestations of a single totality activated within one system, a system that does not overrule the unique characteristics of all the works. If we draw a metaphor from contemporary syntactic studies, we can say that the various literary texts of Naguib Mahfouz are only surface structures set up and sustained by a deeper unifying structure that makes the particular texts one and the same text, with an internally regulated system.

Some critics of Naguib Mahfouz sense the presence of this system and refer to it with various names, such as "the vision of Naguib Mahfouz" or "the revelation of Naguib Mahfouz," just as they call it "the fictional world of Naguib Mahfouz," "the world of Naguib Mahfouz," and so forth. Some associate the name with positive qualities, some with negative qualities. Some get carried away with metaphorical language and speak of an "aesthetic architecture" or "unity of rhythm," or "basic features" or "fixed structures." Yet whatever the name or metaphor, it indicates an understanding of a kind of "self-created system" that is the true cause of the totality or its underlying structure. Furthermore, their recurrent metaphors, borrowed from various fields (e.g., architecture, sculpture, painting, music, and poetry), are attempts at capturing this elusive system from beyond the surface of varied texts. Thus "architecture" conforms, semantically, with "unity of rhythm," and both confirm the existence of "basic features" and "fixed structures" that function as the constitutive elements of a totality made up of relations. This totality is "the fictional world" or whatever "vision" or "revelation" that world produces.

The difference between the words *vision* and *revelation* marks a difference in critical conceptions of the elements making up the world of Naguib Mahfouz. "Vision" leads us to "reality" and lands us on the shores of "realism," as can be seen, for example, in ʿAbd al-Muhsin Taha Badr's *Najib Mahfuz: al-ruʾya wa al-adat* (Naguib Mahfouz: The vision and the means). "Revelation" leads us to the "symbol" and brings us into the presence of the "absolute"—for example, in the way George Tarabishi explains in *Allah fi rihlat Najib Mahfuz al-ramziyya* (God in the symbolic journey of Naguib Mahfouz). Both words herald the realization of a "unified world" and make us feel that it has a system of some sort. Thus we hear one critic say:

> The fictional world of Naguib Mahfouz is a world unto itself, nearly the equivalent of the society outside. Its elements are causally related, each element deriving its own relative value from its relationship with the other parts, and its byways and back alleys lead onto its main street. All its events are regulated in a fixed frame that allots each event its due significance. In such a world, a personal whim may converge with a political treaty; for all that surrounds us has merged with a network of intellectual signs and ready-made stimulations.[16]

We hear another critic say:

> The basic features of the world of Naguib Mahfouz have already taken shape. This is not to charge it with stagnation. No. For how transcendent is the variety of this world, how fertile and how deep is its unceasing renovation! And yet it is, in truth, a homogeneous world and remains as such from the first pulse set in motion in the first work till the last of his unpublished work, and even, in my opinion, in works not yet written. There are in this world major centers, fixities, and basic frameworks that compose its movement and that, no matter how renewed, evolved, developed, and deepened in thought, method or style, embrace a fundamental, integrated artistic vision—despite their continual development—from the beginning till that end that abides in many long years of deep and gratifying creativity.[17]

If we move beyond the surface level of the secondary metaphors or similes used in the above quotations ("byways," "back alleys," "first pulse," "fixed frame," "converge," etc.) to the semantic core that magnetizes all those similes and metaphors, we find ourselves close to the system of which I have been speaking, without quite penetrating its code. The first quotation contains a hidden evaluative tone that sneaks into the sentences and that ascribes to the fictional world certain negative qualities, such as strict formalism leading to automation, but the second quotation contains an evaluative tone that is conveyed by impressionistic excitement ("how transcendent," "how deep") and that assigns this fictional world positive qualities (unity and variety). Both quotations assertively credit the world of Naguib Mahfouz with "internal regularity," suggesting that the texts of Naguib Mahfouz proffer "an integrated vision of human life in whose integrity we are able to meditate on the constant and changing elements."[18]

Such quotations bring us nearer to the primary function of Mahfouz's critics: that of viewing Mahfouz's texts as a whole, governed by a definite system with constitutive elements, manifold centers, and conflicting levels that relate the many axes of his world and bring the levels of his vision into harmony. A critic's understanding of this function is a realization of the principle that attributes aesthetic value to the notion of "unity in variety." But unity in this sense is not the unity of spatially contiguous parts, works temporally consecutive, or texts externally accumulated. It is a unity that would lead those critics aware of it to the system lying behind all the texts of Naguib Mahfouz. We try to penetrate the surface of accumulated texts to the foundation of this unity without getting distracted by variety, and end up with compartmentalization. Instead, we should perceive variety in relationships that lead us to the "living unit" of a system, marked by restlessness rather than stagnation. In this way, unity emerges not as the sum of parts but as the result of combined relations, both among elements of a single text and among elements in all the texts.

The problem is that critics of Naguib Mahfouz stray from this primary function more often than they strive to attain it. It is not difficult to see how critics yield to a partial point of view, evolutionary and historical only in a narrow sense. Thus the texts are divided up and made spatially consecutive without merging into a regulatory, unified system.

One of the simplest forms of this partial point of view is the assumption of two totally different stages through which the texts of Naguib Mahfouz have passed. These two stages may be called realism and neorealism, or the static and the dynamic. Such a division implies contradictory conceptual dimensions on the diachronic plane, a radical change in temperament from one extreme to the other.

This division (which blurs the distinction between levels of the same system) places a group of Mahfouz's novels (such as *al-Qahira al-jadida, Khan al-Khalili,* and *The Beginning and the End*) on a remote island opposed to another island of novels different in nature, topography, and inhabitants (such as *The Thief and the Dogs, al-Tariq* [The path], and *The Beggar*). Apparently, we have no bridge to connect the two islands. There is no harm in pursuing the idea that the first island is an orderly, systematic, shipshape environment where everything fits in with everything else as in the architectonics of an arabesque—where everything is based on recording, description, and cold observation in which the passing of time is much like the falling away of the leaves of a calendar, one by one, hour by hour. We may further imagine the first island to be inhabited by "creatures who are stiff . . . cold, giving the impression that they resent excitement, and the second island to be tumultuous, roaring with motion, violence, and deep, exploding volcanoes, a setting where time and place commingle, an island inhabited by fiery creatures who speak a dense language in which, as Yahya Haqqi has said, behind every other word there is more than one possible meaning. We do not object, either, when another critic, Raja' al-Naqqash, repeats the same axiom, drawing on the artist and major critic Stephan Zweig, and tells us that the creatures of the first island, the static ones, move about "within the limits of the natural systems of their movement . . . without haste," while the inhabitants of the second island, the dynamic ones, "bolt out shouting and yelling, consumed with fire in the arena of their whimsical passions"; they are "martyrs and suicides."[19]

If the inhabitants of the first island in Naguib Mahfouz's fiction remind us of Tolstoy's characters, the dwellers of the second remind us of Dostoevsky's characters—if we are to believe Raja' al-Naqqash. And why not believe Yahya Haqqi when he suggests:

> Artists can be classified according to temperament, I maintain, into two major types . . . : the dynamic type whose works reflect the glare of battles, and the static type that survives battle unaffected, free of excitement and revolt. Laying one stone on top of another patiently in the manner of an architect . . . Naguib Mahfouz, may God preserve him for us, is a perfect testimony to the difference in characteristics between the two types . . . for we encounter both types in him, and in both he has reached the degree of perfection in artistic expression.[20]

But if we believe Yahya Haqqi or Raja' al-Naqqash, there is a sharp division in the works of Naguib Mahfouz. His texts fall into two groups forming two isolated islands, two consecutive stages, which implies two contradictory temperaments for Naguib Mahfouz the man. Naguib Mahfouz would then be transformed into a Dr. Jekyll and Mr. Hyde, with the important difference that Dr. Jekyll first unifies with his staticism, which lasts for a while and then dies only for Mr. Hyde to be resurrected in his stead, with his dynamism, or with "the whip with which he lashes his characters," to use Raja' al-Naqqash's phrase.

The comparison between the static and the dynamic is intelligent and amusing. It is related, as a critical project, to the symbolic opposition with which critics explain differences in the temperaments of writers and to the formations of paradigms that oppose, for example, Apollo to Dionysus, cold intellectuality to blazing emotion, or clarity (the sun) to ambiguity (the moon). Yet such symbolic classifications, though amusing, "are too abstract and schematic to be of much help in the stylistic study of particular texts or authors."[22]

This oppositional duality, if we consider again its manifestations in the texts of Naguib Mahfouz, is dangerous because, on one level, it makes us fancy, as do Yahya Haqqi and Raja' al-Naqqash, a sharp sense of change in the writer's vision of his world, as if it were an alternation from one vision to its opposite. On a second level, it diverts us from following the immediate struggle of the fictional world by making us track only the external successive alternation. On a third level, it diverts us from the fictional text to mere temperament. And on a fourth level, it directs us more toward the differences among the groups of texts than toward their similarities. As a result, we falsify the text instead of helping to realize its possibilities, dividing the fictional world instead of preserving its unity.

We may grant that a certain transformation takes place in the texts of Naguib Mahfouz, moving us from the static to the dynamic, if we wish to retain the two terms of Yahya Haqqi. Yet this transformation comes through, on the one hand, in the form of internal changes within one system and, on the other hand, like a struggle that breaks out among various diachronic and consecutive levels, in both individual and multiple texts at once. Hence, we can observe this struggle and these changes in all the texts of Naguib Mahfouz both in their horizontal and vertical succession. And what takes place in all the texts, as a totality, also takes place in each text separately. We are not confronted with "the static" in *The Trilogy* and then "the dynamic" in

The Thief and the Dogs, but we encounter both in both texts. The difference between the two works does not come about because of an "artistic shift" from one school to another opposing school or because of the "historical overthrow" of one vision in favor of another. It is a difference in the way internal transformations and immediate struggles in one system manifest themselves, and this takes place within each text separately. These statements do not mean that history should be canceled out or that the transformations taking place in a writer should be denied; but they do require viewing the historical position and artistic transformations holistically, not partially, so that we do not divide the artist into compartments or force him to move from one position to another (without his really moving). They mean viewing his texts, in their totality, as a significant system, the significance of which cannot be grasped except through the unity of its texts (as a system).

It is important to realize the synchronicity of the relationship between the static and the dynamic and also to realize its development through time. The static, as a quality that comprises levelness and pairedness is not an absolute contrary utterly cut off from the quality of the dynamic. Nor are the two qualities transformed into attributes experienced in tension in the same text. This is why Luwis ʿAwad was able to realize a certain kind of tension—which he called an abyss or a chasm—terming it "the classicism of form" and "the romanticism of content" in *The Thief and the Dogs.* He also perceived in *The Trilogy* the same tension between classical form and what it hides behind its perfected façade, a content that is "as remote as it can be from classicism."[22] Similarly, Mahmud al-Rabiʿi has identified a conflict between dialogue and monologue in *The Thief and the Dogs,* as well as a conflict between the linguistic units that constitute the text's diction—that is, between the surface and depth of consciousness within it. He pointed out the necessity of simplifying those linguistic units in dialogue while complicating them as much as possible when dialogue shifts back to monologue. He also hinted at the necessity of polishing the diction and of trimming it on the outer surface while giving it free rein and power on the level of interiority.[23]

The two qualities, from this perspective, are but attributes of two different levels belonging to the same system. The manifestations of the relationship between these two levels are subject to regular transformations that take place within one comprehensive context. Hence, the static and the dynamic can be opposed, intersecting, or converging, on one axis or on many axes. In the final analysis, it all depends on the internal transformations taking place within one text; namely, the works of Naguib Mahfouz as a totality. As long as this one total text harbors fixed, unchanging elements, the attribute of regularity is present and that of totality takes shape. It is not the regularity of, say, a "wall" in a building but it is a regularity of levels and efficient fulcra in "the language" (*al-lugha*).

This partial point of view takes up even more dangerous forms than the dualistic form of the dynamic and the static. It is possible to observe these forms when we consider the literary trendiness imposed on the texts of Naguib Mahfouz. Considered from such an angle, his works are grouped in stages. The first stage starts with *ʿAbath al-aqdar* (The absurdity of the fates) and ends with *Kifah Tiba* (The struggle of Thebes); the second stage starts with *al-Qahira al-jadida* and ends with *al-Sukkariyya*; the third stage starts with *Children of Gebelawi* and ends with *Tharthara fawq al-Nil* (Chatter on the Nile); and so on. These stages succeed one another historically, starting with the first published work of Naguib Mahfouz and ending with his last one, as if the measure for these stages were succession in time, which would parallel another succession of sequential literary trends.

Each stage should be endowed with the attributes not of only one trend but of many discordant ones. The first stage, for instance, can be classified as romantic historicism, illusory vision, or correspondence to reality. It can also be labeled the historical stage solely. Or if the conditions of its membership can be expanded, it can include, besides historicism, "the struggle for liberation," just as it can also be placed, finally, under the label of "symbol within the frame of history."[24] As for the second stage, it can be described as critical realism, social realism, photographic realism, or naturalism (as Luwis ʿAwad contends), or it may extend beyond realism (according to Edward al-Kharrat). Each stage is thus thought over and over until its texts are fit for accumulation and ready for insertion under three trends as remote from each other as naturalism is from critical realism.

Our present concern is not so much with the chaos of classifications as it is with the process of classification itself and its threat to the unity of texts. Emphasis on stages and on such methods of classification generates the same limited point of view. It fractures the living unity that holds the texts together and transforms it into accumulated heaps lined up horizontally, along which critics pass, as a train passes through one station after another. In such a case, it is only natural that critics will decline to linger at any group of texts not immediately situated on the lines of their railway, that is, at any group of texts that does not fit easily into their classificatory schema. Even if they do linger over these texts, the critics' concern will be to situate them: either they force them in under the same stage (consider the case of *al-Sarab* [The mirage], located in the social stage) or they ignore their formal attributes altogether or flatten them by confusing, say, representation in *Children of Gebelawi* with symbols that get in the way. All that matters to these critics is that the texts should be piled into outwardly similar heaps, so that the historiographic journey of Naguib Mahfouz's work may proceed smoothly and the heaps of his texts may disembark, as travelers do, each at a different station. As long as the critics are concerned primarily with the differences in succession, they ignore similarities and look at the works only as an essence manifested in the "now."

What Fatima Musa says, for instance, will not differ in essence from what ʿAli Shalaq says. Musa maintains that Naguib Mahfouz "started off with the historical novel, which represents the romantic stage . . . then moved to the realistic stage . . . and, having exhausted the possibilities of the contemporary realistic novel, . . . he passed over to a new stage, which can be called metarealistic."[25] To both critics the texts accumulate into horizontally successive heaps; Naguib Mahfouz starts under a certain label, then moves on to another, then passes over a stage to a new one. But what are the persistent elements and the internal relations of the collective texts, and what is the vertical dimension in "the evolutionary stages of fiction"? All these questions must disappear when the texts are divided among piles forming disjointed islands and stations. Yet this disjunction will not prevent us from pointing out some styles that have progressed by discovering their roots in the past.

If we return to the logic of the division, we have to ask whether one novelist's work can be classified under all these categories, all these labels, and yet remain sound. Would these diverse labels (realistic, naturalistic, etc.) end up estranging the novelist's texts, transforming them into something like a dervish's rags? And if we consider that terms like *realism* are distillations of different systems, would it imply—if we accepted all these terms, the way they are applied to Mahfouz's works—that Mahfouz's career leads to one of two possibilities: a welter of discordant systems (in which case his works would lack value because they would lack cohesion); or a shifting, novelistic vision that sees the world in turn as do the realist (critical-documentary), the naturalist, the existentialist, and the absurdist (in which case his mind would lack soundness)? In that case it is not useful to say that "none of our writers compares with Naguib Mahfouz in his critical understanding of literary theories and his application of them in his works."[26] If this statement were true, Naguib Mahfouz would turn into a critic or a man of letters who writes novels based on all the available measurements and theories.

This division of Mahfouz's texts into stations through which critics pass is not just the result of a partial point of view. It is also the result of a historiographic rather than a historical point of view, one that looks at the works of a writer as things that develop with time. From this perspective, each movement made by the texts of Naguib Mahfouz would be a forward movement involving more craftsmanship and maturity in this worldview, as if he had started off as a child with *ʿAbath al-aqdar,* grown into boyhood in *The Trilogy,* reached maturity in *Children of Gebelawi,* and become a wise old man in *Malhamat al-harafish.* This upward, evolutionary movement of Naguib Mahfouz may stumble a little or waver, yet it persists in its ascent on the ladder of evolution.

If we distance ourselves from the above fallacy of evolution, we discern its lack of a historical perspective, its tendency to measure a writer in years or according to the succession of his works, independent of any other measurements. Moreover, this point of view usually presupposes a starting point for the evolution: a zero point where the least evolved of all creatures reside. Yet this point is of no value except as a mere beginning. Consequently, the starting point has to denote the lowest literary point on the ladder of evolution and thus on the ladder of value. The end point on the scale, therefore, has to be the highest position on the ladder of evolution and, consequently, on the ladder of value. Following this logic, the texts of Naguib Mahfouz end up being arranged temporally according to a sequence based on a hierarchy, at the bottom of which reside the romanticism of *ʿAbath al-aqdar,* whereas at its top there is the realism—or metarealism, according to some critics—of *The Trilogy.*

The first consequence of such classification and subclassification—the trap into which the "realist" critic falls once lured by the novelist—is a descent from the "realism of comprehensive revolution" to "the heart of the night," where certainty does not amount to the 50 percent Abdallah speaks about in "Harat al-ʿushshaq" (Lovers' alley) from *Hikaya bi-la bidaya wa la nihaya* (1971). The metarealist critic faces this dilemma when he is cunningly lured by the novelist into taking a seat in *al-Karnak*'s café. Would the first, realistic critic disavow his previous position? Would the second, metarealist critic accuse Naguib Mahfouz of regression? Possibly they would. But the category of evolution would then be transformed into something vague and would thus become suspect.

The second consequence will be the problem of internal classifications for Naguib Mahfouz's evolving texts. Critics have given the basic stages names and made them into grades, one on top of the other. But what about the internal subclassifications within each grade? Here we might pause at the work of ʿAbd al-Muhsin Taha Badr, whose book on Naguib Mahfouz, despite the enormous efforts he exerted in it, furnishes us with a clear example of the pitfalls of such an evolutionary point of view. This book, *Najib Mahfuz: al-Ruʾya wa al-adat* (Naguib Mahfouz: The vision and the means), presents us with an unfailing duality in which vision appears in sharp opposition to is means. Then both form another opposition to the duality of form and content, an opposition that leads us step by step to a definition of content that molds and then imposes form, then to a definition of form that follows by necessity and influences content. The content nonetheless remains separate and stands by itself. It is a vision, or the offspring of a vision, whose roots begin to form during the stage of childhood (and can easily be derived from Mahfouz's statements about his own boyhood), roots that sprout and develop in the stages that follow. These roots will remain as the constant elements of this vision, where nothing changes except some minor parts that do not affect the whole, or some aspects of the means that become its container.

If we shift from this opposition of vision and means to the fictional texts of Naguib Mahfouz, we find them in a state of evolution on a ladder whose rungs represent various kinds of vision. (A fatalistic illusory vision exists here, an individualistic vision there, and finally, a realistic vision.) Naguib Mahfouz started with the lowest rung, in *ʿAbath al-aqdar* and *Radubis,* and then moved up to the stage of connection with reality in *Kifah Tiba*--which in effect is a dispatch from ancient Egypt to modern Egypt—and then to *al-Qahira al-jadida,* which touches reality. Then Naguib Mahfouz further developed toward realism in *Khan al-Khalili* and *al-Sarab,* and finally consummated his development with the realism of *Midaq Alley* and *The Beginning and the End.*

If we inquire about the real distinction between "connection with reality" and "toward realism" and ask whether this distinction bears any differential significance, the only answer we find is this meticulous care to classify the rungs of the ascending ladder from the lowest to the highest—that is, from illusory vision to realistic vision. Still, one will be quite surprised at the paradox toward the end of the book where the realism of Naguib Mahfouz turns out to be, in truth, an ethical idealism in which fate represents "the most influential of factors on action and characterization, while drive or instinct represents the influencing factor next to fate in importance." Nothing remains for the social factor in the realistic stage, except a "marginal role, despite what many researchers have maintained."[27]

If we return to the first presupposition of Badr's *al-Ru'ya wa al-adat,* namely, the integrity of Mahfouz's vision, we find this integrity shattered and distributed over the rungs of the ladder of evolution, among the categories "illusory vision," "connection with reality," "toward realism," and "realism," which in the end gets lost. Moreover, the fictional world itself is divided among an antecedent vision, a content, and a form, or a vision that is a content separate from "form." This division leads to a rupture of the relationship between vision and means and to the formation of a duality of opposites between constants and variables. If we accept the constants, we would deny Mahfouz's evolution, and the variables to mere incidental transformations in the vision.

Yet we do not encounter just a single vision in Naguib Mahfouz's works, but numerous evolving visions; otherwise, such oppositions as those set up between illusory vision and realistic vision would appear totally nonsensical. And if we accept Mahfouz's evolution, we must accept the validity of variables and deny the constants. Nonetheless, the constants would still remain as solid and as unaffected as blocks of stone, for Naguib Mahfouz has never experienced "a radical upheaval leading to a shift from one extreme to the other. All that happened was that his vision became deeper and more profound."[28]

In either case, however, the struggle between constants and variables has disappeared, and the relationship between them has become more vague than ever. What is constant in the first case emerges in the second more like a Hegelian spirit that exists before the texts and manifests itself in them through the ascending rungs of vision: illusory, idealistic, and realistic. Then the constant becomes an absolute, which had been there since the days of his youth (which can be derived from Mahfouz's first statements, if not from his novels). This constant enables visions to replace one another, as train stations do before the eyes of a traveler. The variable in the second case becomes biological states that evolve, in stages, like a chimpanzee that has become a man. Each stage then has a different vision, with conceptual categories as distinct from one another as the head of the monkey and that of the human being. The constant then disappears altogether. And while vision in the first case turns into an absolute that is different from its graded manifestations in those piles of texts, the visions in the second case, become content clothed in different forms. If we recall the assumptions that content is directly associated with situation and that content is fundamental to vision, the result is an abundance of situations in the texts of Naguib Mahfouz or, rather, breakdowns that threaten the totality of these texts, which indeed will cause the whole totalizing system to scuttle away.

The text in itself cannot be described as constant or restricted to a single, solid meaning. It can become, in Edward Said's words, "a network of often colliding forces," but a text also "in being a text is a being in the world."[29] Because the text exists in the world, it is only logical for its meaning to be reproduced for the benefit of the world. It is logical, too, that the interaction of its internal forces not take place in complete separation from a reader who, in his turn, exists in the world. The text is originally the result of an immediate contact between author and medium in a definite world. And once the author releases the text and allows it to circulate, it engages itself in other processes of production for the benefit of the world in which it now exists. Insofar as the text is attributed to its author, it is also attributable to those who have contributed to the production of its meaning.

We may dive into even deeper waters and turn to the epistemological and ontological nature of the text. As object, the text exists independently of our consciousness, starting with its printed pages and words, all the way through the signifiers contained in its pages. The text is therefore an object of knowledge manifested in a particular ontological entity. The independent existence of the text, however, harbors a paradox that does not destroy its independence but still delimits it. It thereby defines the processes of reading. It is an independent existence inasmuch as it is an object of knowledge. And this independence naturally influences the reader who perceives it. This perceiving reader, in turn, interferes by shaping the object of his perception (namely, the text) and thereby helps in determining its ontological and epistemological dimensions.

Hence, the text is at the same time independent of and tied to is reader. It remains both influencing and influenced, acting and acted upon. The production of meaning, then, becomes a process in which text participates as the primary agent of production and the reader, in the last analysis, takes part as a secondary agent. This process is then called a reading, as long as the reader does not, under any circumstances, sacrifice the read text, and as long as this text remains fundamental in directing the reading process.

Were the case to be reversed and the secondary to become primary, reading would then disappear and even turn into something negative. It would deteriorate gradually into mere reduction on the part of the perceiver who will neither read nor reduce. The logical outcome of such a reversal is the destruction of the text's independence and its transformation into an exhibition of political or social concepts or into an occasion for reviewing religious deliberations. The critical task would then shift from reading to a cluster of impressionistic processes that would start with a discussion of the work's effect on the psyche—consider it as a "psychological performance," to use Anwar al-Maʿaddawi's term—pass through the process of extracting a group of ideas, and isolating them from the text, then end up focusing on religious or political reveries that, in effect, enable us to identify the critic and not the text. In all such cases, we fall away from reading and edge closer to reduction.

If we take all the above into consideration, we find ourselves faced with a twofold position on the criticism of Naguib Mahfouz, a position that oscillates between reading and reduction. Reading is thus a performance of the text and a production of its meaning. It is so definitely both that it makes reading into an articulation of the text, whereas reduction is an articulation of the critic speaking through text. Therefore, reduction is not a process in which text "articulates" but one in which the text is interrogated. Reading is a process of interacting levels in which the text achieves its internal struggle among the various elements whose relationships constitute its system. It is also a process in which the system of the read text contends with that of the perceiving reader, without either of them replacing the other, and in which both systems fall under the influence of larger and more comprehensive systems that intervene as influential factors in the reading process.

We thus identify three interacting levels in the reading process. The manner in which interactions occur among these levels and the outcome of their interactive relationships will distinguish one reading from another. These readings become types that can be described and analyzed. Reduction as a process is a different matter. In it the first level of the text dwindles until nothing is left apart from the critic's system—nothing but his or her critical theory or literary norms corresponding to a larger system (or a world view)—so that there arises, out of the correspondence, this process of interrogating the text to make it conform with the critic's system.

Still, whether it is a case of reading or reduction, the text always contains a constant drift from inside to outside—that is, from the inner world of the text—that actual domain in which reading, or reduction, is effected—to other extratextual terrain. It follows that the movement in the reading process never ceases to alternate between the text's inner system and other outer systems until meaning has been produced. On the contrary, movement in the reductive process is a direct one, and although it may have more than one direction, it remains predestined, starting from the same point to which it returns, with neither mediation nor complexity.

The drift from inside the text to its outside is natural as long as the text by its very nature as a linguistic artifact, makes reference to the world.[30] Because each reading of the text must eventually relate to or interact with something outside the text, it becomes possible to admit that reading, though not innocent, does not negate the autonomous nature of the text. But there are two faces to reading's noninnocence: a negative one that relates to reduction and a positive one that relates to the act of reading itself. The positive aspect is associated with the reader's self, which functions actively in perceiving the text as an independent object of knowledge. It is also associated with the clash between readings, whereas the negative aspect amounts to denying the text's autonomy, thus immersing it in the chaos of reductions and the consequent negative implications of interrogating the text.

Among Mahfouz's critics, this interrogation of the text begins to manifest itself the moment they disregard the complex mediations between the text and the world, when they marginalize the relationship between signifier and signified or confuse the richness of signification and the poverty of intent. Then we find the text transformed into an intellectual document that becomes a testimony to the intentions of Naguib Mahfouz and a symptom among the signifying symptoms of his thought systems. The critic then describes not literary texts but ideas translated in an imaginative language. Such being the case, it is no wonder then to find critics speaking of "Naguib Mahfouz the politician" or searching for "national sentiments in the literature of Naguib Mahfouz," "Egyptian national history in *The Trilogy*," "the crisis of political consciousness in *Autumn Quail*," or even "singing and singers in the literature of Naguib Mahfouz."[31]

The searcher for Naguib Mahfouz the politician will pause before Sawsan Hammad's speech in *al-Sukkariyya* and expound on its straightforwardness and gravity—the cunning of the plot and the elusive manner in which it expresses its opinion. This searcher or interrogator would then identify what Sawsan Hammad says with Naguib Mahfouz, and her statements become a pact by which Naguib Mahfouz has abided ever since he started writing and which expresses his opinions and thoughts. Naguib Mahfouz would emerge from the outset as a political writer, with a clear, historically defined opinion, a solid social position, and an intellectually comprehensive view, no matter how much it may appear to be clothed in narrative artifice or hidden in the cunning folds of his art. There would be no objection to such statements if they were the project of research carried out by a historian who manipulates the literary text, as a document, for definite historical rather than for literary purposes. Yet the literary text would end up being arrested and accused directly, charged with an emphasis on the image of the middle classes rather than that of the working and peasant classes in the course of Egypt's revolution.

Once we are involved in such a process of interrogation, it follows necessarily that we step into the circle of rectifying judgment based on the authority of secondary references, on the thought systems of the critic or interrogator himself. Here we oscillate between the negative and the positive as we begin to face inconclusive oppositions and contradictions. We shall find, on the negative side, one critic saying, "Naguib Mahfouz is the writer of the petite bourgeoisie, but he does not articulate the new social forces striving for self-assertion." Therefore, Naguib Mahfouz "commemorates the tragedy of his own class, beyond which he cannot see."[32] In the same vein, we find another critic saying that Naguib Mahfouz views the world mechanically and that his view "reduces the world to some fixed laws, the discovery of which, it is claimed, would lead to the understanding of this world." This critic concludes that Naguib Mahfouz "hits the surface but not the core" and that "besides not watching for movement and its incessant contradictions, he does not try to put the question in its correct, or possible, formulation and to ask why instead of how." We are thus bound to find in the characters of Naguib Mahfouz "residual traces of the bourgeois mentality that fancies intellect as separated from science, science from intellect . . . both from man, and everyone from particular cultural circumstances."[33] All such statements lead us to a particular system of thought.

Yet it is possible for this same thought system to breed another opposing perspective leading to a judgment of positive value. Then we hear Mahfouz called "the best among writers to understand the middle class, the ablest in articulating its problems and exhibiting the intricacies of its life, enabled by his insight into its reality and deep understanding of its contradictions."[34] He becomes the writer who "intelligently perceived the nature of the middle class," or rather, "the truth of his own cultural and historical circumstances" and "the nature of the social forces and their struggles and evolutionary movement in Egyptian society." By so doing, Mahfouz enables us to "approach social phenomena perceptively and soundly."[35] We also find, in the same vein, other descriptive terms relating to "the progressivism of the idealist thinker," designating his "radical" and "humanitarian" thinking. All are articulated with positive intentions.

We find a critic looking at the same document that was previously devalued and viewed negatively, confirming it positively, and claiming that the works of Naguib Mahfouz embrace "a significant progressivism in an oriental society whose passive dependency has grown out of proportion." We find in the texts of Naguib Mahfouz "premises of a humanitarian credo whose progressively democratic role no one can deny, in an oriental, otherworldly society whose history knows no radical, democratic revolutions."[36] Yet we can still discern some opposition, even on this positive level. One critic may tell us about Naguib Mahfouz "the materialist, socialist writer," but another will not hesitate to say to Naguib Mahfouz himself in the pages of periodicals, "The transition in your political history was from the Wafd to Marxism."[37]

This last conflict soon leads to another contradiction, for the intellectual implication of Mahfouz's text can always be viewed from within a different system. We find Sayyid Qutb on the positive side, praising Naguib Mahfouz for the ethical religious content of his *Khan al-Khalili,* which would make the novel an example of a type of thinking that believes in the sarcasm of fate, "the sarcastic fate towering over all," that fate that "does not even take up a serious countenance in the moments of bitterest irony" because one "reads the story and then puts it down to open up the greater story of humanity, the story of impotent humanity in the hands of mighty fate."[38] In this context, Sayyid Qutb captured one symptom out of many in the same novel and wrenched out of it an ethical value—the same value that made him say about *Kifah Tiba,* "Had it been in my power, I would have put it into the hands of every young man and woman: I would have printed and distributed it in every house for free."[39] This same value induces Sayyid Qutb to affirm that "the critic in the Arab East rises not to reform the measures of art alone but to reform those of ethics also."[40] Indeed, it will induce him to salute Naguib Mahfouz for this inclination in *al-Qahira al-jadida* to "uphold principles at any cost, and to debase self-indulgence, social and ethical deterioration, filth and loose morality."[41]

As we move within the framework of this ethical system to the negative side, we find critics who reproach Naguib Mahfouz for harassing his characters and invariably exposing them to the curses of life so much so that any sense of hope or note of optimism is almost extinguished. It is as if there were a curious enmity between Naguib Mahfouz and his characters. "I do not know the origin of this enmity within him," says Muhammad Fahmi. "He treats them [his characters] so severely that even those rare sparks of happiness and contentment in his stories soon fade away unable to dispel the severity and gloom of their atmosphere."[42]

The same ethical system repeats itself once more, on the positive side, after many long years. We once more hear statements that are but a continuation of the formal elements lurking in Sayyid Qutb, yet in more depth and profundity, in Muhammad Hasan ʿAbd Allah's *al-Islamiyya wa al-ruhiyya fi adab Najib Mahfuz* (Islam and spiritualism in the literature of Naguib Mahfouz). This book came out as an attempt to "reconstitute the logic of its writer's presuppositions by viewing recourse to God as man's only possible, even fated, solution in the face of the mysteries he was unable to resolve."[43] Hence, with such an attempt, Naguib Mahfouz is brought back to the domain of Islam, having almost been expelled from it. Yet the ethical problem persists. The search after the infinite is placed in opposition to the finite, and belonging is placed in opposition to uprootedness.

Thus the process of interrogating the text proceeds in search for "the religious character and the spiritual touch" (ʿAbd Allah, 19) and tells us accordingly that Qurʾanic sources "are more influential and more deeply presented in *ʿAbath al-aqdar* than in its Greek mythological sources" (35). "The Struggle of Thebes" likewise yields "many of the features characteristic of religious life" (55). And in the profound ending to *Midaq Alley,* readers are made to pause before Radwan al-Husayni, the character who represents "the pious self-obligation on the part of the able toward the needy, the sound in mind and body toward the abnormal and disabled, and the disabled and the safely guided toward the misguided" (112). The stature of ʿAbd al-Munʿim Shawkat then rises above that of Ahmad Shawkat, "for he is the productively fertile one whereas the latter is impotent and sterile" (184).

If such is the case, we should not be surprised that ʿAbd al-Wahab ʿIsmail (in *Mirrors*) represents Sayyid Qutb himself. Yet ʿAbd Allah does not let the matter pass without setting up a new trial, for Naguib Mahfouz could have enriched this character "by looking at him from a humanistic standpoint. Even if he were against prejudice, the way he deals with this character betrays his prejudice against him" (131). Yet when Naguib Mahfouz's heart softened and the universe shrank before his eyes, "his spiritual inner tendencies truly took over, and he soared up high—a tragic bard bemoaning human destiny and ridiculing the vanity of man—finite, mortal man" (192). ʿAbd Allah's statements are not so different from those of Sayyid Qutb on fate in *Khan al-Khalili,* an affinity that shows us that we are dealing with the constituent elements of one and the same system;

Regardless of the obvious ideological contrast, the search after the petit bourgeois issues and the search after spiritual values are in fact two facets of one and the same process, the process of interrogating the text. Inasmuch as this process destroys the unique autonomy of Mahfouz's texts, it also exposes them to distortion and causes them to lose that which is most intrinsic to literary texts, their literary nature. Such a process contributes in more than one way to the negative view of literature as mimesis, by reinforcing the implicit assumption that literature imitates ethical values at one time and social events at another. A critic speaking of spiritual values will not then differ from another telling us about the social issues of the petite bourgeoisie. In fact, neither critic will differ from Taha Husayn when he speaks of *Midaq Alley* as "a massive gospel" of great value because "it is a perfect sociological study, carried out as sociologists might have done through field-work, portraying the society under study accurately and investigating it thoroughly." [44]

If we finally move from this interrogation of spiritual values, bourgeois affiliations, and well-researched sociological studies, we find that the text-document transforms with each interrogation—in the manner of Ovid's transformed creatures—so that its generator, Naguib Mahfouz, becomes at once an idealist, a materialist, and a reactionary. Then, on the one hand, his idealism becomes a humanitarian tendency and a mystic socialism; on the other hand, it becomes scientific socialism and Marxism. As for his progressive and reactionary tendencies, they are manifested in the uncovering of the contradictions of a particular class. What we get in the end, or even before the end, is nothing but the chaos of reductions.

I suppose, then, that this intellectual interrogation of meaning represents a fundamental component of all the extratextual systems in which the criticism of Naguib Mahfouz moves. This element may also lead us to be aware of structures in which certain traditionally inherited thought-forms wrestle with one another. And within them proponents of manifest meaning fight with the proponents of hidden meaning over the intent behind the text, and its plurality. The distortion of meaning leads to other thought-forms in the same structures of awareness. Certain forms of belief wrestle with one another and demand interpretation to fill in the gap between them and the text and to achieve a certain degree of congruity that will bestow on them a multidimensional validity. As far as these forms return us to the innermost depths of tradition, they also relate us to other contemporary forms of commitment.

This element of interrogation makes us aware that the criticism of Naguib Mahfouz cannot be viewed separately from the struggle between systems of belief outside it. It also leads us to a major dilemma that still confounds the critic of Naguib Mahfouz: how to achieve a balanced relationship between his reading self and the object of his reading. Such a problematic must be discussed in another place, for we have to start with an analysis of the types of reading, and I have yet to analyze all those types. In the course of that analysis will emerge the other, positive side of the complex tangle of commentaries, explications, and interpretations that constitute criticism on Naguib Mahfouz—the complexity, richness, and variety wrapped up within it.

NOTES
BIBLIOGRAPHY
INDEX

NOTES

1. MAPPING THE WORLD OF NAGUIB MAHFOUZ

1. Besides Fedwa Malti-Douglas's essay, "Mahfouz's Dreams," in this collection, there is still very little treatment in English of Mahfouz's writing since 1967. See the assessment of Mahfouz's formal evolution during that period in Rasheed El-Enany's introduction to his translation of *Hadrat al-muhtaram* (*Respected Sir* [London: Quartet, 1986], xi–xiii).

2. Edward Said, introduction to *Little Mountain*, by Elias Khoury, trans. Maia Tabet (Minneapolis: Univ. of Minnesota Press, 1989), xiv.

3. *al-Liss wa al-kilab* (Cairo: Maktabat Misr, 1961), 9, our trans.; English trans.: *The Thief and the Dogs*, trans. Trevor Le Gassick and Mustafa Badawi rev. John Rodenbeck (New York: Doubleday, 1989), 15.

4. ʿAbd al-Rahman Yaghi, *al-Juhud al-riwaʾiyya min Salim al-Bustani ila Najib Mahfuz* (The novelistic project from Salim al-Bustani to Naguib Mahfouz) (Beirut: Dar al-ʿAwda, 1972), 102–3.

5. Jameson develops the term in "Third-World Literature in the Era of Multinational Capitalism," *Social Text* 15 (Fall 1986): 65–88; this reference would be incomplete without citing also a famous reply to it, Aijaz Ahmad's, "Jameson's Rhetoric of Otherness and the 'National Allegory,' " *Social Text* 17 (Fall 1987): 3–25.

6. Elias Khoury, *Tajribat al-bahth ʿan ufuq* (The experiment of searching for a horizon) (Beirut: Munazzamat al-Tahrir al-Filastiniyya, 1974), 109.

7. The English translation is *Zayni Barrakat*, trans. Faruk Abdel Wahab Mustafa (New York: Penguin, 1988).

3. NAGUIB MAHFOUZ AND THE NOBEL PRIZE: *Reciprocal Expectations*

1. Arnold Tovell, director of the American University in Cairo Press and Mahfouz's publisher, noted that after the award "we have done nothing but represent him around the world to foreign publishers. We have licensed twenty foreign-language editions of varying titles, and there are probably another twenty which we're in the

process of negotiating. In addition, Doubleday in New York has committed itself to publish fourteen books by Mahfouz." Larry Luxner, "A Nobel for the Arab Nation," *Aramco World* 40, no. 2 (Mar–Apr. 1989): 16.

2. J. C. Brandt Corstius, "Writing Histories of World Literature," *Yearbook of Comparative and General Literature* 12 (1963): 5–14; René Etiemble, "Faut-il réviser la notion de *weltliteratur?" International Comparative Literature Association Proceedings* (1986): 5–16.

3. Soyinka is cited in French by Tahar Ben Jelloun as part of the latter's article on Arab writer's lack of recognition ("Le Nobel, le poète, et l'État"; "The Nobel, the Poet, and the State"): "Si l'Afrique crée un prix de la valeur et de la renommée du Nobel, attendra-t-elle quatre-vingts ans pour récompenser un Européen?" *Jeune Afrique* 1403, (25 Nov. 1987): 23. The editors of *Jeune Afrique* included his remarks in their celebration of Ben Jelloun's being the first Arab-African to win the Goncourt Prize.

4. Frank N. Magill, ed., *The Nobel Prize Winners,* 1 (Pasadena: Salem, 1987), 1: 184–85.

5. "Hat die Nobel-Jury in ihrem dunklem Drange, neue Landstriche zu erschliessen, möglicherweise recht entschieden?" Translation of German: "In their obscure urge to open up new regions, did the Nobel jury possibly make a good choice?" *Der Spiegel,* 17 Oct. 1988.

6. Hans-Georg Gadamer, *Truth and Method,* rev. ed., trans. Joel Weinsheimer and Donald Marshall (New York: Crossroad, 1989), 442.

7. "Statutes of the Nobel Foundation," in *Nobel: The Man and His Prizes,* 3d ed. rev., ed. Nobel Foundation and W. Odelberg, coordinating editor (New York: American Elsevier, 1972), 619. Paragraph two of the statutes enlarges the definition of literature so that it may include history and philosophy: "Under the term 'literature' shall be comprised, not only belles-lettres, but also other writings which, by virtue of their form and method of presentation, possess literary value" (620).

8. William Riggan, "The Swedish Academy," *World Literature Today* 55, no. 3 (Summer 1981): 399–405.

9. Ibid., 405 n. 3.

10. Committee evaluation written by writer and academy member Carl David af Wirsén; cited by Anders Ö Sterling in Nobel Foundation and Odelberg, 92.

11. Committee evaluation by Verner von Heidenstam; cited by Österling in Nobel Foundation and Odelberg, 101.

12. Nobel Foundation and Odelberg, 108.

13. Seferis was awarded the prize "for his eminent lyrical writing, inspired by a deep feeling for the Hellenic world of culture." Frank N. Magill, ed., *The Nobel Prize Winners* (Pasadena: Salem, 1987), 3:703.

14. Ibid., 956.

15. Luxner, 15.

16. Cited in Ivar Ivask, "Czeslaw Milosz: 1980 Nobel Prize in Literature," *World Literature Today* 55, no. 1 (Winter 1981): 6.

17. "Pendant la guerre d'Algérie, alors que nous avions signé la déclaration des 121, j'aurais accepté le prix avec reconnaissance, parce qu'il n'aurait pas honoré que moi, mais aussi la liberté pour laquelle nous luttions." Cited in Michel Dansel, *Les "Nobels" français de littérature* (Paris: André Bonne, 1967), 212. Translation of French: "During the Algerian war, when we had signed the Declaration of the 121, I would have accepted the prize gratefully because it would have honored not only me, but also the freedom for which we were struggling."

18. Reed Way Dasenbrock, "Wole Soyinka's Nobel Prize," *World Literature Today,* 61, no. 1 (Winter 1987): 5–9.

19. Cited by Österling in Nobel Foundation and Odelberg, 84. In the same book Ragnar Sohlman describes the extended political and familial controversy over Nobel's will and the proposed foundation (see esp. 39-72).

20. Naguib Mahfouz, *Khitab al-ihtifal bi-tasallum ja'izat Nubil/The Nobel Lecture,* trans. Muhammed Salmawy (Cairo: American University in Cairo Press, 1988). Quotations that follow are from the lecture and are taken from the first four pages of the English text.

21. These same authors are read by "literate people." In an interview with Larry Luxner, Mahfouz makes the surprising statement that after he received the Nobel Prize, "international doors have opened, and that from now on, literate people will consider Arab literature also. We deserve that recognition." Luxner, 15. An ironic echo from the past may be heard in the remark by the Swedish poet and critic Oscar Levertin shortly before the foundation was established: "For the first time foreign specialists in literature will direct their attention to the distant academy in Stockholm." Cited by Österling in Nobel Foundation and Odelberg, 84.

4. NAGUIB MAHFOUZ AND THE ARABIC NOVEL: *The Historical Context*

1. Roger Allen, "Arabic Literature and the Nobel Prize," *World Literature Today* (Spring 1988): 201–3.

2. I explore the phenomenon of the Arabic novel throughout the Arab world region in "The Mature Arabic Novel Outside Egypt," in *Cambridge History of Arabic Literature,* vol. 4, ed. by M. M. Badawi forthcoming.

3. Edward Said, "Goodbye to Mahfouz," *London Review of Books* 10, no. 22 (8 Dec. 1988): 10-11.

4. Edward Said, Introduction to *Days of Dust* by Halim Barakat, trans. Trevor Le Gassick (Wilmette, Ill.: Medina Univ. Press International, 1974), xiii.

5. Quoted in Jonathan Culler, *Structuralist Poetics* (Ithaca, N.Y.: Cornell Univ. Press, 1975), 189.

6. Analyzed and trans. by Roger Allen in *The Worlds of Muslim Imagination,* ed. Alamgir Hashmi (Islamabad: Gulmohar, 1986), 15–33, 212–15.

7. Sasson Somekh, *The Changing Rhythm* (Leiden: Brill, 1973), 44–46.

8. Naguib Mahfouz, *Hams al-junun* ([1938?]; reprint, Cairo: Maktabat Misr, 1969), 4–10. For an English translation, see *God's World,* trans. Akef Abadir and Roger Allen (Minneapolis: Bibliotheca Islamica, 1973), 47–54.

9. Lionel Trilling, *The Liberal Imagination* (1940; reprint, New York: Scribners, 1976), 22.

5. FROM "NAGUIB MAHFOUZ REMEMBERS"

This translation is from Gamal al-Ghitani, *Najib Mahfuz yatadhakkar* (Naguib Mahfouz remembers) (Cairo: Akhbar al-Yawm, 1987), 10–27, with permission.

1. *Waqf* denotes property dedicated to God, the income from which is used for religious or charitable purposes.

2. *Majadhib* (pl. of *majdhub*), meaning possessed by spiritual fervor, is used to describe someone who was not taught by a specific sufi *sheikh* but received enlightenment spontaneously. In this context, it means enthusiasts, or Sufis in general.

3. Zaʿita, the sinister figure in that novel, makes his livelihood through a kind of surgery, supplying professional beggars with real deformities to elicit sympathy from potential donors.

4. "The minaret is the only one which survives from the Ayyubid period, and displays the evolution of minaret forms from late Fatimid to early Mamluk (ca. 1340). It is composed of three stories: square, octagonal, and a fluted keel-shaped cap, known as a mabkhara [*mibkhara*] or 'incense burner.' " Richard B. Parker and Robin Sabin, *Islamic Monuments in Cairo: A Practical Guide,* 3d ed., rev. and enl. Caroline Williams (Cairo: American Univ. in Cairo Press, 1985), 193.

5. The July 23d revolution was the officers' rebellion that overthrew King Faruq in 1952.

6. This monument refers to the *maqʿad,* or "sitting place," of the palace of Amir Sayf al-Din Mamay (A.D. 1496). Parker and Sabin, 230.

7. The name, evidently Turko-Persian in its origin, can be construed to resemble a vulgar phrase in Arabic slang.

6. PLACE AND TIME IN MAHFOUZ'S AL-QAHIRA

1. Also part of the historic monumental nucleus is the area that continues from Bab Zuwayla to the citadel.

2. Al-Gamaliyya is traditionally that area of al-Qahira that extended from Bab al-Nasr to the mosque of al-Husayn, but since the 1950s it has been shown on most maps as extending west to Shariʿ Muʿizz and south to Shariʿ al-Azhar.

3. Ahmad b. ʿAli al-Maqrizi (A.D. 1364–1442), *al-Mawaʿiz wa al-iʿtibar fi dhikr al-khitat wa al-athar* (Reprinted from the Bulaq edition, Cairo: 1270/1853–54), 2:379–81.

4. The "vaulted roof" (*Palace Walk,* 50) is a round tunnel, part of the basement area of the "suspended" madrasa that Amir Mithqal built in 1362.

7. RESPECTED SIR

1. Gamal al-Ghitani, *Najib Mahfuz yatadhakkar* (Naguib Mahfouz remembers) (Cairo: Akhbar al-Yawm, 1987), 9.

2. Ghali Shukri, *al-Muntami* (The committed) (Cairo: Akhbar al-Yawm, 1964).

3. Ghali Shukri, *Najib Mahfuz: min al-Jamaliyya ila Nubil* (Naguib Mahfouz: From the Gamaliyya to Nobel) (Cairo: al-Hay'a al-ʿAmma li al-Istiʿlamat, 1988), 103.

4. Luwis ʿAwad, *Dirasat fi al-naqd wa al-adab* (Studies in criticism and literature) (Cairo: Maktabat al-Anglu-Misriyya, 1964).

5. I am here including Mahfouz's appointment as member of the editorial staff of *al-Ahram* after his retirement in 1971. Mahfouz's first governmental post was in the administration of Fuad I University in 1934. His appointments from then were as follows: 1939, parliamentary secretary to the Minister of Waqf; 1960, chair of the Cinema Institute; 1962, art advisor in the Cinema Organization; 1963, head of the Reading Committee of the General Cinema Organization; 1965, member of the Supreme Council for Arts and Letters; 1966, general supervisor of the General Cinema

Organization; 1968-71, consultant to the minister of culture, Tharwat ʿUkasha. Mahfouz retired in Nov. 1971 and joined the editorial staff of *al-Ahram* in December of the same year.

6. This information is part of an interview conducted with Adham Rajab in Cairo's weekly magazine *Uktubir,* 20 Oct. 1988.

7. My interviews with Naguib Mahfouz at *al-Ahram,* 1989 (hereafter cited as Mahfouz interviews).

8. Ibid.

9. Mahmud Fawzi, *Najib Mahfuz: zaʿim al-harafish* (Naguib Mahfouz: Leader of the riff-raff) (Cairo: Dar al-Jil, 1988), 43.

10. Mahfouz interviews.

11. Ibid.

12. Ibid.

13. My interview with Fathi al-ʿAshri at *al-Ahram,* 1990. Al-ʿAshri is one of the literary critics at *al-Ahram* and was the first to volunteer part of his time to help organize and supervise Naguib Mahfouz's schedule after Mahfouz's receipt of the Nobel Prize. By virtue of this position, al-ʿAshri has been in close contact with Mahfouz himself and has been exposed to most of the issues and controversies that have surrounded Mahfouz since the award.

14. *al-Ahram,* 2 Mar. 1989, 7.

15. *al-Ahali,* 26 Apr. 1989.

16. *al-Ahali,* 3 May 1989.

17. Mahfouz interviews.

18. Ibid.

19. Shukri, *Najib Mahfuz,* 56.

20. Ibid., 56.

21. Mahfouz interviews.

22. Fuad Duwwara, *Najib Mahfuz: min al-qawmiyya ila al-ʿalamiyya* (Naguib Mahfouz: From regionalism to globalism) (Cairo: al-Hayʾa al-Misriyya al-ʿAmma li al-Kutub, 1989), 240.

23. Shukri, *Najib Mahfuz,* 54.

24. Ibid., 55.

25. Ibid., 83.

26. Naguib Mahfouz, *Respected Sir,* trans. Rasheed el-Enany (London: Quartet, 1986), 110–11.

27. *Uktubir,* 11 Dec. 1988.

28. Mahfouz interviews.

29. Shukri, *al-Muntami,* 452.

30. Mahfouz interviews.

31. al-Ghitani, *Najib Mahfuz,* 7.

32. Duwwara, *Najib Mahfuz,* 232.

33. Mahfouz interviews.

34. *Uktubir,* 11 Dec. 1989.

35. Duwwara, *Najib Mahfuz,* 318.

36. Mahfouz interviews.

37. Duwwara, *Najib Mahfuz,* 318.

38. Mahfouz interviews.

39. Shukri, *Najib Mahfuz,* 12.

40. Ibid., 14.

41. Duwwara, *Najib Mahfuz,* 249.

42. Fathi al-ʿAshri, ed., *Najib Mahfuz: hawl al-thaqafa wa al-taʿlim, hawl al-shabab wa al-hurriyya, hawl al-din wa al-dimuqratiyya* (Naguib Mahfouz: Concerning culture and learning, youth and freedom, religion and democracy) 3 vols. (Cairo: Al-Dar al-Misriyya al-Lubnaniyya, 1990).

43. Shukri, *Najib Mahfuz,* 83.

44. Letters to Adham Rajab, *Uktubir,* 11 Dec. 1989.

45. Shukri, *Najib Mahfuz,* 82.

46. Naguib Mahfouz, *Amam alʿarsh: Hiwar maʿ rijal Misr min Mina hatta Anwar al-Sadat* (Before the throne: A dialogue with the rulers of Egypt from Mina to Anwar al-Sadat) (Cairo: Maktabat Misr, 1983), 204.

47. Sonallah Ibrahim, unpublished lecture given in Berlin and Cairo, 1989.

48. Duwwara, *Najib Mahfuz,* 243.

49. al-Ghitani, *Najib Mahfuz,* 9.

8. EXISTENTIAL THEMES IN A TRADITIONAL CAIRO SETTING

1. See, for instance, ʿAbd al-Rahman Badawi, *al-Zaman al wujudi* (Existential time) (Cairo: Maktabat al-Nahda al-Misriyya, 1945); *al-Insaniyya wa al-wujudiyya fi al-fikr al-ʿArabi* (Humanism and existentialism in Arab thought) (Cairo: Maktabat al-Nahda al-Misriyya, 1947); *Min tarikh al-ilhad fi al-Islam* (On the history of atheism in Islam) (Cairo: Maktabat al-Nahda al-Misriyya, 1945); and *al-Insan al-kamil fi al-Islam* (The perfect man in Islam) (Beirut: Dar al-Qalam, 1976).

2. ʿAbd al-Rahman Badawi, quoted in Anouar Abdel Malek, ed., *Anthologie de la littérature Arabe contemporaine* (Paris: Seuil, 1965), vol. 2, 326.

3. Raoul Makarius in Abdel Malek, vol. 1, 47.

4. Eugene Ionesco, *La photo du colonel* (Paris: Gallimard, 1962), 47.

5. Albert Camus, *L'été* (Summer) (Paris: Gallimard, 1954), 135–36.

6. A succinct definition can be found in the chapter on Sufism in the 1963 edition of *Islam.* It describes how the institution of the *tariqa,* the dervish brotherhood, provided a convenient form of social organization, popularized the teachings of the Sufis, and transmitted them to the lowest ranks of the population, "though not without some vulgarization and damaging of the original values Sufism had represented, substituting emotional revivalism for interior devotion." The core of the *tariqa*'s life was the collective *dhikr* at the lodge, or *tekke,* where the dervishes, under the leadership of an adept, would contemplate, chant, or dance in unison until some fell into a trance. John Williams, ed., *Islam* (New York: Braziller, 1960) 155.

7. I am paraphrasing Sartre's famous letter to Camus in *Les temps modernes,* vol. 82 (Aug. 1952), 353.

9. THE MAHFOUZIAN SUBLIME

1. Michael Beard, *Hedayat's "Blind Owl" as a Western Novel* (Princeton: Princeton Univ. Press, 1990), 18.

2. *Mirrors,* trans. Roger Allen, Studies in Middle Eastern Literatures, no. 8, (Minneapolis: Bibliotheca Islamica, 1977), 23; *al-Maraya* (Cairo: Maktabat Misr, 1972), 30.

3. *Respected Sir,* trans. Rasheed El-Enany (London: Quartet, 1986), 4.

4. Kant would call this the mathematical sublime. See *Critique of Judgment*, trans. J. H. Bernard (New York: Hafner, 1951), 89–95. Thomas Weiskel's seminal study of this subject, *The Romantic Sublime: Studies in the Structure and Psychology of Transcendence* (Baltimore: Johns Hopkins Univ. Press, 1976), has reopened the category of the sublime for a new generation of American critics, and since then a Longinian criticism has come to seem eminently well suited for application to Arabic literature, both classical and contemporary.

5. Mattityahu Peled, *Religion, My Own: The Literary Works of Najib Mahfuz* (New Brunswick, N.J.: Transaction, 1983), 145–49 and passim.

6. Jacques Lacan explores this polarity tellingly in "The Agency of the Letter in the Unconscious or Reason since Freud," in *Ecrits: A Selection*, trans. Alan Sheridan (New York: Norton, 1977), 146–75.

7. A. Kamegulov, quoted in "The Metaphoric and Metonymic Poles," in Roman Jakobson and Morris Halle, *Fundamentals of Language* (The Hague: Mouton, 1956), 90–96, 94.

8. *Midaq Alley*, trans. Trevor Le Gassick (Washington, D.C.: Three Continents, 1974), 219.

9. *Children of Gebelawi*, trans. Philip Stewart (London: Heinemann; Washington, D.C.: Three Continents, 1981), 5.

10. Sasson Somekh, *The Changing Rhythm: A Study of Najib Mahfuz's Novels* (Leiden: Brill, 1973), 146.

11. *The Beggar*, trans. Kristin Walker Henry (Cairo: American Univ. in Cairo Press, 1986), 31.

12. From an interview by Mohammad Siddiq with an unidentified writer; cited by Anton Shammas in the *New York Review of Books* 2 Feb. 1989, 20.

13. "Bulbuli khun-e deli khowrd-u guli hasil kard" ("A nightingale wore himself out and harvested a rose"). *Hikayat haratina*, 4, 185. The verse looks like gibberish in the Arabic context.

10. MEN CONSTRUCTED IN THE MIRROR OF PROSTITUTION

1. Hisham Sharabi, *Neopatriarchy* (New York: Oxford Univ. Press, 1989).

2. In his introduction to Maia Tabet's English translation of Elias Khoury's *Little Mountain* (Minneapolis: Univ. of Minnesota Press, 1989), Edward Said has written: "Mahfouz's precedence assures [later generations of Egyptian writers] a point of departure . . . discursive patterns of a narrative structure that was not merely a passive reflection of an evolving society, but an organic part of it. . . . Mahfouz's novels, his characters and concerns have been the privileged, if not always emulated, norm for most other Arab novelists" (xiii).

3. "The State is an exhalation of the spirit of God, incarnate on earth" (Mahfouz, *Respected Sir*, trans. Rashid el-Enany [London: Quartet Books, 1986], 143-44).

4. Fawzia al-Ashmawi-Abouzeid, *La Femme et l'Egypte moderne dans l'oeuvre de Naguib Mahfouz: 1939-1967* (Geneva: Labor et Fides, 1985), 60.

5. Interview with Salwa El-Naimi, "Notre père Mahfouz," *Magazine Littéraire* 251 (Mar. 1988): 28.

6. "The Visit," from *Khammarat al-qitt al-aswad* (The black cat tavern, 1969), explores the terrors and anxieties of a faded beauty who never married and who has no support system. She is physically and psychologically dependent on her callous servant, who is economically dependent on her.

In *Afrah al-qubba* (1981; trans. as *Wedding Song*), two prostitutes confront the same circumstances with different outcomes: one is killed; the other becomes a brothel madame. Tahiyya, the murdered actress, is never given a voice. Her story is recounted by four protagonists, none of whom has ever seen her. The reader glimpses a woman whose only function has been to fulfill men's dreams and desires. But Tahiyya's mother-in-law, Halima al-Kabsh, despite the resentment she feels toward Tahiyya, understands Tahiyya as no man ever had or could. She is able to learn from a woman's experience.

7. See Tarabishi, *Ramziyyat al-mar'a fi al-riwaya al-'Arabiyya wa dirasat ukhra* (Symbolism of women in the Arabic novel and other studies) (Beirut, 1981). After eighteen pages on men, he writes, "Is it not time for us to talk about Zahra herself?" (120), and he does so for just over four pages. Rasheed al-Enany comments: "The maid servant (i.e., Egypt, the common majority, the nonbeneficiaries of the revolution) has to fend for herself all the time against the sexual advances of all lodgers. . . . The girl however proves more than a match for her attackers. . . . Thus Egypt emerges as strong and self-reliant." Later, he writes of Saniyya, the grandmother in *al-Baqi min al-zaman sa'a* (There only remains one hour), that she represents the spirit of Egypt herself." El-Enany, "The Novelist as Political Eye-Witness: A View of Naguib Mahfouz's Evaluation of the Nasser and Sadat Eras," *Journal of Arabic Literature* 21, no. 1 (1990): 76, 80–81.

8. Menahem Milson, "Najib Mahfuz and Jamal 'Abd al-Nasir: The Writer as Political Critic," *Asian and African Studies* 23, no. 1 (Mar. 1989): 10.

9. Mona Mikhail, *Images of Arab Women: Fact and Fiction* (Washington, D.C.: Three Continents, 1978), 92. In a more recent work, *'Ara'is fi al-mawlid dirasat hawl al-mar'a al-'Arabiyya* (Brides at the feast: Studies on Arab women) (Cairo: Dar al-'Arabi, 1987), Mikhail discusses Hamida as a fallen virtuous woman (*saqita fadila*) and as a victim (78). She does insist, however, that Hamida is a strong woman who is rebelling against society.

10. Simone de Beauvoir, *The Second Sex*, trans. H. M. Parshley (New York: Vintage, 1974), 157–223.

11. Amy Katz Kaminsky, "Women Writing about Prostitutes," in *The Image of the Prostitute in Modern Literature*, ed. Pierre L. Horn and Mary Beth Pringle (New York: Ungar, 1984), 120, 125.

12. She is quite unlike the mother in Driss Chraibi's Moroccan novel *La civilisation, ma mère!* (1972), trans. as *Mother Comes of Age* by Hugh A. Harter (Washington, D.C.: Three Continents Press, 1984), whose exposure to the world after protracted seclusion leads to violent self-consciousness and political activism.

13. Cf. also the sheikh and the prostitute in "The Mosque in the Alley" (in *Dunya Allah*, 1962).

14. *al-Maraya* (Cairo: Maktabat Misr, 1972), 174–77.

15. Men's fear of women is a topos in modern Arabic literature. Fiction writers have often described the dangers imagined to be inherent in beautiful women. Cf. Yusuf Idris, "Hadithat al-sharaf" (Affair of honor), in which the merest suspicion of illicit relations is enough for the innocent woman to be punished; and Yahya Haqqi, "al-Firash al-shaghir" (The empty bed), in which a young man is so disturbed by women's sexual responsiveness that he finally resorts to necrophilia.

16. "One can easily tell that Mahfouz gives great importance to his female characters and that he uses them as a mirror in which the evolution of customs is reflected. Through his paper characters, he elaborates the stages in the emancipation of the flesh and blood contemporary woman" (al-Ashmawi-Abouzeid, 160).

17. Like Nafisa, Hasan has a perspective from his marginal position, and he is amused by the irony. When Hasanayn high-handedly demands that Hasan return to the straight and narrow, Hasan retorts: "If you really want me to abandon my tainted life, then you, too, must abandon yours" (294).

18. "How delicious is flirtation even if it is a lie. She was in a shameful situation but this restored the self-esteem and dignity of a woman whose wings had been broken" (165). Note the use of the broken-wings image so common in feminist literature.

19. In *Tharthara fawq al-Nil* (Chatter on the Nile), the mostly male occupants of the houseboat reject Sammara Bahjat when she confronts them with the emptiness of their lives and their social irresponsibility.

20. In *The Beggar,* ʿUmar's daughter Buthayna writes apocalyptic poetry as had her father when he was young. Yet he cannot understand her spiritual yearnings, assuming that women write only about love. The woman who is his mirror hides behind his reflection, whether she wants to or not.

21. As in *Hikayat haratina, Fountain and Tomb,* 38–39 (trans., 30).

22. As in *al-Maraya* (*Mirrors*), 27, 82, 320.

23. "We had become as accustomed to having girls in our midst as to the rumors flying around during the difficult period before marriage" (*al-Maraya,* 294).

11. MAHFOUZ'S DREAMS

1. See, for example, the section on Naguib Mahfouz in *Aramco World,* 40, no. 2 (Mar.–Apr. 1989), esp. 17.

2. Hafiz Ibrahim, *Layali Satih* (The nights of Satih), ed. and introd. ʿAbd al-Rahman Sidqi (Cairo: al-Dar al-Qawmiyya li al-Tibaʿa wa al-Nashr, 1964); Muhammad al-Muwaylihi, *Hadith ʿIsa ibn Hisham* (Cairo: al-Dar al-Qawmiyya li al-Tibaʿa wa al-Nashr, 1964); Ahmad Shawqi, *Shaytan Bintaʾur* (The devil of Bintaʾur), cited in ʿIrfan Shahid, *al-ʿAwda ila Shawqi* (The return to Shawqi) (Beirut: al-Ahliyya li al-Nashr wa al-Tawziʿ, 1986), 569. See also Roger Allen, "An Annotated Translation and Study of the Third Edition of *Hadith ʿIsa ibn Hisham*" (Ph.D. diss., Oxford, 1968); Roger Allen, "*Hadith ʿIsa ibn Hisham* by Muhammad al-Muwailihi: A Reconsideration," *Journal of Arabic Literature* 1 (1970): 88–108; Shahid, 545–66; Fedwa Malti-Douglas, "al-Wahda al-nassiyya fi *Layali Satih*" (Textual unity in *Layali Satih*), *Fusûl* 3, no. 2 (1983): 109–17; Matti Moosa, *The Origins of Modern Arabic Fiction* (Washington, D.C.: Three Continents, 1983), 93–121.

3. On the history of the modern Arabic novel in its early phases, see Roger Allen, *The Arabic Novel: An Historical and Critical Introduction* (Syracuse: Syracuse Univ. Press, 1982), 19–45.

4. For the novel, the best example of this literary trend is without a doubt Gamal al-Ghitani, *Al-Zayni Barakat,* trans. by Faruk Abdel Wahab Mustafa as *Zayni Barakat* (New York: Penguin, 1988). For the short story, see al-Ghitani's masterful "Hidayat ahl al-wara li-baʿd mimma jara fi al-maqshara," in al-Ghitani, *Awraq shabb ʿasha mundhu alf ʿam* (The papers of a young man who lived a thousand years ago) (Cairo: Maktabat Madbuli, n.d.), 83–98.

5. Taqiyy al-Din al-Maqrizi, *Kitab al-Mawaʿiz wal-iʿtibar bi-dhikr al-khitat wa al-athar;* known as *al-Khitat al-Maqriziyya* (The Maqrizian plans) (Beirut: Dar Sadir, n.d.).

6. ʿAli Basha Mubarak, *al-Khitat al-Tawfiqiyya li-Misr al-Qahira* (known as the Tawfiqian plans) (Cairo: Al-Hayʾa al-Misriyya al-ʿAmma li al-Kitab, 1980).

7. al-Ghitani, *Khitat al-Ghitani* (al-Ghitani's plans) (Beirut: Dar al-Masira, 1981).

8. Muhammad Mustajab, *Min al-ta'rikh al-sirri li-Nu'man 'Abd al-Hafiz* (From the secret history of Nu'man 'Abd al-Hafiz) (Cairo: Maktab al-Nil li al-Tab' wa al-Nashr, 1982), 4. See also Fedwa Malti-Douglas, "*Min al-ta'rikh al-sirri li-Nu'man 'Abd al-Hafiz* wa tadmir tuqus al-hayat wa al-lugha" (?), *Ibda'* 1, nos. 6–7 (1983): 86–92.

9. Emile Habibi, *Ikhtayyi* (What a pity) (Cyprus: Kitab al-Karmil, 1985), 9. See also Sa'id 'Allush, *'Unf al-mutakhayyil fi a'mal Imil Habibi* (The dreamer's violence in the works of Emile Habibi) (Casablanca: al-Mu'assasa al-Haditha li al-Nashr wa al-Tawzi', 1986).

10. Mahmud al-Mis'adi, *Haddatha Abu Hurayra qal* (Abu Hurayra related, saying) (Tunis: Dar al-Janub li al-Nashr, 1979). See also Mahmud Tarshuna, *al-Adab al-murid fi mu'allafat al-Mis'adi* (Literature of the seeker in the works of Al-Mis'adi) (Tunis: La Maghrébine pour l'Impression, l'Edition et la publicité, 1989).

11. Linda Hutcheon, *Narcissistic Narrative: The Metafictional Paradox* (New York: Methuen, 1984); Patricia Waugh, *Metafiction: The Theory and Practice of Self-Conscious Fiction* (London: Methuen, 1984).

12. Yusuf al-Qa'id, *Shakawa al-Misri al-fasih* (The complaints of the eloquent Eqyptian), vol. 1 (Beirut: Dar al-Masira, 1981); vol. 2 (Cairo: Dar al-Mustaqbal al-'Arabi, 1983); vol. 3 (Cairo: Dar al-Mustaqbal al-'Arabi, 1985).

13. See Fedwa Malti-Douglas, "Yusuf al-Qa'id wa al-riwaya al-jadida" (Yusuf al-Qa'id and the new novel), *Fusul* 4, no. 3 (1984): 190–202.

14. Alain Robbe-Grillet, *Les gommes* (Erasers) (Paris: Les Editions de Minuit, 1973).

15. Donald Barthelme, *Snow White* (New York: Atheneum, 1986).

16. Italo Calvino, *The Castle of Crossed Destines,* trans. William Weaver (New York: Harcourt Brace Jovanovich, 1977); John Gardner, *Grendel* (New York: Vintage, 1985).

17. See, for example, Hutcheon, 32–34, 82–85; Waugh, 40–00.

18. Naguib Mahfouz, *Layali alf layla* (The nights of a thousand nights) (Cairo: Maktabat Misr, 1982).

19. Naguib Mahfouz, *Rihlat ibn Fattuma* (The travels of ibn Fattuma) (Cairo: Maktabat Misr, 1983).

20. Gamal al-Ghitani, *Najib Mahfuz yatadhakkar* (Naguib Mahfouz remembers) (Cairo: Akhbar al-Yawm, 1987).

21. Naguib Mahfouz, "Ra'aytu fima yara al-na'im" (I saw as the sleeper sees), in *Ra'aytu fima yara al-na'im* (Cairo: Maktabat Misr, 1982), 139–73. When analyzing the dreams in the text, we shall simply refer to them by number—e.g., Dream 1, Dream 2, and so on.

22. Naguib Mahfouz, "Za'balawi," in *Dunya Allah* (Beirut: Dar al-Qalam, 1962), 148.

23. See, for example, al-Kirmani, *Sahih al-Bukhari bi-sharh al-Kirmani* (Al-Bukhari's canon with a commentary by al-Kirmani) (Beirut: Dar Ihya' al-Turath al-'Arabi, 1981), 24:94–143.

24. See, for example, Toufic Fahd, *La divination arabe* (Leiden: Brill, 1966), 329-63; Artémidore d'Ephèse, *Le livre des songes,* trans. from the Arabic of Hunayn ibn Ishaq (Damascus: Institut Français de Damas, 1964); al-Nabulusi, *Ta'tir al-anam fi ta'bir al-manam* (A work on dream interpretation) (Cairo: 'Isa al-Babi al-Halabi, n.d.); Ibn Sirin, *Muntakhab al-kalam fi tafsir al-ahlam,* printed in the margins of al-Nabulusi.

25. See, for example, Ahmad al-Sabbahi 'Awad Allah, *Tafsir al-ahlam* (Interpretation of dreams) (Cairo: Maktabat Madbuli, [1977?]); Ibrahim Muhammad al-Jamal, *Ikhtartu lak min al-turath: Tafsir al-ahlam li al-imamayn al-jalilayn ibn Sirin wa al-Nabulusi* (I have

chosen for you from the tradition: dream interpretations by the two venerable imams Ibn Sirin and al-Nabulusi) (Cairo: Maktabat al-Qurʾan, 1982).

26. See Fedwa Malti-Douglas, "Dreams, the Blind, and the Semiotics of the Biographical Notice," *Studia Islamica* 51 (1980): 144.

27. For the possible ambiguity in Arabic between a vision and a dream, see Fahd, 269–72.

28. al-Kirmani, 24:113.

29. Mahfouz, "Raʾaytu," 145, 148.

30. See, for example, Malti-Douglas, "Dreams."

31. al-Safadi, *Nakt al-himyan fi nukat al-ʿumyan* (A biographical compendium on the blind), ed. Ahmad Zaki (Cairo: al-Maktaba al-Jamaliyya, 1911), 206.

32. Mahfouz, "Zaʿbalawi," 148.

33. On Juha, see ʿAbbas Mahmud al-ʿAqqad, *Juha al-dahik al-mudhik* (Juha, he who laughs and the object of laughter) (Cairo: Dar al-Hilal, n.d.); Charles Pellat, "Djuha," EI².

34. See, for example, al-Qalqashandi, *Maʾathir al-inaqa fi maʿalim al-khilafa* (A work on caliphs and the caliphate), ed. ʿAbd al-Sattar Ahmad Farraj (Beirut: ʿAlam al-Kutub, n.d.), 1:92.

35. Mahfouz, "Raʾaytu," 149.

36. Ibid., 154.

37. Badiʿ al-Zaman al-Hamadhani, *al-Maqamat*, ed. Muhamad ʿAbduh (Beirut: Dar al-Mashriq, 1968); Fedwa Malti-Douglas, "Badiʿ al-Zaman Hamadhani," in *Encyclopaedia Iranica* (London: Routledge and Kegan Paul, 1988), 3:377–79; James T. Monroe, *The Art of Badiʿ al-Zaman al-Hamadhani as Picaresque Narrative* (Beirut: American Univ. of Beirut Center for Arab and Middle East Studies, 1983).

38. This student relationship has been well established by critics. See, for example, Abd el-Fattah Kilito, "Le genre 'Séance': Une introduction," *Studia Islamica* 43 (1976): 36–37; Monroe, 24.

39. al-Ghitani, *Najib Mahfuz*, 14, 25.

40. al-Muwaylihi, 1.

41. Allen, "*Hadith*."

42. Louis Cheikho, ed., *Kitab Kalila wa-Dimna* (Beirut: Dar al-Mashriq, 1969).

43. A. J. Wensinck, "Al-Khadir (al-Khidr)," EI². See also al-Thaʿlabi, *Qisas al-anbiyaʾ* (Beirut: Dar al-Qalam, n.d.), 217–31.

44. See Fedwa Malti-Douglas, "Sign Conceptions in the Islamic World," in *Semiotics: A Handbook on the Sign-Theoretic Foundations of Nature and Culture*, ed. Roland Posner, Klaus Robering, and Thomas E. Sebeok (Berlin: Walter de Gruyter, forthcoming).

45. See Jaroslav Stetkevych, "Spaces of Delight: A Symbolic Topoanalysis of the Classical Arabic *Nasib*," in *Critical Pilgrimages: Studies in the Classical Arabic Tradition*, ed. Fedwa Malti-Douglas, special issue of *Literature East and West* 25 (1989): 5-28.

46. *al-Qurʾan*, Surat al-Kahf, v. 67. The phrase (*lan tastatiʿ maʿi sabran*, {Thou wilt not be able to have patience with me," trans. by Yusuf ʿAli) occurs several times during the Qurʾanic interchange between Moses and al-Khidr.

12. FROM "NAGUIB MAHFOUZ'S CRITICS"

The essay from which this chapter was drawn was originally published in Arabic as "Qiraʾa fi nuqqad Najib Mahfuz: mulahazat awwaliyya" *Fusul* 1, no. 3 (Apr. 1981): 161–79. Translated with permission.

1. Luwis ʿAwad, *Dirasat fi al-naqd wa al-adab* (Studies in criticism and literature) (Cairo: Maktabat al-Anglu-Misriyya, 1964), 345–46.

2. ʿAli al-Raʿi, *Dirasat fi al-riwaya al-Misriyya* (Studies in the Egyptian novel) (Cairo: al-Muʾassassa al-Misriyya al-ʿAmma, 1964), 254.

3. The first noticeable manifestations of the petite bourgeoisie in Mahfouz criticism appeared in 1954 in both the periodical *al-Risala al-jadida* and the newspaper *al-Misri* with Abd al-ʿAzim Anis, who later wrote *Fi al-thaqafa al-Misriyya* (On Egyptian culture) (1955), and Muhammad Mandur, who later wrote *Qadaya jadida fi adabina al-hadith* (New issues in our modern literature) (Cairo, 1958). The same elements later become the basis for full-length studies, as Ghali Shukri's *al-Muntami* (The committed) (Cairo: Akhbar al-Yawm, 1964).

4. Naguib Mahfouz, *al-Sukkariyya* (Cairo: Maktabat Misr, 1957); trans. in Hamdi Sakkut, *The Egyptian Novel and Its Main Trends: 1913*–1952 (Cairo: American Univ. in Cairo Press, 1971), 137. The statement in fact originates with Kamal's nephew Ahmad [eds.].

5. Sabri Hafiz, "al-Ittijah al-riwaʾi al-jadid ʿind Najib Mahfuz" (The new direction of Naguib Mahfouz's fiction) *al-Adab* (Nov. 1963): 19.

6. Naguib Mahfouz, *Qalb al-layl* (The heart of the night) (Cairo: Maktabat Misr, 1975), 131.

7. ʿAwad, *Dirasat,* 346.

8. Mandur, 73.

9. Kamal Yusuf (whom I do not know, unless it is a pen name) has revealed some of the aspects in which ʿAbd al-ʿAzim Anis was influenced by Roger Garaudy in an important essay entitled "Nuqqaduna al-waqiʿiyyun ghayru waqiʿiyyin" (Our unrealistic realist critics), *Al-Risala al-jadida* (June 1956): 14, 17. Meanwhile, Christopher Caudwell's three books: *Illusion and Reality, Studies in a Dying Culture* and *Further Studies in a Dying Culture* have had a marked influence on early Arab realist writing. Perhaps their influence is obvious in Luwis ʿAwad's *Fi al-adab al-Inglizi* (On English literature) (Cairo: al-Hayʾa al Misriyya li al-Kutub, 1950).

10. I should like to acknowledge how indebted I am to the valuable bibliography published by our colleague Ahmad Ibrahim al-Hawari in *Masadir naqd al-riwaya fi al-adab al-ʿArabi al-hadith fi Misr* (Sources of criticism of the novel in modern Arabic literature in Egypt) (Cairo: Dar al-Maʿarif, 1979).

11. Edward al-Kharrat, "ʿAlam Najib Mahfuz" (The world of Naguib Mahfouz), *al-Majalla* (Jan. 1963): 27.

12. Mahmud Amin al-ʿAlim, *Taʾammulat fi ʿalam Najib Mahfuz* (Meditations on the world of Naguib Mahfouz) (Cairo: al-Hayʾa al-Misriyya al-ʿAmma li al-Taʾlif wa al-Nashr, 1970), 64.

13. The history of the term *type* in realistic criticism starts with what Engels wrote to Margaret Harkness in 1888: "Realism to my mind implies, besides truth of details, the truthful reproduction of typical characters under typical circumstances." See Terry Eagleton, *Marxism and Literary Criticism* (Berkeley: Univ. of California Press, 1976), 46. The term was then tossed around among critics of realism until it reached full maturity, as a seminal concept, in the writings of George Lukács; and so it remained until it was obviously shaken by Brecht's attack, which was supported by Walter Benjamin.

14. The "archetype" or *al-namudhaj al-awwal,* or *al-mithal* as translated by Magdi Wahba (*Muʿjam mustalahat al-adab / A Dictionary of Literary Terms: English, French, Arabic* [Beirut: Libraririe du Liban, 1974], 29), goes back to the Cambridge School of Comparative Anthropology and Jung's psychology. Jung's definition of the term was "the pri-

mordial image" or "archetype," "an institution . . . or a process repeated throughout history, when fantasy manifests itself freely; thus it is a mythological institution. If we subject these archetypes to careful inspection, we shall discover in them the effects of typical experiences. They are psychic residua of numberless experiences of the same type." Obviously these archetypes are not the products of one individual, but of all ancestors; and they are inherited as a priori determinants of individual experience. See Maud Bodkin, *Archetypal Patterns in Poetry* (1934; reprint, London: Oxford Univ. Press, 1968), 8. And inasmuch as this criticism relates "symbol" and "archetype," it distinguishes between "symbol" and "representation" and connects the former to myth on the basis that it merges into the archetype to project a different instinctive, universal image or to designate certain types of human behavior indicative of certain primeval forms of belief. For various applications of this criticism, see John B. Vickery, ed., *Myth and Literature: Contemporary Theory and Practice* (Lincoln: Univ. of Nebraska Press, 1969), trans. Jabra Ibrahim Jabra as *al-Ustura wa al-ramz* (Baghdad, 1973).

15. See Nikos Kazantzakis, *The Fratricides,* trans. Athena Gianakas Dallas (New York: Simon and Schuster, 1964).

16. Ibrahim Fathi, *al-ʿAlam al-riwaʾi ʿind Najib Mahfuz* (The fictional world of Naguib Mahfouz) (Cairo: Dar al-Fikr al-Muʿasir, 1978), 6.

17. al-ʿAlim, 6.

18. ʿAbd al-Muhsin Taha Badr, *Najib Mahfuz: al-ruʾya wa al-adat* (Naguib Mahfouz: The vision and the means) (Cairo: Dar al-Thaqafa li al-Tibaʿa wa al-Nashr, 1978), 9.

19. Rajaʿ al-Naqqash, "Udabaʾ muʿasirun" (Contemporary writers), *Kitab al-Hilal* (Feb. 1971): 183–84.

20. Yahya Haqqi, *ʿItr al-ahbab* (The aroma of lovers) (Cairo: Matabiʿ al-Ahram, 1971), 84–85.

21. See Stephen Ulmann, "Style and Personality," in *Contemporary Essays on Style,* ed. G. A. Love and M. Payne (Glenview, Ill.: Scott, Foresman, 1969), 161.

22. ʿAwad, *Dirasat,* 361.

23. Mahmud al-Rabiʿi, *Qiraʾat al-riwaya: namadhij min Najib Mahfuz* (Reading the novel: Excerpts from Naguib Mahfouz) (Cairo: Dar al-Maʿarif, 1974), 15–16.

24. See, respectively, Nabil Raghib, *Qadiyyat al-shakl al-fanni ʿind Najib Mahfuz* (The question of artistic form in Naguib Mahfouz) (Cairo: al-Muʾassassa al-Misriyya al-ʿAmma li al-Taʾlif wa al-Nashr, 1967), 17–18; Taha Badr, 151–52; al-ʿAlim, 25–26; ʿAli Shalaq, *Najib Mahfuz fi majhulihi al-maʿlum* (Naguib Mahfouz in his unknown known) (Beirut: Dar al-Masira, 1979), 146; Sulayman al-Shatti, *al-Ramz wa al-ramziyya fi adab Najib Mahfuz* (Symbol and symbolism in the writings of Naguib Mahfouz) (Kuwait: al-Matbaʿa al-ʿAsriyya), 29–30.

25. Fatima Musa, *Fi al-riwaya al-ʿArabiyya al-muʿasira* (On the contemporary Arabic novel) (Cairo: al-Anglu-Misriyya, 1972), 27.

26. Haqqi, 106.

27. Badr, 451.

28. Ibid., 72.

29. Cf. Edward Said, "The World, the Text, and the Critic," in *Textual Strategies,* ed. Josué V. Harari (Ithaca, N.Y.: Cornell Univ. Press, 1979), 161–88; later included in *The World, the Text and the Critic* (Cambridge, Mass.: Harvard Univ. Press, 1983), 31–53.

30. See Paul Ricoeur, *Interpretation Theory: Discourse and the Surplus of Meaning* (Fort Worth: Texas Christian Univ. Press, 1976), 36–37.

31. See, respectively, Ibrahim ʿAmir, "Najib Mahfuz siyasiyyan min thawrat 1919 ila Yunyu 1967" (Naguib Mahfouz the politician: from the 1919 coup d'état to June

1967), *al-Hilal* (Feb. 1970): 26–27; Fuad Duwwara, "al-Wijdan al-qawmi fi adab Najib Mahfuz" (National emotional life in the literature of Naguib Mahfouz), *al-Hilal* (Feb.1970): 100–109; Jalal al-Sayyid, "Tarikhuna al-qawmi fi *Thulathiyyat* Najib Mahfuz" (Our national history in *The Trilogy* of Naguib Mahfouz), *al-Katib* (Jan. 1963): 70–79; Hilal Ghunaymi, "Azmat al-wa'i al-siyasi fi qissat *al-Summan wa al-kharif*" (The crisis of political consciousness in *Autumn Quail*), *al-Katib* (Jan. 1963): 24–31; Kamal al-Najmi, "Ma' al-ghina' wa al-mughanin fi adab Najib Mahfuz" (Singers and singing in the literature of Naguib Mahfouz), *al-Hilal* (Feb. 1970): 128–35.

32. Mahmud Amin al-'Alim and 'Abd al-'Azim Anis, *Fi al-thaqafa al-Misriyya* (On Egyptian culture) (Cairo: Dar al-Fikr al-Jadid, 1955), 154, 166.

33. Ahmad 'Abbas Salih, "Qira'a jadida li Najib Mahfuz" (A new reading of Naguib Mahfouz), *al-Katib* (Feb. 1966): 64–67.

34. 'Abd al-Mun'im Subhi, "al-Shakhsiyya al-ijabiyya fi adab Najib Mahfuz" (Positive characters in the literature of Naguib Mahfouz), *al-Katib* (Jan. 1963): 64.

35. Hafez, 19, 21.

36. George Tarabishi, *Allah fi rihlat Najib Mahfuz al-ramziyya* (God in the symbolic journey of Naguib Mahfouz) (Beirut: Dar al-Tali'a, 1973), 66, 130.

37. Raja' al-Naqqash, "Bayn al-Wafdiyya wa al-Marksiyya" (Between the Wafd and Marxism), *al-Hilal* (Feb. 1970): 40.

38. Sayyid Qutb, *Kutub wa shakhsiyyat* (Books and characters) (Cairo: Matba'at al-Risala, 1946). See also *al-Risala* (17 Dec. 1945): 1366.

39. Sayyid Qutb, "*Kifah Tiba* li Najib Mahfuz" (The struggle for Thebes by Naguib Mahfouz), *al-Risala* (2 Oct. 1944): 892.

40. Sayyid Qutb, "Khawatir mutasawiqa" (Coherent ideas), *al-Risala* (27 Nov. 1944): 1044.

41. Sayyid Qutb, "al-Qahira al-jadida" (New Cairo), *al-Risala* (30 Dec. 1946): 1441.

42. Muhammad Fahmi, "Zuqaq al-midaqq" (Midaq Alley), *al-Muqtataf* (Dec. 1947).

43. Muhammad Hasan 'Abd Allah, *al-Islamiyya wa al-ruhiyya fi adab Najib Mahfuz* (Islamism and spiritualism in the literature of Naguib Mahfouz) (Cairo: Dar Misr li al-Tiba'a, 1977), 450.

44. Taha Husayn, *Naqd wa islah* (Criticism and reform) (Beirut: Dar al-'Ilm li al-Malayin, 1956), 118.

BIBLIOGRAPHY

WORKS OF NAGUIB MAHFOUZ

All Mahfouz's works except *Awlad haratina* are published in Cairo by Maktabat Misr. When the year of publication is uncertain, we suggest alternative dates in brackets.

Hams al-junun (Whisper of madness). Short stories. 1939. [1938?].

'Abath al-aqdar (The absurdity of the fates). 1939.

Radubis. [1943].

Kifah Tiba (The struggle of Thebes). 1944.

al-Qahira al-jadida (New Cairo). 1945 [1946].

Khan al-Khalili. 1946 [1945].

Zuqaq al-Midaqq. 1947. Translated by Trevor Le Gassick as *Midaq Alley.* Beirut: Khayyat, 1966. Reprint. London: Heinemann; Washington, D.C.: Three Continents, 1974.

al-Sarab (The mirage). 1948 [1949].

Bidaya wa nihaya. 1949 [1951]. Translated by Ramses Awad as *The Beginning and the End.* New York: Doubleday, 1989.

Bayn al-Qasrayn. 1956. Translated by William M. Hutchins and Olive E. Kenny as *Palace Walk.* New York: Doubleday, 1991.

Qasr al-shawq. 1957. Translated by William M. Hutchins, Lorne M. Kenny and Olive E. Kenny as *Palace of Desire.* New York: Doubleday, 1991.

al-Sukkariyya. 1957. Translated by William Maynard Hutchins and Angele Botros Samaan as *Sugar Street.* New York: Doubleday, 1992.

Awlad haratina. In *Al-Ahram,* 1959. Reprint in book form. Beirut: Dar al-Adab, 1967. Translated by Philip Stewart as *Children of Gebelawi.* London: Heinemann; Washington, D. C.: Three Continents Press, 1981.

al-Liss wa al-kilab. 1961. Translated by Trevor Le Gassick and Mustafa Badawi and revised by John Rodenbeck as *The Thief and the Dogs*. New York: Doubleday, 1989.

al-Summan wa al-kharif. 1962. Translated by Roger Allen as *Autumn Quail*. Cairo: American Univ. in Cairo Press, 1985.

Dunya Allah (God's world). Short stories. 1962.

al-Tariq (The path). 1964 Translated by Muhammad Islam as *The Search* [Cairo: American Univ. in Cairo Press, 1987.

Bayt sayyi' al-sum'a (House of ill repute). 1965.

al-Shahhadh. 1965. Translated by Kristin Walker Henry as *The Beggar*. Cairo: American University in Cairo Press, 1986.

Tharthara fawq al-Nil (Chatter on the Nile). 1966.

Miramar. 1967. Translated by Fatma Moussa-Mahmoud. London: Heinemann, 1978.

Khammarat al-qitt al-aswad (The black cat tavern). Short stories. 1969.

Taht al-mizalla (Under the bus-stop shelter). Short stories. 1969.

Hikaya bi-la bidaya wa la nihaya (Story without beginning and without end). Short stories. 1971.

Shahr al-'asal (Honeymoon). Short stories. 1971.

al-Maraya. 1972. Translated by Roger Allen as *Mirrors*. [Minneapolis: Bibliotheca Islamica, 1977.

al-Hubb taht al-matar (Love under the rain). 1973.

al-Jarima (The crime). 1973.

al-Karnak. 1974. In *Three Contemporary Egyptian Novels*, translated by Saad Al-Gabalawy. Fredricton, New Brunswick: York Press, 1984.

Hadrat al-muhtaram. 1975. Translated by Rashid El-Enany as *Respected Sir*. [London: Quartet, 1986.

Hikayat haratina. 1975. Translated by Soad Sobhy, Essam Fattouh, and James Kenneson as *Fountain and Tomb*. Washington, D. C.: Three Continents, 1988.

Qalb al-layl (Heart of the night). Short stories. 1975.

Malhamat al-harafish (The epic of the riff-raff). 1977.

al-Hubb fawq hadbat al-haram (Love on Pyramid Plateau). 1979.

al-Shaytan ya'iz (Satan preaches). 1979.

'Asr al-hubb (Time of love). 1980.

Afrah al-qubba. 1981. Translated by Olive Kenny and revised by Mursi Saad El Din and John Rodenbeck as *Wedding Song*. New York: Doubleday, 1989.

al-Baqi min al-zaman sa'a (There only remains one hour). 1982.

Layali alf layla (The nights of a thousand nights). 1982.

Ra'aytu fi-ma yara al-na'im (I saw as the sleeper sees). 1982.

Amam al-'arsh: Hiwar ma'a rijal Misr min Mina hatta Anwar al-Sadat (Before the throne: A dialogue with the rulers of Egypt from Mina to Anwar al-Sadat). 1983.

Rihlat ibn Fattuma (The travels of ibn Fattuma). 1983.

al-Tanzim al-sirri (The secret order). 1984.
al-ʿAysh fi al-haqiqa (Life in reality). 1985.
Yawm qutil al-zaʿim. 1985. Translated by Malak Hashim as *The Day the Leader Was Killed.* Cairo: General Egyptian Book Organization, 1989.
Hadith al-sabah wa al-masa' (Morning and evening talk). 1987.
Sabah al-ward (Morning of roses to you). 1987.
Khitab al-ihtifal bi-tasallum Jaiʾzat Nubil / The Nobel Lecture. Translated by Muhammed Salmawy. Cairo: American Univ. in Cairo Press, 1988.
Qustumur. 1989.
al-Fajr al-kadhib (The false dawn). 1989.

TRANSLATIONS OF MAHFOUZ'S SHORT STORIES

"The Conjurer Made off with the Dish," In *Egyptian Short Stories,* translated by Denys Johnson-Davies, 61–67. Arab Authors Series, no. 8. London: Heinemann, 1978.
God's World. Short stories from various collections of Mahfouz. Translated by Akef Abadir and Roger Allen. Minneapolis: Bibliotheca Islamica, 1974. Contents: "God's World," "The Happy Man," "A Photograph," "An Extraordinary Official," "The Whisper of Madness," "Child's Paradise," Shahrazad," "The Drug Addict and the Bomb," "The Singing Drunkard," "The Barman," "A Dream," "Passers-by," "The Black Cat Tavern," "Under the Bus Shelter," "Sleep," "The Heart Doctor's Ghost," "The Window on the Thirty-Fifth Floor," "The Prisoner of War's Uniform," "An Unnerving Sound," "The Wilderness."
"Investigation." Translated by Roger Allen. *Edebiyat* 3, no. 1 (1978): 27–44.
"A Man and a Shadow," "Under the Bus Shelter," and "The Time and the Place." In *Flights of Fantasy,* edited by Ceza Kassem and Malek Hashem, 47–52, 91–98, 207–16. Cairo: Elias, 1985.
"The Mosque in the Narrow Lane" and "Hanzal and the Policeman." In *Arabic Writing Today: The Short Story,* edited by Mahmoud Manzalaoui, 117–36. Cairo: American Research Center in Egypt, 1968.
"The Mummy Awakes." Translated by Roger Allen. In *The Worlds of Muslim Imagination,* edited by Alamgir Hashmi 15–33, 212–15. Islamabad: Gulmohar, 1986.
"An Old Photograph." Translated by Roger Allen. *Nimrod* 24, no. 2 (Spring–Summer 1981): 91–100.
"The Tavern of the Black Cat," Translated by A. F. Cassis. *Contemporary Literature in Translation* 19 (Summer–Fall 1974): 5–8.
"A Visit." Translated by Ismail I. Nawwab. *Aramco World* 40, no. 2 (Mar.–Apr. 1989): 20–25.
"Zaabalawi." In *Modern Arabic Short Stories.* Translated by Denys Johnson-Davies, 137–47. London: Heinemann, 1974.

TRANSLATIONS OF MAHFOUZ'S PLAYS

"Harassment." Translation by Judith Rosenhouse. *Journal of Arabic Studies* 9 (1978): 105–37.

"The Chase." Translated by Roger Allen. *Mundus Artium* 10, no. 1 (1977): 134–62.

RELATED BOOKS AND ARTICLES

ʿAbd Allah, Muhammad Hasan. *al-Islamiyya wa al-ruhiyya fi adab Najib Mahfuz* (Islamism and spiritualism in the literature of Naguib Mahfouz). Cairo: Dar Misr li al-Tibaʿa, 1977.

Abdel Malek, Anouar, ed. *Anthologie de la littérature arabe contemporaine.* 3 vols. Paris: Seuil, 1964, 1965, 1967.

Ahmad, Aijaz. "Jameson's Rhetoric of Otherness and the 'National Allegory,' " *Social Text* 17 (Fall 1987): 3–25.

al-ʿAlim, Mahmud Amin. *Taʾammulat fi ʿalam Najib Mahfuz* (Meditations on the world of Naguib Mahfouz). Cairo: Al-Hayʾa al-Misriyya al-ʿAmma li al-Taʾlif wa al-Nashr, 1970.

al-ʿAlim, Mahmud Amin and ʿAbd al-ʿAzim, Anis. *Fi al-thaqafa al-Misriyya* (On Egyptian culture). Cairo: Dar al-Fikr al-Jadid, 1955.

Allen, Roger. "An Annotated Translation and Study of the Third Edition of *Hadith ʿIsa ibn Hisham.*" Ph.D. diss., Oxford Univ., 1968.

———. "Arabic Literature and the Nobel Prize," *World Literature Today* (Spring 1988): 201–3.

———. *The Arabic Novel: An Historical and Critical Introduction.* Syracuse: Syracuse Univ. Press, 1982.

———. "*Hadith ʿIsa ibn Hisham* by Muhammad al-Muwaylihi: A Reconsideration." *Journal of Arabic Literature* 1 (1970): 88–108.

———. "The Mature Arabic Novel Outside Egypt." In *Cambridge History of Arabic Literature.* Vol. 4. Edited by M. M. Badawi. Forthcoming.

ʿAllush, Saʿid. *ʿUnf al-mutakhayyil fi aʿmal Imil Habibi* (The dreamer's violence in the works of Emile Habibi). Casablanca: Al-Muʿassassa al-Haditha li al-Nashr wa al-Tawziʿ, 1986.

ʿAmir, Ibrahim. "Najib Mahfuz siyasiyyan min thawrat 1919 ila Yunyu 1967" (Naguib Mahfouz the politician: From the 1919 coup d'état to June, 1967), *al-Hilal* (Feb. 1970): 26–27.

al-ʿAqqad, ʿAbbas Mahmud. *Juha al-dahik al-mudhik* (Juha, he who laughs and the object of laughter). Cairo: Dar al-Hilal, n.d.

Asfour, Gaber. "Qiraʾa fi nuqqad Najib Mahfuz: Mulahazat awwaliyya" (A reading of Naguib Mahfouz's critics: Preliminary observations). *Fusul* 1, no. 3 (Apr. 1981): 161–79.

al-Ashmawi-Abouzeid, Fawzia. *La Femme et l'Egypte moderne dans l'oeuvre de Naguib Mahfouz, 1939–1967.* Geneva: Labor et Fides, 1985.

al-ʿAshri, Fathi, ed. *Najib Mahfuz: hawl al-thaqafa wa al-taʿlim, hawl al-shabab wa al-hurriyya, hawl al-din wa al-dimuqratiyya* (Naguib Mahfouz: Concerning culture and learning, youth and freedom, religion and democracy). 3 vols. Cairo: al-Dar al-Misriyya al-Lubnaniyya, 1990.

ʿAwad, Luwis. *Dirasat fi al-naqd wa al-adab* (Studies in criticism and literature). Cairo: Maktabat al-Anglu-Misriyya, 1964.

———. *Fi al-adab al-Inglizi* (On English literature). Cairo: al-Hayʾa al-Misriyya li al-Kutub, 1950.

ʿAwad Allah, Ahmad al-Sabbahi. *Tafsir al-ahlam* (Interpretation of dreams). Cairo: Maktabat al-Madbuli, [1977?]

Badawi, ʿAbd al-Rahman. *al-Insan al-kamil fi al-Islam* (The perfect man in Islam). Beirut: Dar al-Qalam, 1976.

———. *al-Insaniyya wa al-wujudiyya fi al-fikr al-ʿArabi* (Humanism and existentialism in Arab thought). Cairo: Maktabat al-Nahda al-Misriyya, 1947.

———. *al-Zaman al-wujudi* (Existential time). Cairo: Maktabat al-Nahda al-Misriyya, 1945.

———. *Min Tarikh al-ilhad fi al-Islam* (On the history of atheism in Islam). Cairo: Maktabat al-Nahda al-Misriyya, 1945.

Badr, ʿAbd al-Muhsin Taha. *Najib Mahfuz: al-ruʾya wa al-adat* (Naguib Mahfouz: The vision and the means). Cairo: Dar al-Thaqafa li al-Tibaʿa wa al-Nashr, 1978.

Barthelme, Donald. *Snow White.* New York: Atheneum, 1986.

Beard, Michael. *Hedayat's "Blind Owl" as a Western Novel.* Princeton: Princeton Univ. Press, 1990.

de Beauvoir, Simone: *The Second Sex.* Translated by H. M. Parshley. New York: Vintage, 1974.

Bodkin, Maud. *Archetypal Patterns in Poetry.* 1934. Reprint. London: Oxford Univ. Press, 1968.

Brandt Corstius, J. C. "Writing Histories of World Literature." *Yearbook of Comparative Literature* 12 (1963): 5–14.

Brittan, Arthur. *Masculinity and Power.* London: Blackwell, 1989.

Calvino, Italo. *The Castle of Crossed Destinies.* Translated by William Weaver. New York: Harcourt Brace Jovanovitch, 1977.

Camus, Albert. *L'été* (Summer). Paris: Gallimard, 1954.

Caudwell, Christopher. *Further Studies in a Dead Culture.* London: Bodley Head, 1949.

———. *Illusion and Reality: A Study of the Sources of Poetry.* London: Macmillan, 1937.

———. *Studies in a Dying Culture.* London: John Lane, 1938.

Cheikho, Louis, ed. *Kitab Kalila wa Dimna.* Beirut: Dar al-Mashriq, 1969.

Chraibi, Driss. *Mother Comes of Age.* Translated by Hugh A. Harter. Washington, D. C.: Three Continents, 1984.

Cossery, Albert. *Men God Forgot.* Translated by Harold Edwards. San Francisco: City Lights, 1963.

Culler, Jonathan. *Structuralist Poetics.* Ithaca Cornell Univ. Press, 1975.

Dansel, Michel. *Les "Nobels" français de littérature.* Paris: André Bonne, 1967.

Dasenbrock, Reed Way. "Wole Soyinka's Nobel Prize." *World Literature Today* (Winter 1987): 5–9.

Duwwara, Fuad. "al-Wijdan al-qawmi fi adab Najib Mahfuz" (National emotional life in the literature of Naguib Mahfouz), *al-Hilal* (Feb. 1970): 100–109.

———. *Najib Mahfuz: Min al-qawmiyya ila al-ʿalamiyya* (Naguib Mahfouz: From regionalism to globalism) Cairo: Al-Hayʾa al-Misriyya al ʿAmma li al-Kutub, 1989.

Eagleton, Terry. *Marxism and Literary Criticism.* Berkeley: Univ. of California Press, 1976.

El-Enany, Rasheed. "The Novelist as Political Eye-Witness: A View of Naguib Mahfouz's Evaluation of the Nasser and Sadat Eras," *Journal of Arabic Literature* 21, no. 1 (1990): 72–86.

d'Ephèse, Artémidore. *Le livre des songes.* Damascus: Institut Français de Damas, 1964.

Etiemble, René. "Faut-il réviser la notion de *weltliteratur?" International Comparative Literature Association Proceedings* (1966): 5–16

Fahd, Toufic. *La divination arabe.* Leiden: Brill, 1966.

Fahmi, Muhammad "Zuqaq al-midaqq" (Midaq Alley). *al-Muqtataf* (Dec. 1947).

Fathi, Ibrahim. *al-ʿAlam al-riwaʾi ʿind Najib Mahfuz* (The fictional world of Naguib Mahfouz). Cairo: Dar al-Fikr al-Muʿasir, 1978.

Fawzi, Mahmud. *Najib Mahfuz: zaʿim al-harafish* (Naguib Mahfouz: Leader of the riff-raff). Cairo: Dar al-Jil, 1988.

Gadamer, Hans-Georg. *Truth and Method.* Rev. ed. Translated by Joel Weinsheimer and Donald Marshall. New York: Crossroad, 1989.

Gardner, John. *Grendel.* New York: Vintage, 1985.

al-Ghitani, Gamal. *Awraq shabb ʿasha mundhu alf ʿam* (Papers of a young man who lived a thousand years ago). Cairo: Maktabat Madbuli, n.d.

———. *Khitat al-Ghitani* (Al-Ghitani's plans). Beirut: Dar al-Masira, 1981.

———. *Najib Mahfuz yatadhakkar* (Naguib Mahfouz remembers). Cairo: Akhbar al-Yawm, 1987.

———. *Zayni Barakat.* Translated by Faruk Abdel Wahab Mustafa. New York: Penguin, 1988.

Ghunaymi, Hilal. "Azmat al-waʿi al-siyasi fi qissat *al-Summan wa al-kharif*" (The crisis of political consciousness in *Autumn Quail*). *al-Katib* (Jan. 1963): 24–31.

Gordon, Haim. *Naguib Mahfouz's Egypt: Existential Themes in His Writings.* Contributions to the Study of World Literature, no. 38. New York: Greenwood, 1990.

Habibi, Emile. *Ikhtayyi* (What a pity). Cyprus: Kitab al-Karmil, 1985.

Hafiz, Sabri. "al-Ittijah al-riwaʾi al-jadid ʿind Najib Mahfuz" (The new direction of Naguib Mahfouz's fiction), *al-Adab* (Nov. 1963).

Hamadhani, Badiʿ al-Zaman. *al-Maqamat.* Edited by Muhammad ʿAbduh. Beirut: Dar al-Mashriq, 1968.

Haqqi, Yahya. *ʿItr al-ahbab* (The aroma of lovers). Cairo: Matabiʿ al-Ahram, 1971.

al-Hawari, Ahmad Ibrahim. *Masadir naqd al-riwaya fi al-adab al-ʿArabi al-hadith fi Misr* (Sources of criticism of the novel in modern Arabic literature in Egypt). Cairo: Dar al-Maʿarif, 1979.

Husayn, Taha. *Naqd wa islah* (Criticism and reform). Beirut: Dar al-ʿIlm li al-Malayin, 1956.

Hutcheon, Linda. *Narcissistic Narrative: The Metafictional Paradox.* New York: Methuen, 1984.

Ibn Sirin. *Muntakhab al-kalam fi tafsir al-ahlam* (The choicest words in dream interpretation). Printed on the margins of al-Nabulusi, *Taʿtir al-anam fi taʿbir al-manam.*

Ibrahim, Hafiz. *Layali Satih* (The nights of Satih). Edited by ʿAbd al-Rahman Sidqi. Cairo: al-Dar al-Qawmiyya li al-Tibaʿa wa al-Nashr, 1964.

Ionesco, Eugène. *La photo du colonel.* Paris: Gallimard, 1962.

Ivask, Ivar. "Czeslaw Milosz: 1980 Nobel Prize in Literature." *World Literature Today* 55, no. 1 (Winter 1981): 6.

Jakobson, Roman, and Morris Halle. *Fundamentals of Language.* The Hague: Mouton, 1956. Reprint. 1980.

———. "Two Aspects of Language and Two Types of Aphasic Disturbances." In Jakobson and Halle, *Fundamentals of Language,* 69–96. Also collected in Roman Jakobson, *Selected Writings,* 2: 239–59. The Hague: Mouton, 1971.

al-Jamal, Ibrahim Muhammad. *Ikhtartu lak min al-turath: Tafsir al-ahlam li al-imamayn al-jalilayn ibn Sirin wa al-Nabalusi* (I have chosen for you from the tradition: Dream interpretation by the two venerable imams, ibn Sirin and al-Nabulusi). Cairo: Maktabat al-Qurʾan, 1982.

Jameson, Frederic. "Third-World Literature in the Era of Multinational Capitalism." *Social Text* 15 (Fall 1986): 65–88.

Kaminsky, Amy Katz. "Women Writing About Prostitutes." In *The Image of the Prostitute in Modern Literature,* edited by Pierre L. Horn and Mary Beth Pringle, 119–31. New York: Ungar, 1984.

Kant, Immanuel. *Critique of Judgment.* Translated by J. H. Bernard. New York: Hafner, 1951.

Kazantzakis, Nikos. *The Fratricides.* Translated by Athena Gianakas Dallas. New York: Simon and Schuster, 1964.

al-Kharrat, Edward. "ʿAlam Najib Mahfuz" (The world of Naguib Mahfouz). *Majallat al-Majalla* (Jan. 1963).

Khoury, Elias. *Tajribat al-bahth ʿan ufuq* (The experiment of searching for a horizon). Beirut: Munazzamat al-Tahrir al-Filastiniyya, 1974.

Kilito, Abd el-Fattah. "Le genre 'Séance:' Une introduction." *Studia Islamica* 43 (1976): 36–37.

al-Kirmani. *Sahih al-Bukhari bi-sharh al-Kirmani* (Al-Bukhari's canon with a commentary by Al-Kirmani). Beirut: Dar Ihyaʾ al-Turath al-ʿArabi, 1981.

Lacan, Jacques. "The Agency of the Letter in the Unconscious or Reason Since Freud," In *Ecrits: A Selection.* Translated by Alan Sheridan, 146–75. New York: Norton, 1977.

Le Gassick, Trevor, ed. *Critical Perspectives on Naguib Mahfouz.* Washington D.C.: Three Continents, 1991.

Luxner, Larry. "A Nobel for the Arab Nation." *Aramco World* 40, no. 2 (Mar.–Apr. 1989): 14–19.

Magill, Frank N., ed. *The Nobel Prize Winners: Literature.* 3 vols. Pasadena: Salem, 1987.

Malti-Douglas, Fedwa. "al-Wahda al-nassiyya fi *Layali Satih.*" (Textual unity in *Layali Satih*), *Fusul* 3, no. 2 (1983): 109–17.

———. "Badi' al-Zaman al-Hamadhani." In *Encyclopedia Iranica,* 3: 377–79. London: Routledge & Kegan Paul, 1988.

———. "Dreams, the Blind, and the Semiotics of the Biographical Notice." *Studia Islamica* 51 (1980), 137–62.

———. "*Min al-tarikh al-sirri li-Nu'man 'Abd al-Hafiz* wa tadmir tuqus al-hayat wa al-lugha" ("From the Secret History of Nu'man 'Abd al-Hafiz" and the destruction of the rituals of life and language). *Ibda'* 1.6–7 (1983): 86–92.

———. "Sign Conceptions in the Islamic World," In *Semiotics: A Handbook on the Sign-Theoretic Foundations of Nature and Culture,* edited by Roland Posner, Klaus Robering, and Thomas E. Sebeok, Berlin: Walter de Gruyter, forthcoming.

———. "Yusuf al-Qa'id wa al-riwaya al-jadida," (Yusuf al-Qa'id and the new novel). *Fusul* 4, no. 3 (1984): 190–202.

Mandur, Muhammad. *Qadaya jadida fi adabina al-hadith* (New issues in our modern literature). Cairo, 1958.

al-Maqrizi, Taqiyy al-Din. *al-Khitat al-Maqriziyya* (The Maqrizian plans). Beirut: Dar Sadir, n.d.

———. *al-Mawa'iz wa al-i'tibar fi dhikr al-khitat wa al-athar* (known as "The Maqrizian plans"). Cairo: Dar al-Taba'a, 1853.

Mikhail, Mona. *'Ara'is fi al-mawlid: dirasat hawl al-mar'a al 'Arabiyya* (Brides at the feast: Studies on Arab women). Cairo: Dar al-'Arabi, 1987.

———. *Images of Arab Women: Fact and Fiction.* Washington, D.C.: Three Continents, 1978.

Milson, Menahem. "Najib Mahfuz and Jamal Abd al-Nasir: The Writer as Political Critic." *Asian and African Studies* 23, no. 1 (Mar. 1989), 1–22.

al-Mis'adi, Mahmud. *Haddatha Abu Hurayra qal* (Abu Hurayra related, saying). Tunis: Dar al-Junub li al-Nashr, 1979.

Monroe, James T. *The Art of Badi' al-Zaman al-Hamadhani as Picaresque Narrative.* Beirut: American Univ. of Beirut Center for Arab and Middle East Studies, 1983.

Moosa, Matti, *The Origins of Modern Arabic Fiction.* Washington, D.C.: Three Continents, 1983.

Morier, Henri. *La psychologie des styles.* Geneva: Georg, 1959.

Mubarak, ʿAli Basha. *al Khitat al-Tawfiqiyya li-Misr al-Qahira* (Known as the Tawfiqiyya plans). Cairo: al-Hayʾa al-Misriyya al-ʿAmma li al-Kitab, 1980.

Musa, Fatima. *Fi al-riwaya al-ʿArabiyya al-muʿasira* (On the contemporary Arabic novel). Cairo: al-Anglu-Misriyya, 1972.

Mustajab, Muhammad. *Min al-taʾrikh al-sirri li-Nuʿman ʿAbd al-Hafiz.* (From the secret historiography of Nuʿman ʿAbd al-Hafiz) Cairo: Maktab al-Nil li al-Tabʿ wa al-Nashr, 1982.

al-Muwaylihi, Muhammad. *Hadith ʿIsa ibn Hisham.* Cairo: al-Dar al-Qawmiyya li al-Tibaʿa wa al-Nashr, 1964.

al-Nabulusi. *Taʿtir al-anam fi taʿbir al-manam* (A work on dream interpretation). Cairo: ʿIsa al-Babi al-Halabi, n.d.

El-Naimi, Salwa. "Notre père Mahfouz." *Magazine littéraire* 251 (Mar. 1988): 28.

al-Najmi, Kamal. "Maʿ al-ghinaʾ wa al-mughanin fi adab Najib Mahfuz" (Singers and singing in the literature of Naguib Mahfouz), *al-Hilal* (Feb. 1970): 128–35.

al-Naqqash, Rajaʾ. "Bayn al-Wafdiyya wa al-Marksiyya" (Between the Wafd and Marxism). *al-Hilal* (Feb. 1970).

———. *Udabaʾ muʿasirun* (Contemporary writers). Cairo: al-Anglu-Misriyya, 1968.

Nobel Foundation and W. Odelberg, coordinating ed. "Statutes of the Nobel Foundation." In *Nobel: The Man and His Prizes.* 3d ed., rev. New York: American Elsevier, 1972.

Parker, Richard B. and Robin Sabin. *Islamic Monuments in Cairo: A Practical Guide.* 3rd ed., rev. and enl. by Caroline Williams. Cairo: American Univ. in Cairo Press, 1985.

Peled, Mattityahu. *Religion, My Own: The Literary Works of Najib Mahfuz.* New Brunswick, N.J.: Transaction, 1983.

al-Qaʿid, Yusuf. *Shakawa al-Misri al-fasih* (The complaints of the eloquent Egyptian), vol. 1. Beirut: Dar al-Masira, 1981; vol. 2 and 3. Cairo: Dar al-Mustaqbal al-ʿArabi, 1983, 1985.

al-Qalqashandi. *Maʾathir al-inaqa fi maʿalim al-khilafa* (A work on caliphs and the caliphate). Edited by ʿAbd al-Sattar Ahmad Farraj. Beirut: ʿAlam al-Kutub, n.d.

Qutb, Sayyid. "al-Qahira al-jadida" (New Cairo). *al-Risala* (30 Dec. 1946): 1441.

———. "Khawatir mutasawiqa" (Coherent ideas). *al-Risala* (27 Nov. 1944): 1044.

———. "*Kifah Tiba* li Najib Mahfuz" ("The struggle for Thebes" by Naguib Mahfouz). *al-Risala* (2 Oct. 1944): 892.

———. *Kutub wa shakhsiyyat* (Books and characters). Cairo: Matbaʿat al-Risala, 1946.

al-Rabiʿi, Mahmud. *Qiraʾat al-riwaya: Namadhij min Najib Mahfuz* (Reading the novel: Excerpts from Naguib Mahfouz). Cairo: Dar al-Maʿarif, 1974.

Raghib, Nabil. *Qadiyyat al-shakl al-fanni ʿind Najib Mahfuz* (The question of artistic form in Naguib Mahfouz). Cairo: al-Muʾassassa al-Misriyya al-ʿAmma li al-Taʾlif wa al-Nashr, 1967.

al-Raʿi, Ali. *Dirasat fi al-riwaya al-Misriyya* (Studies in the Egyptian novel). Cairo: Al-Muʾassassa al-Misriyya al-ʿAmma, 1964.

Ricoeur, Paul. *Interpretation Theory: Discourse and the Surplus of Meaning.* (Fort Worth: Texas Christian Univ. Press, 1976).

Riggan, William. "The Swedish Academy." *World Literature Today* (Summer 1981): 399–405.

Robbe-Grillet, Alain. *Les gommes* (Erasers). Paris: Editions de Minuit, 1973.

Rushdi, Rashad. *Ma huwa al-adab* (What is literature?). Cairo: al-Anglu-Misriyya, 1960.

———. *Mukhtarat min al-naqd al-adabi al muʿasar* (Selections from contemporary criticism). Cairo: al-Anglu-Misriyya, 1951.

al-Safadi. *Nakt al-himyan fi nukat al-ʿumyan* (A biographical compendium on the blind), Edited by Ahmad Zaki. Cairo: al-Maktaba al-Jamaliyya, 1911.

Said, Edward. "Goodbye to Mahfouz." *London Review of Books* 10, no. 22 (8 Dec. 1988): 10–11.

———. Introduction to *Days of Dust,* by Halim Barakat. Translated by Trevor Le Gassick. Wilmette, Ill.: Medina Univ. Press International, 1974.

———. Introduction to *Little Mountain,* by Elias Khoury. Translated by Maia Tabet. Minneapolis: Univ. of Minnesota Press, 1989.

———. "The World, the Text, and the Critic." In *The World, the Text, and the Critic, 31–53.* Cambridge, Mass.: Harvard Univ. Press, 1983.

Sakkut, Hamdi. *The Egyptian Novel and Its Main Trends: 1913–1952.* Cairo: American Univ. in Cairo Press, 1971.

Salih, Ahmad ʿAbbas. "Qiraʾa jadida li Najib Mahfuz" (A new reading of Naguib Mahfouz), *al-Katib* (Feb. 1966): 64–67.

al-Sayyid, Jalal. "Tarikhuna al-qawmi fi *Thulathiyyat* Najib Mahfuz" (Our national history in *The Trilogy* of Naguib Mahfouz), *al-Katib* (Jan. 1963): 70–79.

Shahid, ʿIrfan. *al-ʿAwda ila Shawqi* (The return to Shawqi). Beirut: al-Ahliyya li al-Nashr wa al-Tawziʿ, 1986.

Shalaq, ʿAli. *Najib Mahfuz fi majhulihi al-maʿlum* (Naguib Mahfouz in his unknown known). Beirut: Dar al-Masira, 1979.

Shammas, Anton, "The Shroud of Mahfouz." *New York Review of Books* (2 Feb. 1989): 19–21.

Sharabi, Hisham. *Neopatriarchy.* New York: Oxford Univ. Press, 1989.

al-Shatti, Sulayman. *al-Ramz wa al-ramziyya fi adab Najib Mahfuz* (Symbol and symbolism in the writing of Naguib Mahfouz). Kuwait: al-Matbaʿa al-ʿAsriyya.

Shukri, Ghali. *al-Muntami* (The committed). Cairo: Akhbar al-Yawm, 1964.

———. *Najib Mahfuz: min al-Jamaliyya ila Nubil* (Naguib Mahfouz: From Jamaliyya to Nobel). Cairo: al-Hayʾa al-ʾAmma li al-Istiʾlamat, 1988.

Somekh, Sasson. *The Changing Rhythm: A Study of Najib Mahfuz's Novels.* Leiden: Brill, 1973.

Stetkevych, Jaroslav. "Spaces of Delight: A Symbolic Topoanalysis of the Classical Arabic *Nasib.*" In *Critical Pilgrimages: Studies in the Classical Arabic Tradition,* edited by Fedwa Malti-Douglas, special issue of *Literature East and West* 24 (1989): 5–28.

Subhi, ʿAbd al-Munʿim. "al-Shakhsiyya al-ijabiyya fi adab Najib Mahfuz" (Positive characters in the literature of Naguib Mahfouz). *al-Katib* (Jan. 1963): 64.

Tarabishi, George. *Allah fi al-riwaya rihlat Najib Mahfuz al-ramziyya* (God in the symbolic journey of Naguib Mahfouz). Beirut: Dar al-Taliʿa, 1973.

———. *Ramziyyat al-marʾa fi al-ʿArabiyya wa dirasat ukhra* (Symbolism of women in the Arabic novel and other studies). Beirut, 1981.

Tarshuna, Mahmud. *al-Adab al-murid fi muʾallafat al-Misʿadi* (The seeker literature in the works of al-Misʿadi). Tunis: La Maghrébine pour l'Impression, l'Edition et la Publicité, 1989.

al-Thaʿalibi. *Qisas al-anbiyaʾ* (Accounts of the Prophets). Beirut: Dar al-Qalam, n.d.

Trilling, Lionel. *The Liberal Imagination.* New York: Scribners, 1940. Reprint. 1976.

Ulmann, Stephen. "Style and Personality." in *Contemporary Essays on Style,* edited by G. A. Love and M. Payne. Glenview, Ill.: Scott, Foresman, 1969.

Vickery, John B., ed. *Myth and Literature: Contemporary Theory and Practice.* Lincoln: Univ. of Nebraska Press, 1969. Translated into Arabic by Ibrahim Jabra as *al-Ustura wa al-ramz.* Baghdad, 1973.

Wahba, Magdi. *Muʿjam mustalahat al-adab/A Dictionary of Literary Terms: English, French, Arabic.* Beirut: Librairie du Liban, 1974.

Waugh, Patricia. *Metafiction: The Theory and Practice of Self-Conscious Fiction.* London: Methuen, 1984.

Weiskel, Thomas. *The Romantic Sublime: Studies in the Structure and Psychology of Transcendence.* Baltimore: Johns Hopkins Univ. Press, 1976.

Williams, John, ed. *Islam.* New York: Braziller, 1960.

Yaghi, ʿAbd al-Rahman. *al-Juhud al-riwaʾiyya min Salim al-Bustani ila Najib Mahfuz* (The novelistic project from Salim al-Bustani to Naguib Mahfouz) Beirut: Dar al-ʿAwda, 1972.

Yusuf, Kamal. "Nuqqaduna al-waqiʿiyyun ghayru waqiʿiyyin" (Our unrealistic realist critics). *al-Risala al-jadida* (June 1956): 14, 17.

INDEX

NAGUIB MAHFOUZ
was composed in 10 on 12 Palatino on a Mergenthaler Linotronic 300
by Partners Composition;
with display type in Legend by Dix Type;
printed by sheet-fed offset on 55-pount, acid-free Antique Cream,
Smyth-sewn and bound over binder's boards in Joanna Arrestox B,
by Maple-Vail Book Manufacturing Group, Inc.;
with dust jackets printed in 2 colors by Johnson City Publishing Co., Inc.;
and published by
SYRACUSE UNIVERSITY PRESS
SYRACUSE, NEW YORK 13244-5160